SAVING THE FUTURE

SAVING THE FUTURE

How Social Partnership Shaped Ireland's Economic Success

TIM HASTINGS, BRIAN SHEEHAN
AND PADRAIG YEATES

BLACKHALL
Publishing

This book was typeset by Ark Imaging for

Blackhall Publishing
33 Carysfort Avenue
Blackrock
Co. Dublin
Ireland

e-mail: info@blackhallpublishing.com
www.blackhallpublishing.com

ISBN (PBK): 978-1-84218-135-5
ISBN (HBK): 978-1-84218-140-9

A catalogue record for this book is available
from the British Library.

Printed in Ireland by ColourBooks Ltd

Contents

Foreword

As Ireland heads for 21 years of social partnership, new questions are being asked about the role of social partnership in transforming Ireland from an economic basket case to a model of economic development and full employment.

Saving the Future: How Social Partnership Shaped Ireland's Economic Success tells – for the first time – the inside story of this unique period through the eyes of the men and women who made it happen. Drawing on new insights from ministers, business leaders, top civil servants and trade union leaders, it charts the background to the first national agreement in 1987 and the acceptance among these diverse groups of a deceptively simple economic formula and new articles of faith, which brought Ireland back from the economic brink.

It's a book for people who want to fully understand the success of the Irish economy, and the contribution of the unique social partnership model to that success. The book does not claim that social partnership was solely responsible for the Irish economic miracle. Rather it suggests that it is now part of the fabric of our political, economic and social life and it has made a significant contribution to shaping modern Ireland. *Saving the Future* seeks to fill a significant gap in the discourse about our recent economic and social history, which often ignores or downplays the importance of social partnership from the mid-1980s to the present day.

Written by the leading industrial journalists who tracked the ups and downs of the period, the book describes the most dynamic years of Ireland's economic development through the eyes of those who helped to shape it. The authors uncovered a rich seam of material as they interviewed 40 of the top politicians, business leaders, civil servants, and trade unionists who conceived and developed Irish social partnership. The authors' focus has inevitably been on the economy, especially pay, employment, living standards and industrial relations. They tell the story of social partnership from the inside, providing insight into key developments and themes that marked the period.

The story begins in the dark days of the early 1980s and Charles Haughey's attempts at fiscal rectitude, and continues through Alan Dukes' crucial bipartisan approach, Ray McSharry's attack on public spending and Bertie Ahern's role as a pillar of the process. It also charts the conversion of the State's second largest party, Fine Gael, to the process, and its former leader John Bruton's role in expanding the partnership to include the community pillar. Along the way, the book explores why leaders from business and government, as well as the unions, deemed social partnership preferable to another option available in the 1980s – an Irish version of Thatcherism.

The first significant national agreement yielded the era of so-called 'jobless growth', when the economic indicators improved but the dole queues lengthened. Later agreements provided the stability that encouraged major new foreign direct investment and fostered new approaches to tackling inequality, unemployment, public sector pay and reform, and the development of Ireland as a leading European economy.

In its penultimate chapter, the book analyses the hidden dynamics that allowed a highly disparate collection of individuals and organisations to successfully work together in a way that remains unique. It argues that social partnership was never an alternative to conflict. Its architects and supporters often had – and continue to have – very different views of society and how it should develop. But social partnership worked because leaders from different backgrounds were able to find a consensus on the fundamental economic and social challenges, and then negotiate and implement practical solutions that were acceptable to their very different constituencies.

The people who first conceived and developed the model in the 1980s believed it could solve the then pervasive malaise of unemployment and emigration, paving the way for more fundamental changes in Irish society. While it was successfully doing this in the first decade, the outside world was changing almost beyond recognition.

The Berlin Wall came down, shifting the centre of gravity of world politics. The emergence of China and India as economic powers had a similarly dramatic impact on the nature of the global competitive economy. New technologies continued to redefine consumer demand and workplace realities. The accelerating speed of life raised expectations of public and private services and reduced tolerance of incompetence or disruption. As the gap between rich and poor widened, the as yet untapped power of consumers emerged as a potentially huge force in society. More recently, the emergence of climate change as a primary global concern has changed things again.

Social partnership had bought us back from the brink, but we emerged into a tougher world where we have to constantly and quickly adapt to sustain our success. To use a soccer analogy, it was as if we'd avoided a disastrous relegation to the third division, only to find ourselves competing with the world's best in an international champions' league. How well we compete and achieve at this level remains to be seen.

The book questions whether Irish social partnership is capable of adapting to deal with the massive challenges facing a successful Ireland in a changing and ever more demanding global environment. In other words, can it continue to 'save the future'? The thought-provoking conclusion reflects on whether social partnership was simply a constructive factor in creating the new and vibrant Ireland of today, or whether it can help deal with tomorrow's challenges for our modern dynamic economy – challenges like sustaining competitiveness and social justice in a globalised economy and labour market. It argues that reaching the consensus necessary to sustain the successful social partnership model poses big challenges to the emerging new generation of Irish political, business and labour leaders – and to society itself.

Peter McLoone
General Secretary
IMPACT trade union

Acknowledgements

The authors were approached by the Irish Municipal Public and Civil Trade Union (IMPACT) to write this book in mid-2006. The union's Central Executive Committee had discussed ways of marking the fact that IMPACT General Secretary Peter McLoone held the presidency of the Irish Congress of Trade Unions (ICTU) between 2005 and 2007, and decided that sponsoring this discussion of 21 years of social partnership was the appropriate way to do it.

The authors wish to express their thanks to IMPACT's Executive for backing the project, to its General Secretary Peter McLoone for empowering the work, providing extensive assistance with contacting interviewees and offering key insights at crucial junctures. We would also like to thank IMPACT's Information Officer Bernard Harbor, for his extensive and patient work on editing and his advice. The authors are also grateful to Julie Healy for her work on transcribing the interviews, many at short notice.

The following people were interviewed as part of the research for this book. The bulk of the interviews took between September 2006 and April 2007. The authors wish to thank sincerely all who gave freely of their time to be interviewed.

Bertie Ahern, Taoiseach and leader of Fianna Fáil
Mike Allen, secretary of the Labour Party and former general secretary, INOU
Billy Attley, former general secretary, SIPTU
David Begg, general secretary, ICTU
Michael Berkery, general secretary, IFA
John Bruton, former leader Fine Gael and EU ambassador
Rosheen Callender, national equality officer, SIPTU

Peter Cassells, executive chairman, the National Centre for Partnership and Performance

Bernard Collins, chairman of the VHI

Mel Cousins, former advisor to the Department of Social and Family Affairs

Liam Doherty, former divisional director IBEC, now a consultant

Kevin Duffy, chairman of the Labour Court

Alan Dukes, former leader of Fine Gael

John Dunne, former director general of IBEC and currently chairman of IDA Ireland

John Dunne, chief executive, Chambers Ireland

Brian Flynn, director and chief appeals officer, Department of Social and Family Affairs

Phil Flynn, former general secretary IMPACT

Des Geraghty, former general president SIPTU

Fr. Sean Healy SMA and co-director of the Justice Commission, CORI

Blair Horan, general secretary, CPSU

Patricia King, regional secretary, SIPTU

Con Lucey, economist, IFA

Dan McAuley, former director general, Federated Union of Employers (later IBEC)

Dermot McCarthy, secretary general, Department of the Taoiseach and current chairman of NESC

Charlie McCreevy, former Minister for Finance and EU commissioner

Kieran McGowan, former chief executive IDA

Peter McLoone, general secretary, IMPACT

Ray McSharry, former Minister for Finance and EU Commissioner

Tom Mulherin, assistant secretary, Department of Social and Family Affairs

Kieran Mulvey, chief executive of the Labour Relations Commission

Dan Murphy, general secretary, Public Services Executive Union (PSEU)

Kevin Murphy, former secretary for Public Service Management and Development, Department of Finance and former ombudsman

Jack O'Connor, general president, SIPTU

Rory O'Donnell, director of the NESC

Breege O'Donoghue, HR director, Penneys and Primark

Eoin O'Driscoll, chairman, forfás

Jim O'Leary, economist and lecturer, National University of Ireland, Maynooth

Brian O'Raghallaigh, assistant secretary, Department of Social and Family Affairs

Turlough O'Sullivan, director general, IBEC

Paddy Teahon, former secretary general, Department of the Taoiseach and former chairman, NESC

Padraig White, former chief executive, IDA

Professor Gerard F. Whyte, TCD

The authors also used material from other interviews conducted over the last ten years or so with some of the above, and others, including the late Charles J. Haughey, former Taoiseach. In this context they would particularly like to thank John Carroll, former general president of SIPTU, Padraig O'hUiginn, former secretary general, Department of the Taoiseach and former chairman of the NESC.

The authors availed of various newspaper and periodical archives. The extensive database available from the weekly specialist industrial relations publication *Industrial Relations News* (IRN) was especially useful.

The views and analyses of the authors are theirs alone. Any errors or omissions are their responsibility.

CHAPTER 1

Background and History

[Ireland was] a nation ... hard done by in the race for prosperity.
Dermott McAleese, Professor of Economics,
Trinity College Dublin

The Ireland of the early 1980s saw itself as being 'hard done by' in the international race for prosperity and better living standards. The two key questions dominating political and economic conversation were, firstly, who was responsible for this economic mess and, secondly, how could we get out of it?

In time, economic transformation supplied its own answer to both these conundrums but not before significant hardship, high emigration and something akin to national depression had taken their toll. Understanding the background to the evolution of social partnership in Ireland in the late 1980s requires a clear grasp of the economic landscape that preceded it, the relative position of employers, unions and farmers, and the national mindset.

ECONOMIC CONTEXT

Lack of jobs and high levels of personal taxation were the outward manifestations of the slowdown which the country faced in the early years of the 1980s. Unemployment in Ireland averaged a steady 4.7 per cent between 1961 and 1973 and gradually rose to 8.1 per cent between 1974 and 1980. By 1986, it had risen to 18 per cent on the back of a serious economic slowdown. In fact the real level of unemployment was widely seen as being significantly higher because many groups, such as married women who lost their jobs, rarely bothered to 'sign on', while 20,000 older workers were

1

transferred from the Live Register to a pre-retirement allowance. This was a tacit admission that the vast majority of them would never work again. Even massaging suppressed demand out of the official figures, the numbers out of work jumped from 91,000 in 1980 to 226,000 in 1985, an increase of almost 150 per cent in the space of five years.

A 25 per cent drop in employment in manufacturing occurred between 1980 and 1987. This caused emigration to resume at a time when Irish living standards were about 70 per cent of the EU average. The huge jump in the scale of unemployment prompted a number of commentators to try and explain the rise. Early explanations put it down to bad luck rather than bad management and saw it as the outcome of external economic shocks and demographic developments. Later studies, however, suggested the problem had its roots in taxation policy.

In fact, Ireland's unemployment rate exceeded the EU average by less than one percentage point in 1980 but, by 1985, the Irish jobless rate was 6.5 per cent above the higher European average. Leading economist Paul Tansey found that the marginal rates of tax for single people earning average manufacturing wages rose from 39.5 per cent in the 1980–81 period to 56.6 per cent five years later. In effect the 'tax wedge' for workers increased from 33.4 per cent to 42 per cent of employers' direct payroll costs over the same period.

At the end of 1986, national debt stood at £24 billion, three times larger than in 1980, and represented 148 per cent of annual GNP. Fiscal and monetary policy in the 1980s was described as entering a 'crushing spiral of constriction' within which taxes, both direct and indirect, remained high, while interest rates depressed investment and, in the process, impacted on the productive sector of the economy. Things were so bad that the London *Times* famously wrote that the international moneylenders were going to 'pull the shutters down on Ireland'.

Ray McSharry, a pivotal figure in the path to recovery through slashing public expenditure as Minister for Finance in the late 1980s, felt that no government had really set out to tackle the debt situation following the oil crises of the 1970s. This also applied to the Haughey-led Government in 1980. No one, he argued, was willing to confront the debt issue in the way it required: 'When I left the Department of Finance in December 1982 the national debt was £12 billion and when I came back in 1987 it was near to £24 billion and there was something like 80,000 less workers in jobs.'

McSharry had an unusual background for a man whose job it was to cut debt and shrink the public service when the crunch actually came. As junior minister in the Department of Public Services in Jack Lynch's Government in the late 1970s, he had been charged with trying to create public service jobs. He recalls: 'My job was ringing ministers saying they had not reached their targets but I think we knew that the public service pay bill was too high and something had to be done.'

NOT SO NEW

Negotiating and concluding national agreements on pay and wider issues was nothing new to Ireland, even in advance of 1987. Agreements had been struck at various points in the 1940s, 1950s and 1960s but, according to Professor Bill Roche of UCD in the book *Industrial Relations in Practice* (1997), these were little more than 'broad agreements on the increases permissible'. National agreements had been concluded at a central tripartite level in 1977 and 1978 and these had been followed by two National Understandings in 1979 and 1980. Unions used such agreements to protect earnings and the basic ingredients of such deals usually included price indexation and wage floors. In spite of this, Roche concludes that the unions just managed to achieve 'modest improvements' in real pay. And many of these gains were eroded by the rising burden of taxation. The unions faced repeated warnings from Government and employers that serious wage restraint was necessary to improve competitiveness and maintain employment.

On the broader industrial front, work days lost to industrial action reached a peak in 1979 when the one million mark was surpassed for the first time. In broad terms, strike activity peaked during the 1960s on the total work days lost index; the early 1970s saw a downturn with a return to higher figures in the late 1970s and early 1980s (see Table 1.1).

TABLE 1.1: STRIKES 1962–91

Year	Number of Strikes	Workers Involved	Works Days Lost
1962–66	418	141,664	2,219,011
1967–71	606	194,100	2,805,715
1972–76	817	168,899	2,038,178
1977–81	712	174,968	3,424,294
1982–86	686	306,388	1,951,079
1987–91	272	68,415	766,519

Source: Roche, William and Murphy, Tom (eds) (1998), *Irish Industrial Relations in Practice* (2nd edition), Dublin: Oaktree Press.

TABLE 1.2: PRICE AND WAGE INFLATION, 1979–85

Year	Price Inflation (%)	Wage Inflation (%)
1979	13.2	15.7
1980	18.2	21.4
1981	20.4	16.7
1982	17.1	14.7
1983	10.5	11.5
1984	8.6	10.9
1985	5.4	8.0

Source: Tansey, Paul (1998), *Ireland at Work*, Dublin: Oaktree Press.

In terms of trends and sector measurement, private sector strikes in the period 1960–89 fell considerably while the incidence of public service disputes increased.

Pay rises tended to follow inflation in the late 1970s and early 1980s. Under the National Understandings of the late 1970s, pay chased inflation upwards at a fairly rapid rate. Inflation stood at 13.2 per cent in 1979, while hourly earnings rose by 15.6 per cent. However the domestic downturn of the early 1980s saw a sharp drop in inflation and a subsequent moderation in pay rates (see Table 1.2).

The following sections will consider the key roles and positions of the main actors – employers and unions – through the early to mid-1980s in advance of the emergence of a new form of social partnership which was to be enshrined from 1987 in a dynamic and decisive way. Key to their eventual coming together and the development of a shared under standing was the National Economic and Social Council (NESC), a long-standing 'think tank' with its own independent secretariat and research arm. The NESC was to prove pivotal in assisting the parties towards what later came to be seen as a straightforward and simple formula aimed at controlling debt and cutting spending to resuscitate the economy and pull it out of its 1980s torpor.

THE EMPLOYER PERSPECTIVE

The failure in 1981 to negotiate a further national pay agreement to follow the second National Understanding of 1980 led to a return to decentralised pay determination after a decade of centralised arrangements. While employers hailed the benefits of a return to localised bargaining as 'freeing up management to communicate with their own workers and introduce change', others saw it differently. As one observer noted: 'The Federated Union of Employers (FUE), having moved away from national arrangements for agreeing wages, began operating a local direct employee involvement strategy [by] getting out there and dealing with the employees. They had a very clear strategy that this was how they were going to see the future.'

Professor Bill Roche notes that one factor which contributed to the breakdown of the cycle of national agreements was a hardening of the negotiating stances of both private employers and of the State itself. A further factor was the changed political climate following the arrival of the first Fine Gael-Labour Coalition of the decade in June 1981, some of whose members were reported not to be totally convinced of the value of tripartite national-level agreements. Government adopted a hands-off policy towards industrial relations and instead concentrated on the runaway public finances of the time.

Dan McAuley, then director general of the Federated Union of Employers – later to become the national employers' organisation, the Irish Business and Employers' Confederation (IBEC) – recalls that talks broke down in 1981 after there was an initial agreement between private employers and the Government as employer. The Government got into negotiations with the public service unions and came to an agreement on terms they had not conceded in centralised negotiations. McAuley recalls:

> Having come to that agreement, they called the employers in and said, 'We would like you to sign this agreement.' We said, 'No thank you very much, we don't want to sign it, we want to have local bargaining now.' So local bargaining took place during most of the 1980s and, contrary to what many people think, it was quite a constructive period in industrial relations. I think real issues were dealt with at company level. Fixed-term agreements were made. There were serious industrial disputes during that period but I think they were over real issues. They were over the question of change, the relocation of industry; a great deal of transformation was taking place in industry and business at the time and problems were dealt with at that level in a reasonably satisfactory manner. It was external events that were causing the major economic problems at that stage.

Tom Toner, who was president of the FUE from 1984 to 1986, recalls the period as one of transition from old style national and industry-wide agreements to free collective bargaining, which involved company-by-company agreements (this was also to become known as 'free-for-all' bargaining). Initially some companies had feared that this might lead to 'disruption and pressure for unwarranted demands and claims' (see *Federation of Irish Employers 1942–1992*, edited by Basil Chubb). However this did not prove to be the case, partly 'because of the clearly thought out strategy of many companies'. And a further factor, according to Toner, was the co-ordinating role of the executive of the FUE itself, which in many instances extended to direct assistance when negotiating with unions.

Minutes from FUE meetings of the time recall the frustration of the Federation at what it perceived was the Government's unwillingness to issue guidelines on pay policy. However, in late 1983, the Federation again discussed pay policy and the minutes record a preference for centralised pay arrangements with plant-level bargaining as the fall-back position. The minutes also noted the 'desirability of seeking common ground with Government and Congress'. But the return to centralised bargaining was not to take place until 1987.

The Confederation of Irish Industry (CII) (then a separate body which later went on to form part of the Irish Business and Employers Confederation) was apprehensive that public expenditure was rising too fast in the early 1980s. The CII was seriously concerned that there was a mistaken impression among politicians and the general community that government had a source of revenue of its own which did not have to be earned by the community and which could be used to an unlimited extent to award services and even to create jobs. Con Power, their own main economic spokesman at the time and the former director of economic policy at the CII, noted: 'What we were pointing up was the need for good order in the public finances, something which social partnership came to embody. Government was seen to be spending wildly. Borrowing was being used to fund current expenditure.'

Power recalled the depth of the economic woes facing the country: 'We highlighted that one of the major problems facing the economy was the dramatic increase in public sector spending as a proportion of the total spending of government, which had steadily increased from 43 per cent of national output in 1965 to 65 per cent in 1981. The rise of the government

6

share in national output has almost been entirely due to increases in current spending.'

Heading into 1987, the employers were not keen to get into another national agreement. They were reasonably happy about the way things had gone at local level, partly as a result of company-by-company bargaining. The level of wage increases had moderated, although average pay rises remained stubbornly above the rate of inflation. The employers' perception of the unions at the time was that the unions felt 'sidelined'. The employers were surprised by how well 'free-for-all' bargaining had worked during the period. Quite a number of American firms had come into Ireland and not recognised unions, and the employers believed that union influence seemed to have waned at a national level.

The employers' concern was that, if they signed up to a new national pay agreement, they would have the sort of experiences they felt they had in the past, when additional local bargaining increases were sought on top of those agreed at national level. This amounted to signing up for what was meant to be a 'nominal pay increase' but actually ending up with what they viewed as two-tier bargaining. A second major concern was the ICTU proposal to reduce the working week by an hour. Looking back, Dan McAuley says that it was quite clear that the main driving force behind the proposal for a new agreement was Charles Haughey and Padraig O'hUiginn. According to McAuley, Haughey had intimated that 'if we didn't go along with it he would do the same deal with the unions in the public sector and that would set a headline for the private sector. In effect, he was saying they would do the deal anyway.'

HR Director of Penneys in Ireland Breege O'Donohue, looking back to 1987, says that her biggest recollection was of a country that was 'almost bankrupt with high debt and where the IR was adversarial'. In terms of bargaining, her perception was that 'the trade unions lacked order and the employers were weak.' However, she believes that there was a determination on both sides 'to avoid doing any Thatcherite damage like they had in the UK'. And there were clear economic pressures on all parties to 'push for some kind of settlement'.

Meanwhile for those charged with maintaining jobs, the difficulties were mounting. For Padraig White, former chief executive of the Industrial Development Authority (IDA), the closure of the Telectron plant in Tallaght was emblematic of the difficulties the industrial authority faced trying to maintain jobs in what was a difficult industrial relations climate with high employment and high inflation. Telectron had been acquired by ATT as their major plant in Europe and employed 800 people. White feels now that, in retrospect, there was a very complex situation and that there was fault on both sides. He recalls:

> The IDA went to a major meeting with ATT and their heads in Palm Springs in 1983 and we were desperate to prevent closure. Along with David Hand of the IDA and Minister for State Eddie Collins, we told them they would get the co-operation of the workers in the future. We went over on a mission to save [Telectron] and as we wanted to keep the link with ATT.

The IDA put their case to the then Vice-Chairman of ATT James Olsen in the La Quinta hotel complex:

> They retired to think about it and we sat for what seemed like an eternity praying and hoping that we would save it, fearful of the impact for Ireland of losing jobs. They came back after half an hour and told us they did not have sufficient confidence that they would get the co-operation of the workforce in turning that plant around. It was that lack of confidence and the industrial relations climate of the times. It was a classic case of a union faced with change [and] not being able to adapt.

The contrast with the later environment created by the Programme for National Recovery (PNR) could not have been more stark in White's eyes. By then there was confidence that the major issues of high taxation and debt were being tackled and the country had set itself on the route to economic stability.

THE TRADE UNION PERSPECTIVE

Heading into a period of free collective bargaining in the early 1980s, unions were fearful of losing influence both in the workplace and at national level. Former Services, Industrial, Professional and Technical Union (SIPTU) President and earlier General Secretary of the Federated Workers Union of Ireland (FWUI) Billy Attley remembers the collapse of the National Understandings heralding something of a bleak period:

> From 1979 onwards, after the collapse of the National Understanding, things were extraordinary bleak here and we had eight or nine incredible

8

years. I think the statistics were that people were leaving here at nearly 80,000 a year. In the period we lost 250,000 manufacturing jobs. Also, if you look at the pay side of it, we were pushing pay up over and above the level of inflation which was at enormous heights and yet, at the end of all of that period, people were 7 per cent worse off than when they had started. In addition to that, the industrial relations were best described as poisonous. We lost 250,000 man days per year, every year. So nobody wanted to invest here or nobody wanted to do anything. There was a general feeling of 'last out – turn out the lights.'

Attley believes there was an emerging view in some quarters that unions were the source of the problem, rather than the solution. He recalls:

Thatcher was rampant in England. She had beaten the miners and was systematically dismantling what was left of the trade union movement in terms of adding influence. She only met them once, just after being elected, and she just simply read the manifesto, said that was what she would govern on, and stood up and walked out. John Perry, who was the President of the TUC, told me she never met even an official from that moment onwards. So it was a pretty bleak time. Against that background you either had to do something radical [or] you literally just couldn't continue.

More fundamentally, a view was gaining acceptance in business and indeed in wider circles that, ultimately, the Irish political system might not have the ability to address the situation. Unemployment was seen as a major national crisis and an issue which touched every level of Irish society as it seemed to be forcing people at all levels to flee the country. Attley recalls:

I remember talking to somebody from Trinity in 1986 where the whole engineering class of that year went first-post out of the country. There was no work for them, simply no work. So it was like a plague, every house was touched by it and when you talked to people at these meetings and functions, all they were talking about was don't mind about pay if you could get a job for your son or daughter, if you could get them into employment of any description and keep them home.

Unions feared a pincer movement where strong pressure would come on at national level for strong and possibly unpalatable action on the economy just when employers at local level 'were beginning to do things for themselves'.

Phil Flynn, then general secretary of the Local Government and Public Services Union (LGPSU), says what marked the early years of the decade was that 'every single economic indicator was going steeply in the wrong direction.' Wages and conditions were under attack, the employment situation was 'very, very bad' and there was an 'ideological situation' across the water which had the potential to spill over here as it inevitably did. He adds: 'So from the early 1980s, as early as 1982, we were going to have to revisit the whole question of [union] strategy and ask how we are going to deal with this? How are we going to cope?'

In terms of the likely outcome of the dire economic situation, Peter Cassells of ICTU recalls there was a great danger that, at national level, 'you were going to become part of the problem and that, at the level of individual employment, you were going to become marginalised', while in the public service they risked that government were going to 'take them on' regarding pay.

Wider economic issues like the history of emigration were also important. Flynn argues that emigration was not just the sort of traditional working-class emigration whereby people went to work in the UK or America, but rather 'you had such large numbers of young people coming out of school. People were seeing their neighbours' children and their own children all emigrating. This gave a huge momentum to something being done.'

Dan Murphy, general secretary of the Public Services Executive Union (PSEU) and an influential economic thinker within ICTU, feels that one of the reasons why the employers were reluctant to get back into centralised bargaining was because they were managing fine without the unions and because a number of new companies had come into the country who were able to manage their businesses without trade unions. He adds:

> I think, aside from any other consideration, they probably thought that a national process might breathe life back into the trade unions that might not otherwise be there. I think they were somewhat reluctant. The thing that ultimately made them less reluctant was the size of the money that they were expected to bring to the party in terms of wage increases

10

because, there is no doubt about it, the actual wage increases were probably less than we could have secured in decentralised bargaining.

There was a consensus emerging within the union movement that the growth of the right-of-centre Progressive Democrats would mean that 'someone was going to come out and grab the thing by the scruff of the neck' and instigate radical changes in policy at a national level. The danger for the unions was that 'if we were not quick enough on our feet, we would be seen as the source of the problem and would not figure in the solution.' This insight itself was to lead to a major shift in policy which later won wider support.

Kevin Duffy, then general secretary of the Building and Allied Trades' Union (BATU), highlights how people in the Irish trade union movement were acutely aware of what was happening to the UK trade union movement and, in particular, the trend towards marginalisation which was in motion at the time:

> The Conservatives came to power in 1979 and quickly moved to marginalise and weaken the trade union movement, and by the mid-1980s had largely succeeded in doing that. The trade union movement in Ireland, to a significant degree, had always looked with admiration to the British trade union movement. It was influential and powerful. But, by the mid-1980s, it was reduced to nothing more than an ineffective lobby group. In Ireland politics were changing as well because those were the days when the Progressive Democrats were going around the country recruiting significant numbers of people. So there was a view abroad that, just as the trade unions in Britain were seen as part of the problem, there was a concern that trade unions could be seen as part of the problem in Ireland as well. And that could happen if there was a shift to the right in politics.

Dan Murphy recalls the backwash from the politics of British trade unionism making its presence felt in Ireland. Some of this was rooted in the position adopted by the British trade union movement, as far back as the 1970s, of opposition to any form of incomes policy. For Murphy, this approach was based on the 'delusional view' that they could conduct their business without reference to government. Some of these approaches emerged via the engagement of British Unions in Northern Ireland but it

11

also surfaced in the ICTU executive in the Republic. In Murphy's view some of this firm ideological opposition to any form of centralised bargaining may have been communist inspired but, regardless of its origins, it produced tensions. The lessons of the miners' strike in the UK had not been lost on Irish trade unions either. Murphy recalls:

> As time went on, the experience of watching the British trade union movement became more and more educative. The British unions said they had nothing to do with an incomes policy and the British Government, in the form of Mrs Thatcher, said that it had nothing to do with an incomes policy and that everything was decided by the market. This was most certainly a load of 'bunkum' because [Thatcher] most certainly did operate an incomes policy and she operated by means of controlling the money supply.

The ultimate lesson for Murphy was watching Arthur Scargill – who led the 1984–85 miners' strike in the UK – and the National Union of Mineworkers with something approaching horror as the British trade union movement 'committed hari-kari on the altar of one man's ego'.

Peter Cassells recalls a key review carried out by ICTU in the mid-1980s period to assess the period of pay determination, inflation and industrial action they were living through:

> Around 1985–86 we did this exercise. One startling figure that came out [of it] showed that from 1980 to 1986 we had negotiated wage increases of about over 75 per cent and yet, at the end of the period, people were worse off than they were at the beginning. Inflation was running fairly high. Taxation had increased significantly to pay for the national debt, so that was one big problem we were facing. [Another problem was] unemployment, because the lifeblood of trade unions is people at work. Unless they are at work they're not going to be joining unions [and] you're not going to be representing them.

On the ground within the trade union movement, the emphasis had shifted away from extra money to maintaining job security. The concern was, firstly, with the state of the general economy and, secondly, the health or vitality of the business or industry people worked in. As Duffy recalls, this new dawning reality posed specific challenges for the trade union movement and ones which they could not shrink from: 'A view emerged

12

that there was a bigger picture we had to address. It was against that background that people started thinking and talking about a different way of doing business.'

Phil Flynn remembers that, in the climate which existed at the time, there was a major danger that the 'trade union movement's influence was just "drifting away" '. There was an emerging view among the key leadership grouping, people like Dan Murphy, Peter Cassells and Flynn himself – along with Attley – that there would have to be a shift in strategy. Sometimes these internal debates just amounted to 'ideas and critiques'. In time, the 1986 report from the NESC, *A Strategy for Development 1986–90*, would facilitate a much wider debate, not just among the unions but within the other parties as well.

POLITICAL MOVES

The trade unions had tried to engage the Fine Gael-Labour Coalition Government of 1982–87, but their efforts met with little success. Alan Dukes, the Minister for Finance at the time, recalls that, for most of his time in the role, the level of debt the country was carrying was roughly equivalent to the total intake from income tax. In effect this meant that there was a 'huge chunk of State revenue that you could not do anything constructive with because it was all going to service debt'. Dukes recalls:

> One of the issues we had in government was how far we should go with the kind of deflationary action which was required to deal with our situation. I took the view that we should have gone for a more determinedly deflationary approach in the earlier period of that Government to stop building up the debt to the degree that we did.

Dukes feels that it took the Labour Party 'a long time' to realise that taxes were too high, even for their typical voters and supporters. The response of the Labour Party to any turn of the screw was to propose some new kind of taxation. The level of industrial unrest in the early 1980s and the huge depth of feeling about the high level of taxation, first reflected in the tax marches, made it a particularly difficult time to be in power. When the then Government discussed things with the social partners, it emerged that they all had a number of things in common: 'They all wanted the Government to take less tax or take more of it from someone else. They all wanted the Government to be more creative in the way that they spent money which we did not really have,' Dukes recalls.

Dukes was convinced that one stimulus to the economy would be a single rate of VAT pegged at 12 per cent. Ultimately, the money went into increasing personal allowances. And it was very difficult to see that there was going to be any kind of understanding of the interaction of the forces at play by the employers or the trade unions.

Kevin Duffy, now chairman of the Labour Court, recalls that there was little Government enthusiasm for any sort of concordat or agreement to chart a joint path out of the economic morass. Garret FitzGerald was regarded as being sceptical about the unions being part of any solution. Duffy recalls: 'Ruairi Quinn, who was Minister for Labour at the time, was enthusiastic but there appeared not to be a broad consensus. There was a view that they didn't believe that the trade unions could deliver what they would have to deliver for it to work.'

The Government probably realised that any new situation would require the unions to maintain a certain discipline over their members, particularly as regards terms of pay increases, and more generally to accept things that they would find difficult to accept. Given that the trade union movement at the time was outside the process, was looking to 'chase inflation' and was committed to ensuring that there was no reduction in numbers or standards within the public or private sector, the Government probably took the view that the unions would find it difficult to deliver. Ruairi Quinn himself was to complain about the way in which the Labour Party had been 'castigated savagely' by the unions while in power and he compared this with the later 'cave-in' by the unions to the terms of the Programme for National Recovery in 1987 (see *Federation of Irish Employers 1942–1992*, edited by Basil Chubb).

In the 1980s, John Carroll was general secretary of the largest union in the State, the Irish Transport and General Workers' Union (ITGWU), and was Vice President of ICTU in 1986. He feels that the FitzGerald Government did not really have a strategy: 'There was a lot of repartee between myself and Dick Spring at the time. The focus of the Government was on low wage levels and reducing unemployment. They wouldn't gamble as Charlie [Haughey] did on low inflation and tax cuts to offset moderate pay increases.'

John Carroll highlights that there was an underlying fear among unions that the Coalition Government wanted to curb union influence. More pointedly, both the Federated Union of Employers and the Confederation of Irish Industry were 'in the ascendant' as far as views on the economy were concerned.

Peter Cassells recalls that the National Planning Board, which had been established by the FitzGerald Government, made a recommendation that the best way to get out of the crisis was to develop an incomes policy based on a wage freeze. The view was that if 'you could not get it by agreement with the unions then you should legislate for it'. As a result there was a general mindset which suggested that the Government of the day was moving towards strong action. And strong action, as Cassells recalls, generally meant curtailing the unions and wage increases. He remembers one particular set of discussions with the FitzGerald Government:

> One meeting ended up more as a discussion and argument in terms of the national debt between Garret FitzGerald and Donal Nevin, as to whether we were talking about GNP or GDP or what was the scale of the problem and all the rest of it. I think that at that stage people just threw their hat at it on the basis that if this was the level at which we were discussing the problem, it was not on.

The issue of teachers' pay and, in particular, the non-payment of a 10 per cent special pay rise was to cause particular difficulty and act as an early rallying call for the unions who were still fearful of the reverberations from Thatcher's Britain. Unusually, the Government had secured the vote of the Dáil to freeze the pay award, a rare action. This decision brought teachers onto the streets and led to a major rally in their defence in Croke Park, the main stadium of Ireland's Gaelic Athletic Association (GAA). The fear was that similar action could be applied to other pay increases and that an award which was made through the formally agreed processes might never be paid, producing an unacceptable precedent.

Kieran Mulvey, then general secretary of the Association of Secondary Teachers of Ireland (ASTI), says that the experience of that dispute, which went on for twelve months, signalled that there had to be a better way of doing business. He recalls that there were a number of people in the trade union movement who felt that, unless they came to an accommodation with

15

the Government, they would be facing a long war of attrition which no side could win:

> There was beginning to be an understanding between those like myself (who were the new kids on the block) and the old guard of the trade union movement like Paddy Cardiff, John Carroll [and] Christy Kirwan. Certainly on the big union side I would have felt that there was myself, Gerry Quigley (of the INTO) and the teachers and Phil Flynn in the Local Government Union and Dan Murphy within the civil service. There was a burgeoning of people who I feel [were] coming from widely diverse views, and we all considered ourselves to be on the left but it was not the ideo-logical left. We felt we were moving pragmatically in a direction where, subsequently, a lot of others moved.

THE POLITICAL PERSPECTIVE

Alan Dukes recalls meeting leaders of the trade unions in 1986. He remembers that ICTU's Donal Nevin was clearly in sympathy with what the then Taoiseach Garret FitzGerald wanted to achieve. This was to get a common understanding of the nature of the problem and the direction they might take to find a common resolution. On the Government side, prepa-rations were underway for the 1987 Budget, which was going to produce a number of crunch issues with the Labour Party in particular.

At these meeting Dukes was also struck by the tensions between the Labour Party and the trade unions. There was an unstated feeling around, he believes, that the union leaders felt they would get a better deal with Fianna Fáil. He feels that the employers also believed they would 'get a better hearing from Fianna Fáil'. Ultimately, despite being contributors to the Labour Party, there was a perception that unions were more friendly to Fianna Fáil, Ireland's largest political party.

Dukes does not recollect the unions or employers having any fixed ideas about what would resolve the economic crisis at the time. Both sides wanted 'creative ideas' but inevitably differed on what the term actually meant. Dan Murphy recalls the various meetings with the then Taoiseach and his cabinet team. He says that he never got the impression that FitzGerald was interested in a national deal: 'He wasn't unsympathetic to some of the things we wanted but I don't think he ever saw trade unions as having any particular role in that field.'

In the end there was a bust-up over budgetary policy between the Coalition parties and Labour walked out of government in January 1987, only to see the incoming Fianna Fáil Government largely implement the Alan Dukes' Budget. But by this time the unions and the employers realized that they were going to have a different approach from McSharry and Haughey than they had from FitzGerald and Spring.

A NEW GENERATION

Trade union leadership in Ireland underwent significant changes in the 1980s. Much of this change was to facilitate a greater openness to new approaches and a greater willingness to ask new questions in the face of a crisis. Within the public service, leaders such as Phil Flynn of the LGPSU and later IMPACT, Dan Murphy of the PSEU and David Begg of the Postal Telecommunications Workers' Union (PTWU), which later became the Communications Workers' Union, were particularly influential. The appointment in 1988 of a new Assistant General Secretary, Peter Cassells, who openly favoured a tripartite approach along Nordic lines, also facilitated new approaches. The decision to reorganise the ICTU secretariat, including the appointment of two assistant general secretaries to deal with industrial relations and social policy, would also free up Cassells to take a more strategic view.

This new generation of leaders were perceived by both private sector employers and indeed some civil servants as being more attuned to the dynamics of an increasingly competitive economy and also to the impact of global competition. This new generation seemed capable of adopting a more strategic view than their predecessors. They grasped the importance of the European Community and understood that the conventional union wisdom of 'chasing inflation' through successive pay demands had been a failure. More fundamentally, they understood the dynamics of global competition and the challenge posed by Europe and the UK, our main trading partner.

Trade unions in Ireland are credited with adopting a very pragmatic stance towards centralised agreements during the 1970s and 1980s. A number of British-based unions and a small number of Irish craft unions had always opposed such agreements largely on ideological grounds. But, by 1986, some of the Irish craft unions had begun to reassess their traditional opposition to such agreements. Peter Cassells recalls the publication of the

17

ICTU's *Confronting the Jobs Crisis*, which aimed to get the unions focused on what needed to be done:

> *Confronting the Jobs Crisis* was actually a very polemical type document. It didn't read like a submission. It was aimed more at the unions themselves on what needed to be done. We needed to get engaged at a national level and show people that we were serious. In that document we did propose a national effort, a national programme to try and tackle this crisis.

This approach was born out of two perceptions of the problem: first, 'a genuine sense on the part of people that something needed to be done' and, secondly, that they wanted to contribute to a resolution. The second motivator was that, if they did not take this approach, they would be considered a serious part of the problem. Pressed on whether there was a universal view on the best route forward for the unions, Cassell's belief is that, at the time, they viewed their approach as a high risk strategy in terms of pushing things out and bringing people along:

> I suppose you could say that there were sort of three groupings. There were the people who were bogged down in the day-to-day just trying to cope and deal with what was there and particularly the rows that were happening in public service and in the private sector. There were the people who were totally opposed to any sort of incomes policy or dealing with things in this way. And then there were the key leaders who felt that something needed to be done. So I would have thought that, even at the beginning of that process, there probably wasn't a majority of people in favour of it. I think it did require strong leadership to bring it to that phase.

Cassells recalls the Belfast ICTU Annual Conference. A crucial motion from the LGPSU (later to become IMPACT) which called for talks with the Government did not actually feature much debate. Looking back now, Cassells believes that this was because 'I don't think anybody believed it was going to happen.' According to current ICTU General Secretary David Begg, there was a view within trade union circles that the problem had to be dealt with and the main challenge was to act: 'Somebody had to take it by the scruff of the neck.' He said there was a concern that people would embrace proposals that the Thatcher Government had introduced.

So, by 1986, key figures within the trade union movement took the view that the period of free collective bargaining since 1981 had not delivered real take home pay increases or improvements. More fundamentally, it had done nothing to resolve the issue of rising unemployment at a time when trade union membership itself was in decline. A further key issue was that, if anything, trade union influence on government had lessened, despite the presence of the Labour Party in the Government. An independent academic writer at the time, Niamh Hardiman, noted that the trade union movement was likely to enter any talks on a new agreement in a much weaker position than it had been in the 1970s.

NESC AND THE ROAD TO CONSENSUS

The strategy report by the NESC in 1986 provided the platform for agreement on the essential policies needed to address the crisis. The NESC included employer, union and civil service representatives, and it was to play a major part in welding a consensus over economic strategy. The 1986 study, *A Strategy for Development 1986–90*, pinpointed the key requirement for an urgent action plan to tackle the unsolved problem of public expenditure. This unique forum was a 'think tank', not a bargaining arena. Padraig O'hUiginn, its then chairman, was to become secretary of the newly empowered Department of the Taoiseach under the incoming minority Fianna Fáil Government led by Charles Haughey. The NESC was to play a major role in producing the consensus on which the 1987 Programme for National Recovery (PNR) would be based. It concluded that what it termed the twin problems of mass unemployment and chronic fiscal imbalance would have to be tackled at the same time. The NESC was to play this role prior to each of the programmes that followed.

The 1986 report pointed out that, even in the face of a modest upturn in the world economy, the consequent rise in national output would be insufficient to reduce unemployment or to generate a significant improvement in the public finances. Indeed, it added, 'under the more pessimistic scenario for growth output, both unemployment and fiscal imbalances could deteriorate appreciably.'

In time, an economic formula to tackle the national debt, in tandem with cutting expenditure aimed at boosting growth, was debated and later accepted by all sides of the table. Peter Cassells recalls: 'A person who might not like getting part of the credit was Jim O'Leary who was working with the NESC at the time. He was the one who came up with this formula that the way to tackle national debt was to reduce the debt-GNP ratio, which at that stage was about 130 per cent.'

The beauty of this formula was that it could be approached by the parties from either side. Its acceptability to the employers was based on the argument about controlling debt. Alternatively, the resulting impact on growing the gross national product (GNP) appealed to the unions. Cassells recalls that both sides could actually go along with the formula because up to then the FitzGerald Government and others had focused on the current budget deficit each year:

> With this new idea you were concentrating on the overall national debt but saying you can do it by a combination of stimulating growth and cutting the expenditure. So the employers could go along with it on the basis that [they] could argue they cut the debt. We could go along with it by arguing that you really needed to be stimulating as much growth as possible. So, by the time you had the change of government, you had the NESC report. It had actually come out before that change.

By the time the new minority Fianna Fáil Government came in, the key challenge was persuading them to go down that road along the lines recommended by the NESC. According to Peter Cassells, 'I think that if you take the make-up of the NESC, the key person on the employers side at the time was Tom Toner who was the President of IBEC and who had a sense of very strong almost "patriotic duty", or a feeling that where there were big arguments within NESC meetings and that we have to stop cancelling each other out.' Cassells says there was feeling that something had to be done and that 'if we did not stop, we were going to lose a whole generation to emigration. The IMF or somebody would have to come in.' Cassells says it must be remembered that there had been all sorts of changes of government: '. . . all the elections of the 1980s and all the rest of it. I think that we had just a strong sense of "we have to do it now." '

FUE Director General John Dunne notes that the NESC was unique and played a very special role: 'It was important because of its expertise and because of the options it developed in relation to the main policy issues, which were not necessarily shared by all of the parties. But its greatest advantage was that it allowed the main parties to engage without having to commit their organisations.'

This style of debate and interaction depended largely on the trust which was beginning to develop between the key players. It led to the members of the Council being much more open in the NESC about recognising a problem or a direction that was needed. In effect, Dunne remembers that they could be much more open about a problem area than they would necessarily be in the negotiation process itself. Dunne recalls: 'In the formal negotiation itself you were committing and carrying the full weight of your organisation. Nobody would ever quote what you said in the NESC against you, it was that sort of an arrangement. You could say something without it being wrapped around your neck; people could be more open about recognising a problem or a direction that was needed.'

Significant credit is also given by all the parties concerned to then Chairman Padraig O'hUiginn. Con Power recalls him as having 'an extraordinary ability to get people working together. Jim O'Leary, now a lecturer in St Patrick's College Maynooth but then a researcher with the NESC, recalls the workings of the Council in those days: 'At the time, the NESC report itself did not amount to a series of recommendations on pay and determination. The employers at the time stressed that this must be kept at firm level.'

What struck Power most was the common purpose of the people who were involved: 'I remember coming out of some committee meeting one day saying to Liam Connellan (Former Director General of the CII) that "if a person from Mars looked in they would wonder what person represented which organisation." '

In his view the whole process, which lead to the PNR and subsequent agreements, started in the NESC. In retrospect, Power says that he did not see a huge operational role for the politicians: 'I saw a Government giving acceptance to the NESC prescription and then giving the operational role of delivery to Padraig O'hUiginn and the Central Review Committee [the monitoring arm of the PNR].' Looking back he believes it was 'an extraordinarily unusual constituency coming together. From a CII point of view, as economic policy director, I can say hand on heart, that there was a feeling that no government would make the decision.' Power argues that it was the NESC and the social partners coming together which empowered the incoming Government to deal with the country's burgeoning fiscal and monetary problems. In this context, the NESC and the process underlying it became a vehicle for economic transformation. This was to include the development of transport infrastructure, health and education.

O'hUiginn had moved out of the Department of the Taoiseach to take over as chair of the NESC, based on the view that he had become isolated from the Garret FitzGerald-led Fine Gael-Labour Government. Peter Cassells recalls the way O'hUiginn worked with unions and employers in trying to work out the meaning of the strategy in reality. A collection of people who were involved in the process give credit to economist Jim O'Leary – who later attracted controversy for his role in the Government's public pay Benchmarking Body – for coming up with the core economic formula that allowed both union and employer sides to sign up to it.

John Carroll recalls that, when Fianna Fáil came to power in 1987, they initially accepted the policies of the outgoing Fine Gael-Labour Government. But the unions had convinced Charles Haughey that an agreement was essential to move forward, Carroll says. The mood of the country also made it easier to secure an agreement. There was increasing emigration and a sense of disillusionment: 'A lot of left-wing groups, both political and trade unions, felt that outright opposition was the way to go. There was a tendency to reject everything as part of an establishment bureaucracy. And this was reinforced by the rise of Thatcherism, Reaganism and Monetarism which had created a climate which people do not appreciate today.'

ASSESSING THE THATCHERITE INFLUENCE

In reflecting on the policy focus of the 1980s, a key issue is an assessment of the impact of Thatcherite thinking in the UK on the Irish body politic, and indeed on the administrative and civil service system. It is already clear from the remarks of Billy Attley and others that they were much attuned to the danger to them of the Iron Lady's policies surfacing in Ireland and of the downside if the recipe was followed here. But a more central question is to try to gauge the impact of Thatcher's policies among the power mandarins in the most senior government departments. It is clear from the views of some of the politicians themselves that that they did not perceive there was any great advantage to doing a new-style deal with the unions.

The current Taoiseach Bertie Ahern recalls that, on taking office as Minister for Labour in 1987, people at a high level within that Department tried to dissuade him from an engagement with the unions on shaping a national agreement. His response was to simply ignore the advice and instead he went off to meet the unions and employers in the Mansion House, the home of the Lord Mayor of Dublin, an office he held in the same year. Explaining the approach of the civil service, Mr Ahern says that the line 'of the service' would be that 'a lot of these agreements would have been looked at before and that the parties to them weren't real' or, in other words, were not really committed to them. As far as he is concerned, Fianna Fáil were supportive of organised labour and that was the main belief which guided them in their approach.

Paddy Teahon, the former secretary to the Department of the Taoiseach, also recognises that the existence of Thatcher and Thatcherite policies in the country of an immediate neighbour was a significant motivating factor in the Congress support for a new approach. Pressed on whether or not there was some Thatcherite thinking circulating in the Irish administrative system, he replies that that was certainly not the case in the Taoiseach's Department. But he adds: 'I think there were people, including people in the Department of Finance, who would have said, "Where we are is impossible – the labour relations situation, the number of strikes that were taking place. Really, we have to sort that now." ' But he added: 'It would be wrong to say that anybody had developed any kind of Thatcherite programme. That wasn't the case, certainly as far as I'm aware. But there was that crisis-type situation emerging and, who knows, if we hadn't acted on our own part together, if it then became clear that Thatcherite solutions were working after a fashion across the water, who knows whether somebody would have been prepared to put that in place in Ireland.'

For instance, there were fears at the time among people not involved in the trade unions at a senior level that the 'Tallaght Strategy' – named after a speech made by the Fine Gael leader Alan Dukes in the Dublin suburb of Tallaght in which he promised his party's support for the minority Fianna Fáil Government, so long as it pursued spending cutbacks designed to reduce borrowing – could have laid the foundations for a Thatcherite approach. Current SIPTU leader Jack O'Connor is one of those who feels that this might have been the case.

As was widely recognised at the time, even privately by Irish politicians, Thatcherism and its underlying philosophy of restricting union power and opening markets was exerting a major influence on a host of countries. It was seen as a way to shake-up the post-war model of government and consensus building. In the context of tightening public finances across Europe, the Thatcher approach was seen as having potential attractions even for countries that did not have the type of political system which would support or underpin it. But, as we shall see, this was not the path chosen in Ireland, where the main employer and trade union bodies were to forge a new type of consensus, known as social partnership.

CHAPTER 2

The First Programme – Achieving the Breakthrough

NESC deserves the credit for producing the prescription, ICTU deserves the credit for being the catalyst for the political action that followed.

Leading employer figure

The breakthrough that led to the agreement known as the Programme for National Recovery (PNR) was by no means inevitable. It required a unique confluence of events, circumstances and the interplay of influential leaders to forge the first of what turned out to be seven successive national-level partnership agreements.

Trade unions and other representative bodies can respond to a crisis by agreeing to forego immediate gains if the outcome produces growth and recovery. This had occurred in the former Federal Republic of Germany, Austria, the Scandinavian countries and later the Netherlands, when trade unions made sacrifices needed for reconstruction in the aftermath of the Second World War. Ireland's breakthrough agreement in 1987, at the very least, provided a similar platform for the economic and social transformation that followed.

Former Secretary in the Department of the Taoiseach Paddy Teahon suggests that the difference between the time the PNR was achieved (1987) and the period prior to that, is that the Government, the employers, the trade unions and the farmers had at last agreed on a set of broad policies. Everyone was 'pointing in the same direction'. The thrust of these policies had been set out by these same social partners in the National Economic and Social Council's (NESC) 1986 document, *A Strategy for Development, 1986–90*. It had, however, taken a major shift in mindsets, triggered by the financial and economic crisis the country faced, to persuade these often opposed 'social partners' to come together and strike a deal that gave the NESC report a practical form. The report was 'ideology free', according to one of its authors, Jim O'Leary. Later to become a critic of the social partnership process, O'Leary said that the NESC report 'had a relentless internal logic. It concentrated minds.'

The scale of the crisis in the 1980s up to that pivotal year has been well documented. It was as if a permafrost had settled on the political landscape. Former Finance Minister Ray McSharry believes the reason for inaction was simply a matter of 'politics' and no-one was blameless. The Fine Gael-Labour Government of 1983–87 simply could not agree to introduce the sort of savage cuts that economists had been demanding. Nor was it likely that they would have secured a national deal even if they had vigorously pursued it.

The story of how the PNR was achieved ranges over much of 1986 and 1987, covering the final days of the Garret FitzGerald-led Fine Gael-Labour Coalition, the minority Fine Gael administration, Fianna Fáil in opposition and, finally, the early phase of the minority Fianna Fáil Government, led by Charles Haughey.

THE LANDSCAPE OF CRISIS

The severe economic and fiscal crisis of the 1980s, which peaked in 1986–87, essentially forced the social partners and in particular the trade unions into a strategic re-evaluation of incomes policy agreements or the National Understandings, as they had become known.

The crisis threatened the financial stability of the country, even undermining belief in the ability of the political system to cope. Kieran Mulvey, then general secretary of the ASTI, feels that union leaders like John Carroll (ITGWU) and Billy Attley (FWUI) 'were shaping up to a mutual understanding on what needed to be achieved'. They were 'haemorrhaging members', he said. 'People seem to forget that through the late 1970s and into the 1980s it was not unusual to hear of two or three factories closing, usually on a Friday morning. It seemed to be black Friday, every Friday.'

This view was shared by Con Power, the CII's director of policy, who said that in the autumn of 1986 'crisis time' had arrived. Grim unemployment figures and low living standards relative to the EU in general were combined with an 'apparent loss of confidence in the business community in the ability of any government to manage the economy,' Power recalled.

No-one could be found who was other than deeply depressed at the state of the Irish economy, but many believed that it didn't have to be terminal. A combined effort was required, but one that would have to ensure that the interests of each of the main players could also be advanced, insofar as that was achievable. The NESC, which fortunately involved all of the main interest groups, was able at this critical historical juncture to produce a consensual report.

Peter Cassells says previous efforts had always ended up 'with us or the employers having a minority report . . . we suggested, rather than having an annual report, we should go for a three or four year strategy which would include curbing the debt/GNP ratio . . . the employers and ourselves were able to agree on this.' The 1986 report stressed the need to tackle public expenditure and unemployment in an integrated way, involving expenditure cuts and reform of the tax system. The report was the first tangible evidence that this could be done with the backing of influential bodies like IBEC and ICTU.

So why did the NESC not provide the platform for the Fine Gael-Labour Coalition and a breakthrough deal that might have kick-started an earlier economic recovery and breathed some much needed life into an ailing Government?

A TENTATIVE AFFAIR

A tentative effort was made by ICTU and the Fine Gael-Labour Coalition in 1986 to consider whether there was some basis for forging a national approach to the crisis. Ultimately it came to nothing, perhaps because neither side was ready for it. Peter Cassells (then acting general secretary of ICTU) admits that, while the Government of Garret FitzGerald is often criticised for the fact that the PNR didn't happen on their watch, 'to be fair to both sides, I don't think either side was probably capable of pulling it off at that stage because the conditions weren't right.' Or perhaps it was the case that, by then, ICTU had decided that Fianna Fáil was almost certainly going to be the dominant political party in government after the next general election.

27

Garret FitzGerald himself later acknowledged that a consensus would have been unlikely in the prevailing circumstances: 'We would like to have achieved an agreement like that of 1987 [the PNR] while in office, but the subject could not have even been broached until we had completed the process of winding down the inflation we had inherited. Quite apart from that, the unions were too hostile during our period in office; we got absolutely no co-operation from them' (see Chubb's *Federation of Irish Employers 1942–1992*). Former IMPACT General Secretary Phil Flynn denies that the unions were overly hostile: 'Some of us had private discussions with [Labour's] Ruairi Quinn and we would tease out issues with him. Quinn couldn't deliver because FitzGerald, as an orthodox economist, couldn't get his head around it.' Flynn, however, is at one with Cassells in not entirely blaming FitzGerald for this: 'The previous types of national agreements were more honoured in the breach than in the observance. You couldn't blame him to some extent.'

A clue to FitzGerald's attitude, which may have made a corporatist approach well-nigh impossible, is contained in his memoir, *All in a Life*. Looking back from the perspective of 1990, he wrote that his main reason for joining Fine Gael rather than the Labour Party was a belief that the latter's 'dependence on the trade union movement was a negative factor so far as I was concerned. I did not like the idea of a political party being tied to a sectoral interest, even one representing as large a group as the organised labour force.' Later still, Padraig O'hUiginn, a senior civil servant under both FitzGerald and Haughey, claimed that 'Fine Gael and Labour opposed it [the PNR] on the basis that it gave too much power to the social partners. That fault line ran through everything.'

Alan Dukes – former Minister for Finance and, as leader of Fine Gael in opposition after FitzGerald, the instrument of the Tallaght Strategy – remembers a series of tentative talks in the summer of 1986, just prior to publication of the NESC report. He wasn't at the talks, 'being in a sense a "red rag to a bull" to both the unions and employers who found me entirely unsympathetic!' He puts his unpopularity down to the fairly thankless role he played as Minister for Finance at a time of financial stringency. However, Alan Dukes recalls that senior trade union leaders were 'doing their level best to keep the lid on a fairly disgruntled membership.' He also believed that the same union leaders were feeling the pressure from emerging groups like the Irish National Organisation of the Unemployed (INOU).

So why didn't the Fine Gael-Labour talks get anywhere? According to Alan Dukes, 'Looking back, history illustrates this – my suspicion is that both the trade unions and the employers felt that if they came to any kind of understanding it wouldn't last because the Government wouldn't be around for long. We had arguably left it too late in the life of the Government.'

LABOUR AND THE UNIONS

The tension between Labour and the trade unions was also palpable. Some years later, Ruairi Quinn, as part of a considered explanation of the problems between the two traditional 'arms' of the labour movement, touched on their poor relationship: 'When we were in government, the trade union movement had castigated the Labour Party savagely, and in some cases personally' (see Chubb's *Federation of Irish Employers 1942–1992*). Alan Dukes says that these tensions surprised him: 'There was a feeling that the unions took the view that they would get a more sympathetic hearing from Fianna Fáil than they were getting from Fine Gael and Labour.' He also believes that the employers thought the same way.

Looking back at that period, Ruairi Quinn says that, in the aftermath of the breakthrough on the Programme for National Recovery, he told his parliamentary party colleagues to 'leave aside feelings of personal hurt and accept why trade union leaders had co-operated so enthusiastically with Fianna Fáil.' The union leaders had, he believes, received 'the shock of their lives' with the emergence of the Progressive Democrats, while in the UK the economy was booming and 'Maggie Thatcher was riding very high.'

Both Dukes and Quinn consider the emergence of Margaret Thatcher in Britain as a significant factor in conditioning trade union thinking in Ireland. Trade union leaders have consistently confirmed this view. Dukes recalls that one of the favourite terms of abuse when he was in office was the 'Thatcherite' aphorism, which was often applied to him. He maintains that Garret FitzGerald, even after Labour had rejected the Coalition's last Budget leaving Fine Gael to 'go it alone', never had any intention of copying the British Prime Minister.

The then ITGWU General Secretary John Carroll believes that the FitzGerald Government didn't have a strategy: 'They wouldn't gamble, as Charlie [Haughey] did, on low inflation and tax cuts to offset moderate pay increases. He took that decision against his advisors, and he deserves credit for that.'

A QUESTION OF TIMING?

At any rate, the NESC report may simply have arrived just too late for the Fine Gael-Labour Coalition Government. It was already straining at the seams in 1986 due to fundamental differences over how to tackle the worsening financial and general economic crisis. Negotiating a national pact in the context of such division and uncertainty was not a pragmatic option. The Fine Gael-Labour Government was in deep disarray, facing inevitable break-up over proposed budgetary cuts sought by Fine Gael but opposed by Labour. Alan Dukes believes that the real time for that Government to have worked on a national pact would have been in its early years. One senior employer figure recalled that Dukes, 'if he had the power to do so, would have acted some years before'.

This opens up the tantalising prospect that earlier action could have triggered a recovery much sooner than 1987. This 'what if?' question, Ray McSharry suggests, could equally be asked of the 1982 Fianna Fáil administration, which was defeated on its mini-budget of that year. The approach taken in that mini-Budget was really a prototype of that which McSharry adopted as Minister for Finance in far less severe national circumstances five years later.

According to John Carroll, the crisis reached the stage where the FitzGerald Government was going to do 'all sorts of dire things' to bring the public finances under control. Against that background they asked his Government to take a national approach, 'not just to address wages policy but social policy as well, on the understanding that trade union members would endure such a policy.' Carroll suggests that the old ITGWU was 'in essence' the prime mover in this regard: 'The public sector unions were secondary to the general union approach.'

Perhaps the Fine Gael-Labour Government (1983–87) also lacked the sort of personalities that the trade unions felt at ease with. SIPTU's Jack O'Connor certainly takes this view. The PNR 'would not have happened without Haughey. Full stop. He and Bertie Ahern understood the subtlety of Irish politics.' Haughey, whose business connections have been well documented, was also very comfortable around trade union leaders like the ITGWU's Mickey Mullen and John Carroll, with whom he lunched regularly. Carroll himself played an unassuming but influential role in the move towards consensus. Phil Flynn says the attitude of many trade union leaders towards Fianna Fáil was a pragmatic one: 'They just had to deal with the Government and represent their members and get on with it.' These important relationships and the pragmatic, rather than ideological, approach of a majority of Irish trade unions were two elements that would now coalesce in circumstances of national crisis.

John Carroll believes that, when the minority Haughey-led Fianna Fáil Government came to power in 1987, despite Haughey's orientation towards some national-level agreement, the economic crisis also meant that 'they were on the same wavelength as Fine Gael. The Tallaght Strategy meant there was a common approach by Fianna Fáil, Fine Gael and the PDs.' Carroll says that the persuaders on the union side who believed that a national approach was the best way for the country to work its way out of the crisis 'broke through the crust and convinced Charlie, and then he had the courage to go against his advisors'. According to Carroll, they had also to persuade the doubters on their own side: 'It was hard to convince people to go back to national agreements. A lot of left-wing groups felt outright opposition. There was a tendency to reject everything as part of an establishment bureaucracy.'

Charlie McCreevy, Haughey's one-time opponent in Fianna Fáil and later an admirer, recalls: 'You must remember the times we were in. We were banjaxed and everyone knew it, including the lads in the trade unions.' He believes it would not have happened but for Haughey: 'Charlie knows what makes big lads get up in the morning, knows what ordinary people think about. This will offend everyone: Haughey had a great rounded social view of life. He might have lived in the big house but he understood how important it is to keep people together.' Phil Flynn recalls a private conversation with Haughey at the time about what needed to be done and how to turn the economy around: 'He said to me, "Young man, you are absolutely right, except there is one essential ingredient missing. It's hard to quantify, difficult to identify with, but without it we go nowhere." And I said to him, "What's that?" He replied, "Confidence. That's the real merit of what we are trying to do. We are trying to instill confidence in the country, in the economy. And if we do it properly then it will take off".'

A SHARED BLUEPRINT

The unanimity of the social partners gave the 1986 NESC strategy report an important moral authority. The incoming minority Fianna Fáil Government also endorsed it, and then used it as a basis for negotiating an agreement for which there could be widespread support. Even before the NESC report was published, however, the opposition Fianna Fáil party and its leader Charles Haughey and labour spokesman Bertie Ahern, building on long established contacts and relationships, had been making overtures to the trade unions.

Haughey's view of social partnership was deeply influenced by the thinking of his father-in-law and former Taoiseach, Sean Lemass. During his wilderness years after the Arms Trial – when he was accused of attempting to import arms for the IRA and was sacked from the Fianna Fáil front bench for several years, despite his subsequent aquittal – Haughey devoted considerable thought to economic issues. He did not allow his return to the Fianna Fáil front bench in 1975 as spokesman on health to inhibit him from addressing wider concerns. That same year he told the Dublin Society of Chartered Accountants that it was a futile exercise to 'formulate an economic plan without the wage-bargaining process built into it, to propose courses of action and hope that the trade unions will be persuaded by exhortation and admonition to fall in line.' He added that

> [to] stabilise wage claims we must channel the expectations and strength behind them towards co-operative effort to achieve economic expansion. The vehicle for that effort can only be participative economic planning, which clearly demonstrates what real growth in living standards and employment can be attained in future if wage claims are contained now. If the planning process does not permit trade union power to be exercised in developing the economic system we must not be surprised if it seeks its own ends independently (see Martin Mansergh's 1986 book *The Spirit of the Nation*).

This exposition was, in essence, a rationale for social partnership. The experience of the 'free-for-all' of the mid-1980s did nothing to alter his views and, from the 1970s onwards, he had made a point of meeting regularly with leading figures in the trade unions, and to keep in touch with thinking in the movement. The first of these was then ITGWU General

Secretary Mickey Mullen. Haughey became interested in forging a new, more structured, social contract between the Government, unions and employers during his brief terms as Taoiseach in the early 1980s. During this period he came into contact with EU leaders who had corporatist systems for dealing with industrial relations problems. In an interview in early 2001, Haughey recalled being particularly impressed by the German Chancellor and SPD leader Helmut Schmidt, whom he questioned at length about the German model of industrial relations.

THE COURTSHIP BEGINS

Towards the end of the so-called pay 'free-for-all' period 1981–87, stronger signals had started to emerge that a return to centralised bargaining could be on the cards. In the shadow of the almost inevitable general election of February 1987, Fianna Fáil had proposed the creation of 'a national consensus', which in itself was regarded as a response to earlier initiatives made by ICTU. The influential 1985 ICTU document, *Confronting the Jobs Crisis*, had been around sometime and was followed by a motion at the 1986 annual ICTU conference in Belfast, which backed entry into national talks.

Bertie Ahern recalls that a party 'think tank' had been established by him and sympathetic trade unionists as far back as 1985. They were interested in the success of the Nordic model. After ICTU came out with its Jobs Crisis document, Ahern says his group decided to 'feed into' it, seeking out Haughey and securing his commitment to engage with the unions. Ahern also recalls that Fianna Fáil, which had not met the trade unions 'as a political party' for 35 years, met with an ICTU delegation at Raglan Road, led by Haughey and his front bench. This meeting was an important milestone and indicated that a government-trade union-employer consensus was a real possibility after the 1987 election, which returned a minority Fianna Fáil administration.

Kieran Mulvey recalls that the message from Haughey essentially was: 'if I am elected, my door is open to the trade union movement if a deal needs to be done.' Haughey and his colleagues knew that if they achieved office they had some hard decisions to make. 'They needed to be able to take them in the context of a structured agreement with the unions, [so] that in the likelihood of a potential bust-up, they had a forum in which to negotiate.'

A CHAMPION OF CONSENSUS

Bertie Ahern remembers that when the prospect of a national agreement was first raised after the minority Fianna Fáil Government assumed office, the advice within the civil service was to 'stay away from it.' However, the concept had a major champion in Padraig O'hUiginn, secretary in the emerging Taoiseach's Department, who had already played a crucial role as chairman of the NESC. O'hUiginn was regarded as a person with an extraordinary facility to get people working together and get them to focus on solutions. Without him it is possible that the talks would have foundered.

One leading employer said O'hUiginn 'could walk on water. I mean that, it's not a throwaway remark.' This is a view strongly shared by all shades of opinion, not least by the former Minister for Finance Charlie McCreevy, who later recalled: 'O'hUiginn is the smartest civil servant, the smartest person I ever met. If he didn't have a solution, then there "ain't no solution". His role was at least equal to [Ken] Whittaker, if not greater.'

In other words, O'hUiginn was an invaluable player in the search for a national pact built around the NESC report. He was also the first in a succession of talented secretary generals in the Taoiseach's Department, all with a firm grasp of and commitment to what gradually became known as the partnership model.

INFLUENTIAL DEVELOPMENTS

Billy Attley, who had proposed entering talks at an FWUI meeting in Salthill, explains what was stirring among like-minded colleagues such as Peter Cassells, John Carroll, Eddie Browne, Phil Flynn and Dan Murphy at the time: 'We were really impressed with the Scandinavian model. They had a 'virtuous circle' which led to improved living standards and they took on all the headcases.' This was a reference to those who loved, as he colourfully put it, 'this free collective bargaining rubbish and [who] were stuck in the past.'

The CII, another participant in the NESC, had even used the term 'programme for national recovery' in a document it had issued as far back as November 1986. Fianna Fáil used it as the title for its own general election manifesto in 1987. So the scene looked set for a possible return to central level agreements of the type that had not been seen since 1980, at least if the 'price' for all sides was right. Haughey's minority Fianna Fáil Government lost no time in putting the trade unions in the picture in this regard. Bertie

Ahern recalls that the new Finance Minister Ray McSharry met the Public Services Committee of ICTU and told them 'the place was bust.'

Ahern recalls, as Minister for Labour, being warned off a deal with the unions by some civil servants. But he ignored that advice. There was also some resistance to the idea within his own Department of Labour: 'I think the line would have been that a lot of these agreements had been looked at before and the parties to them weren't [being] real.' This skepticism mirrored the concern of private sector employers who didn't believe the trade unions would stick to a pay deal. Rosheen Callender, then in SIPTU's research department, recalls a 'general contempt for trade unions'. In the mid 1980s, 'you didn't get to meet ministers. National agreements later changed the perception of the trade union movement within the civil service.' The upgrading of the Department of the Taoiseach was crucial, given that its Secretary General Padraig O'hUiginn was chairman of the NESC, a firm supporter of the concept of social partnership and was very much in tune with the new Taoiseach Mr Haughey.

The trade unions, as we have seen, were also acutely aware of their own vulnerability at this time, given the battering which the unions in Britain had been taking since the election of the Thatcher Government in 1979. Dan Murphy says the Irish trade union movement, with the important exception of the British based unions here, had a more pragmatic approach than their colleagues in the UK: 'The Government is the Government, you deal with it. Fianna Fáil is pragmatic, not ideological. There was no appetite for conflict in society.' Employer leaders like John Dunne and Con Power strongly shared the view that the 'Thatcher approach' was not the way to go about resolving the Irish crisis.

The trade unions were under pressure. Declining membership, falling living standards, rising taxation, and fears about privatisation and possible tough labour legislation persuaded many of the leading trade union thinkers that a return to national agreements would also be the best option to protect their institutional interests and the interests of the membership. However, the Fianna Fáil Government, despite ICTU's commitment to the NESC strategy, knew that the unions would have to face up to some tough decisions on public spending. The minority Government also had to be convinced that the trade unions were ready to swallow some unpalatable medicine. As Peter Cassells explains: 'They did not really believe that we had the capacity to deal with the national debt problem. We deliberately entitled our document [ICTU's proposal to the Government] in such a way

35

that it dealt with the four issues of national debt, tax reform, jobs, social services. We inter-linked them. I specifically recall that Haughey's reaction was, "well, are you serious about dealing with the national debt?"'

CLEAR SIGNALS

A significant harbinger of developments to come occurred in May 1987 when the General Secretary of the Local Government and Public Services Union (LGPSU) Phil Flynn invited the new Taoiseach to the union's annual dinner. The invitation came after the new minority Government's first Budget in April 1987 which, given the level of spending cuts it contained, had shocked the trade unions. It was the sort of budget that the unions would have found inconceivable a few years earlier.

The new Fianna Fáil Minister for Finance went even further than his Fine Gael predecessor John Bruton had proposed to go, aiming for a current budget deficit of 6.9 per cent – a full 0.5 per cent below Mr Bruton's target. A 2 per cent pay increase due under the old pay round system (the 25th) for public servants was to be honoured, but there were to be no 'special' pay increases other than those already approved; no provision for a 26th round increase; no filling of civil service vacancies without the Minister's permission; and no recruitment in the health boards. The public service unions were also faced with a highly significant watershed when the Minister announced a voluntary severance and early retirement package for public servants. (Some 20,000 public servants were to leave under the package with no shortage of volunteers, as it turned out.)

Ray McSharry says that as Minister for Finance he was 'always the bad boy, saying "we could not do this or that" and trying to put the breaks on things, because we were in serious trouble'. The International Monetary Fund (IMF) was knocking on the door. 'So it wasn't easy, that's why I say politics has as much to do with it as anything else.' Everybody realised after the 1987 election things had to change. According to McSharry 'It was a minority Government. Fine Gael or the PDs could have turned around any day and put us out. We were in there with that Finance Bill through June and July, balancing Fine Gael against the PDs. There were hundreds of amendments. To give in to some would be to give in to all.' The Tallaght Strategy, when it came in, made it a 'little easier on the political side'.

It is in the context of this financial stringency that the LGPSU's invitation to Mr Haughey to attend its conference dinner must be placed. It came not long after the very harsh Budget of 1987, with cutbacks in health particularly tough. The union's leader Phil Flynn had been left out in the cold by the previous Fine Gael-Labour Coalition Government because of his membership of Sinn Féin. Haughey had no such quibbles and told union delegates at the dinner – the first ever attended by a Taoiseach – that, as recommended by the NESC, the proposed recovery programme would be based on four principal elements: fiscal policy, tax reform, social equity and development measures. The levels of pay and conditions of employment that would be obtained during the period of the programme 'will be an essential element to be settled within the framework of the general economic programme.'

IMPACT's Peter McLoone recalls that the Minister for Health Rory O'Hanlon was also there but was greeted with 'stony silence' due to the savage cuts in health that were already underway. Padraig Flynn was invited to address the union's local government section, and fared little better than his colleague in Health. But it was different in the case of Haughey. According to McLoone:

> I was put in charge of making sure he got in and out of the place safely. I couldn't get him away from the table after the dinner. For nearly three quarters of an hour members were queuing up to have their photographs taken with him or get his autograph. He turned to P.J. Mara [his press advisor], saying to him, 'you told me I wasn't popular with people because of all this [the expenditure cuts].' There was just something about him. He retained peoples' confidence, despite the fact that they were enduring a lot of suffering and pain. It was an extraordinary period.

GETTING THE EMPLOYERS ON BOARD

The new Government, while it independently made these tough decisions, including a raft of other almost daily expenditure cuts (as Ray McSharry later recalled), was careful not to alienate the trade unions. McSharry had ruled out new 'special pay' claims given the state of the national finances, but he still adhered to the principle of consultation. It was a distinction that the trade unions appreciated. Discussions were arranged with the unions involved, a form of protocol which, on the face of it, may seem trivial. But it was to prove to be a consistent government policy in subsequent years and set down a way of doing business that remains today.

Therefore, by the late summer of 1987, it remained for the Government to persuade the employers to come to the negotiating table to discuss the one key element needed to cement a national agreement – a pay deal. Even after the Government had signalled its intentions in the 1987 Budget, some commentators were of the view that the FUE could not be persuaded to negotiate a centralised pay arrangement, given its negative reaction to employer experiences under the National Understandings of 1979 and 1980. Chapters 5 and 6 explore this more fully. But suffice to say that, for private sector employers, the issue of adherence to the strict terms of agreed pay deals would be a *sine quo non* this time around.

Haughey indicated to the unions that arrangements were being made to hold talks with employer and farming bodies on such a programme. The initial emphasis would be on bilateral talks between the Government and ICTU. A Ministerial ICTU group was to meet monthly to deal with pay and other income matters, and three joint government-ICTU working parties, meeting at least weekly, were established to deal with employment and development measures, taxation and social welfare.

The Government's firm action in tackling the country's fiscal problems had a big impact on the employer organisations. What may loosely be described as moral or personal persuasion, which the Government placed on the FUE, also helped to convince the employer body to participate in a pay agreement. The tough Budget of 1987 and the voluntary severance deal in the public sector had sent an unmistakable message to employer leaders who had been demanding such measures for years. They knew that the new Government was serious.

The employer side also appreciated the efforts made by ICTU leaders. As one senior figure who understood the politics of the emerging consensus says: 'We had been preaching to successive governments since 1981 but our voice had fallen on deaf ears. The clout to "rivet" the attention of the politicians was the involvement of ICTU, not the CII, not the old FUE or the farmers.'

How could the employers refuse to conclude a pay deal, even if they had grown used to dealing on a 'free-for-all' basis? They didn't want a return to what FUE Director General Dan McCauley describes as their 'experience' in 1981, during the breakdown of the National Understanding. But eventually 'the view was held that, if there is going to be an effective overall national policy for economic recovery, then we'd better be part of it and we should be part of it.' Former President of the FUE Tom Toner was one employer leader in particular whom Peter Cassells recalls as having a very strong sense of 'patriotic duty' at that time.

THE HAUGHEY FACTOR

It would appear the FUE was also put under a considerable degree of pressure to enter the talks on a pay deal. Then, once it became involved in the actual pay negotiations, the FUE had to be persuaded to take a more flexible approach after it had initially adopted a stance that Billy Attley describes as 'hard as nails'. According to this account of the negotiations, the FUE's official negotiators were effectively bypassed, with the Taoiseach calling in the 'big boys', a reference to major and influential employers. Apparently the Taoiseach told them: 'You want to make no contribution to this. He went for them baldheaded. Next day things started to move.' Phil Flynn recalls that the employers were concerned a pay deal wouldn't hold: 'They had concerns that whatever was agreed would become a floor. It was legitimate enough, given their experience.'

The employer leaders of the period have subtly different recollections of this critical stage of the breakthrough that gave birth to the PNR. They all agree the negotiating team was representative of a large cross-section of the membership, with the core team comprised of key FUE executives, as well as the President and Vice-President of the organisation. Director General Dan McCauley recalls that the only pressure brought to bear was when the Taoiseach said the pay deal on the table would be offered to the public sector unions if the employers refused to do business. This meant it would act as a sort of 'benchmark' for the private sector.

Turlough O'Sullivan, then a key negotiator on the FUE team, says Haughey had come into the FUE headquarters. Did he play a major role in 'delivering' the employers? 'It would be fair to say that', recalls O'Sullivan, 'because we were skeptical. Employers were affected by the national interest and by the persuasiveness of Haughey at the time.' Therefore, a combination of tough government action on the economy, a tinge of disappointment with the outcome of the 'free-for-all' period and a level of moral pressure helped to convince the FUE and its membership to re-engage with national agreements for the first time since 1980.

Haughey himself said that 'once the Government and the unions had agreed on a common approach, the employers had to go along with it.' His political instinct to make a play for the union constituency while in opposition had paid off. He had a big impact on the trade union negotiators too. Billy Attley recalls that 'he would walk in, go swanning around shaking hands and then make a big speech [and tell us] about how important this is historically and that we would look back on the day that we pulled the country around.'

The PNR talks were not overly complicated; certainly they were a lot more straightforward than the process was to become in later agreements. Nonetheless, some core principles were laid down and these still apply today. The following description by Billy Attley sums up the essence of the approach, which was later to become strongly associated with then Labour Minister and future Taoiseach, Bertie Ahern:

> Negotiations go through three or four phases. The first is the programme on behalf of the proletariat, thumping each other, then it's down to business and then there's the hard graft, trying to sort this out. And suddenly this change happens where it becomes problem-solving rather than negotiations, a recognition of the problems on either side and trying to construct formulae to deal with the problems. Then it gets to the point where people have put so much time and effort into it they can't conceivably allow it to collapse because they have invested so much time in the process. So the longer it goes on, the better chance you have of success.

The pay deal was, of course, a modest 2.5 per cent a year over three years, a 'no brainer' as employers like Dan McCauley and Turlough O'Sullivan later agreed, at least once the issue of compliance was addressed. Of course, this was ultimately not as minimalist as it seemed at the time, given the parallel tax reductions and a rapid fall in inflation. The negotiation of a one hour reduction in the working week was a stumbling block for the FUE, but for ICTU this was a considerable concession at the time.

Critically, the public service unions were kept 'onside'. It was agreed that the public service pay arrangements in the deal would not impinge on the integrity of the conciliation and arbitration (C&A) system, which covered the majority of civil servants. A timetable to cover payment of any 'special' pay awards made under the C&A system was also part of the deal.

'MISE ÉIRE'

The launch of the PNR was a fairly formal affair for the time, although in retrospect it would come to seem quite modest. Charles Haughey understood public relations instinctively. To the strains of Sean O'Riada's 'Mise Éire', the social partners and media assembled in the conference rooms of the Burlington Hotel. However, right up to the late afternoon launch time there was a concern that some players on the trade union side would try to lever a last minute concession by refusing to 'sign'.

Billy Attley recalls taking a call from Peter Cassells just hours before the event: 'He told me they're not going to recommend it. I said, "what?!"' Apparently there was a problem about lay-offs somewhere in the public sector and some unions were ready to hold up the launch. But it went ahead anyway, with those 'in the know' waiting to see what would happen next. Attley describes the scene:

> The ministers were already there, sitting in front. The next thing the doors swing open and O'hUiginn walks in and says, 'the Taoiseach has arrived.' And he [Haughey] would walk in like Julius Fucking Caesar and everyone would stand up. And he would be shaking hands [saying], 'Gentlemen how are you? What's the problem?' When Haughey was told what the problem was, he said 'that's very helpful.' He went 'rhubarb, rhubarb, rhubarb'. I was sitting there watching all this and I was think-ing, 'this is a like a fucking play.'

Attley says that the union people with 'the problem' said nothing at all in the end and the announcement of what was to become an historic deal was made. Despite this hiccup, which dared not speak its name, the union leaders who had been advocating a new approach to the crisis had won the day. Their work in helping to leverage this milestone has been acknowl-edged by many. Perhaps the remark by FUE Director John Dunne, all the more powerful as it came from the employer 'side', sums up the scale of their achievement: 'The same people, if they hadn't been in the trade union movement, would have been CEOs of some of Ireland's biggest companies. That's a reality. They were substantial people. They showed and demon-strated very significant leadership qualities.'

CHAPTER 3

The First Ten Years – The 'Virtuous Circle' starts to Turn

The national agreements were a huge help when selling Ireland to foreign companies. The UK could not offer the same sort of assurances about the stability of the environment.
Kieran McGowan, IDA chief executive, 1991–1998

The entire social partnership experience has spanned over twenty years, roughly divided into two phases. The period with which this chapter is concerned, from 1987 up to the end of 1996, brought about three agreements: the PNR (1987–90), the Programme for Economic and Social Progress (PESP) (1990–93) and the Programme for Competitiveness and Work (PCW) (1994–96). The second phase, from 1997 to the present day, delivered four subsequent agreements: Partnership 2000, the Programme for Prosperity and Fairness (PPF), Sustaining Progress (SP) and Towards 2016.

Partnership 2000 in 1997 can be said to mark the real beginning of the so-called Celtic Tiger phenomenon, which has attracted so much international attention to the 'Irish model'. The economy had already taken off, but it was only after 1996 that our huge jobs boom truly occured, an achievement that saw Ireland's unemployment rate fall from the 18 per cent high watermark of 1987 to just over 4 per cent today. In 1996, this was hardly foreseeable. Indeed, what had been achieved up to that point had been remarkable enough. Something approaching a national redemption had already occurred. Ireland had not 'gone under', its political system and society proving more resilient than was feared in the dark days of 1986 and 1987.

One senior civil servant was later to remark that the ability of the political institutions to cope with the scale of the problem was seriously questioned during that earlier period: 'There was talk of presidential systems, cabinets [being] brought in from outside and so on. It was a very disheartening period because, as civil servants, you felt helpless to deal with it.' The social partners played a pivotal role in helping the State escape this trough, an achievement that paved the way to helping Ireland at last 'join the world', as political scientist Tom Garvin puts it in his insightful and brilliant book, *Preventing the Future*.

Successful economic and industrial relations outcomes are an essential requirement for the success of any social partner-style system, whether it is in Ireland or in other countries associated with what has become known in the academic literature as corporatism, or neo-corporatism. Countries like Germany, Switzerland, Austria, Norway, Sweden and the Netherlands, where various models of this sort operated, were marked by low levels of strike activity, low inflation, high employment, the maintenance of steady increases in living standards and the continuation of the 'social wage' as a key part of the corporatist 'trade-off'.

Most of these criteria were to be broadly fulfilled in the first ten years of Ireland's twenty-year social partnership story. The economic recovery since 1987 placed the Irish economy among the top performers in several international league charts. Sustained growth, low inflation, rising living standards, employment growth, a strong international balance of payments and a consolidation of the fiscal position were the most noteworthy positive features. But the most critical 'win' of all – the ending of mass unemployment – had to wait until the second ten years, and the emergence of the 'Tiger' economy. It is the first ten years that concern us here, the years that followed on from the crucial first PNR agreement in 1987.

Secretary General of the Department of the Taoiseach Dermot McCarthy believes social partnership was immediately responsible for the 'very successful, sharp, but painful fiscal adjustment in the late 1980s'. It was inconceivable, in his view, that this could have happened without a societal consensus, and 'buy-ins that enabled trade unions, with great courage, to sign up to very moderate deals which looked daft by comparison to what they had been pushing for in earlier deals. It required the employers to go along with that too.'

Any assessment of the outcomes must consider how the programmes squared up to the objectives that all 'sides' held in common and how objectives specific to each of the social partners were met. Agreed or common objectives have proven to be crucial in ensuring that difficult issues or disputes involving any of the partners have not led to the break-up of the agreements. Nonetheless, no one party would stick with a process without their own interest group-specific perspectives also being met. Each, in turn, had to manage their respective constituencies.

WHAT THEY EXPECTED TO GET

The trade union movement, or the majority of ICTU unions who backed partnership, had a number of distinct but related objectives on entering social partnership: the goals of improved living standards through rising real disposable income; lower taxation on members; improved levels of social spending; greater social equity; increased employment and the alleviation of the plight of the unemployed; (initially) the prevention of privatisation; and to ensure that any changes in labour legislation were not inimical to the interests of the trade union movement as a whole. There were also what are perhaps best described as 'institutional' objectives, such as the maintenance of trade union membership levels; the retention of, or improvements in, existing pay systems (with particular emphasis on the public sector); the avoidance of the 'British experience' of the 1980s; and an attempt to ensure that the trade union movement – through ICTU – would continue to have an input into government decisions where these impinged directly on the interests of the movement.

These issues were regularly debated at ICTU conferences, including the special conferences held to ratify the decision made by union members, mostly by secret ballot. Scepticism about the PNR ran deep in some unions. While opposition was concentrated mainly in the private sector, in British-based and in some Irish craft unions, it also included a significant minority of members in the ITGWU and the FWUI. When Jim Eadie, Irish Secretary of the National Union of Journalists (NUJ), proposed a motion at the 1989 ICTU annual conference that affiliates 'consider' withdrawal from the PNR, it was carried by 139 votes to 125, despite vehement opposition from the top table. Billy Attley, then general secretary of the FWUI, attributes the upset to the fact that

> It was the only sunny day of the week and they [the delegates] were all down in the pub. It was Peter Cassells' [ICTU General Secretary] first

conference and he was trying to reply to the debate. I looked around and knew we were fucked. So I said to him, 'I'm going to reply to this debate', and he said, 'why?' I told him: 'This is your first conference, your first speech and you can't be defeated. It won't damage me as much as you.' All the people who would have voted for us were in the pub and we lost narrowly.

The vote at the subsequent Special Delegate Conference calling to withdraw from the PNR was far from a foregone conclusion. The vote to stay in was 180 and the vote to withdraw was 141, the narrowest margin on any national agreement. It was also the last Special Delegate Conference where delegates from Northern Ireland were allowed to vote on social partnership agreements in the Republic. The debate exposed a growing divergence in outlook and strategies between North and South. When Goretti Horgan of the Derry Trades Council denounced the PNR and said, 'the Irish working class haven't created the economic crisis. We should not pay for it,' she was heckled by southern delegates. The debate showed that differences between unions North and South were, in some ways, bigger than between unions and employers in the Republic.

Another important change south of the border in the 1987–96 period, was the degree of rationalisation within the Irish trade union movement. The most important merger was the formation of the Services, Industrial, Professional and Technical Union (SIPTU) through the coming together of the ITGWU and the FWUI. It was Ireland's largest general union with members spread across the private and public sectors. Traditionally, both the FWUI and the ITGWU had been favourably disposed towards centralised bargaining. Another important merger was that of three public service unions to form IMPACT. Both SIPTU and IMPACT staunchly backed the centralised bargaining strategy. Paradoxically, the actual number of votes in favour of agreements did not rise proportionately because votes at special ICTU decision-making conferences are weighted proportionally against larger affiliates. However, if the votes of SIPTU and IMPACT were less than the sum of their parts in voting terms, their informal influence increased because they came close to representing the majority of unionised workers in both the public and private sectors, had some of the most democratic internal decision-making processes and could draw on greater reserves than anyone else of potential industrial muscle and expertise in areas such as research and communications.

(This process seems set to continue. Not alone have a number of smaller craft-based unions merged to form organisations such as BATU and the Technical, Engineering and Electrical Union (TEEU), but we may be witnessing the emergence of the first global union to have an Irish dimension. This is the amalgamation of Amicus and the Transport and General Workers' Union (TGWU), which both have a strong base in Ireland with the US-based United Steel Workers. The Amalgamated Transport and General Workers' Union (ATGWU), as the TGWU is better known in Ireland, has consistently opposed national agreements. The support of Amicus for centralised bargaining has been conditional and the emergence of a large union reflecting the predominantly adversarial industrial relations culture of Britain and the US, could have implications for the internal dynamics of ICTU over the longer term.)

The enormous size of SIPTU in membership terms, relative to the rest of the movement, placed the union in a very powerful position as regards centralised bargaining. At any point from the PNR onwards, if SIPTU members had chosen not to want an agreement then there would have been little chance of a deal, or no point in the employer side agreeing one. It must be remembered that ICTU could not impose sanctions on constituent unions if they breached the terms of a national pay agreement. So even if an agreement was passed by a majority of ICTU delegates, but with SIPTU voting against, the prospect of it working would be slim.

Over the period 1987–96 SIPTU, IMPACT and several public sector unions continued to bolster support for social partnership. But there was also a gradual shift away from traditional outright hostility on the part of some, by no means all, craft and white collar unions toward centralised bargaining. Much of the opposition was located in British-based unions like the ATGWU and the Association of Scientific, Technical and Managerial Staffs (ASTMS – later the MSF), reflecting a strong ideological distaste for incomes policies among UK trade unions generally. In 1993, however, the MSF decided to back negotiations on a new programme (the PCW) and, while the subsequent terms were rejected by the union, the MSF eventually became a staunch supporter of the process.

By the 1990s, craft workers, due to a variety of technological changes, were no longer in a position to be as powerful a force within the trade union movement. Their ability to pursue higher than average pay increases was already diminishing by 1987. Indeed, some of the smaller craft unions were persuaded that their interests would be best served within the context

47

of national agreements. Billy Attley says the construction unions in particular became quite adept at securing their interests in national talks. Former Electrical, Electronic, Telecommunications and Plumbing Union (EETPU) General Secretary Mick Brennan, addressing delegates at the special ICTU conference in early 1991, said their reasons for backing the Programme for Economic and Social Progress (PESP) were unashamedly pragmatic. Billy Attley recalls: 'Between 1981 and 1987 the construction worker was the lowest paid craftsman in the private sector. They [the building craft unions] had a problem they had to address and that brought them all on board in the PESP.'

Shift in Attitudes

The 1980s saw a change in trade union attitudes, strongly influenced by outside factors such as the fiscal crisis and the discipline imposed by the seeming threat of IMF intervention and EU convergence criteria; the inexorable rise of unemployment; the return of alarmingly high levels of emigration; and a realisation that, after an era of 'chasing after inflation', take-home pay had actually fallen. But there was another factor, namely the emergence of a new generation of union leaders who were more economically literate and who focused not just on domestic matters but were able to grasp the importance of EU developments. They also understood the threat to the future of the trade union movement posed by the crisis of the 1980s and the ideological shift to the right in the Western World generally and embodied by the Thatcher administration in Britain. Former Director of IBEC John Dunne puts it this way: 'Some of these people had a great sense of the strategic. They believed that the old style confrontational approach would be negative from their own members' point of view. It required a fair amount of leadership to bring that [change] about.'

ICTU decided that the formal decision-making process, laborious and all as Peter Cassells believed it to be, was crucial in securing buy-in and legitimacy for the various agreements. Getting a mandate to even enter talks, followed by a ballot of the members affected by the outcome, was essential. A minority of trade unions took some time to get this democratic ballot of the members organised. 'People looking in', as Cassells puts it, might ask, 'could they not do this faster? But look at the mistake they made in Britain.' This was a reference to a pay deal in the UK that Cassells said sparked the infamous 'winter of discontent' in 1979, which certainly contributed to the election of the Conservatives under Margaret Thatcher. The ICTU negotiating team had to be extended to make smaller unions feel at home. There was also a need, however, not to get too close to the other side and to remember that 'we are actually representing the union side.'

It was no accident that some of the strongest union advocates of the consensus model were the public sector unions. Given the horrendous state of the public finances by the mid-to-late 1980s, weighed down by a burgeoning public paybill and the general financial and economic crisis facing the country, their immediate interests had come under threat. Public service trade union leaders have since admitted that the umbrella of broad centralised agreements like the PNR, the PESP and the PCW helped to maintain their system of pay determination intact at a time when it was coming under siege from the sort of forces described earlier.

In regard to the general unions, and specifically SIPTU, there were a number of reasons why centralised agreements were a logical way to proceed in respect of pay. Their ability to secure flat rate or 'floor' increases to protect the lower paid was increased. The effect of global competition on their ability to pressurise key employers meant, as Billy Attley says, there were no easy 'targets' anymore. With a large proportion of members within the commercial State companies, a rational approach to pay increases in these companies has helped to prevent pay fragmentation.

CAPACITY FOR STRATEGY

Meanwhile, the capacity of the trade union leadership for adopting a more strategic response to the challenges they faced was also evident in their embracing of the concept of the 'social market' economy. They were influenced in a positive way in this regard in the early 1990s by developments in Europe and in a more negative and defensive manner by events in Britain. How ICTU fundamentally changed its stance on privatisation in 1990 is a striking example of this, a change which its 'natural' ally, the Labour Party, did not embrace until well into the 1990s.

The ICTU position was spelled out in a report entitled *Public Enterprise and Economic Development – A Policy Statement on Privatisation*. While remaining opposed to selling-off all government shares in public enterprises 'except in exceptional circumstances', ICTU said that traditional opposition to all forms of privatisation was no longer an adequate response. According to the document, each case would have to be considered on its own merits, with job preservation as a key criterion. It accepted that a minority level of private sector investment or the sale of a minority interest in public enterprises might be necessary.

ICTU also formally embraced the need for change to meet the challenge posed by international competition in particular. Kevin Duffy was directly involved in drawing up the ICTU document *Managing Change: Review of Union Involvement in Company Restructuring,* which essentially was a policy statement by ICTU, 'saying we are in favour of change but we want to be part of it, we want to manage it, we want to be involved in its implementation and we're certainly not interested in having it imposed.'

Social partnership was also to give the trade unions relevance. 'That in reality made us the envy of European trade unions,' according to Kevin Duffy. It wasn't quite 'a seat at the cabinet table', as it was so often referred to by critics. As Duffy says, 'government remained government.' But it did provide a forum where they could have an input and get the attention of ministers and department officials.

A central role in the early programmes was played by the Central Review Committee (CRC), which was made up of key civil servants and social partner nominees. The CRC monitored the agreements and dealt with difficult issues as they arose. It was regarded as an important innovation in ensuring that commitments made in the agreements were tracked. But, in keeping with the nature of social partnership in Ireland, the CRC also had a strong degree of informality. Phil Flynn, IMPACT General Secretary at the time, described how it could work: 'What happens with the CRC is that we raise an issue and, out of that, a meeting is set up with the Minister. We would meet the Minister privately. If it is resolved it does not necessarily show up on the minutes of the CRC as such.' Getting things done under Haughey, according to Phil Flynn, often meant the close involvement of his Secretary General Padraig O'hUiginn. Sometimes a secretary from another government department might baulk at implementing something that had been agreed under the agreement. Flynn says that O'hUiginn would say: 'My good man, the Taoiseach wants this done. Be back at the next meeting with progress to report.'

THE EMPLOYERS BUY IN, AND STAY THERE

In 1987, the employer's body the FUE was persuaded to enter into an agreement on pay in the PNR and thereafter remained a strong advocate of the centralised bargaining approach, chiefly on the basis that the overall 'price' of the pay arrangements had generally been attractive. Like their former colleagues in the CII (the two were to merge), the FUE did so because the country's fiscal and economic crisis had been addressed to a degree considered inconceivable from the perspective of the mid-1980s. According to former FUE leader John Dunne: 'We always had a pragmatic view about it. We would only sign up if we thought it was better for us than any other way of doing things.' At the end of the day, 'for us it was less political, a small "p" compared to [government dealing with] the unions. I think that will always be the way with business.'

The achievement of the first reduction in working time since the 1960s, without industrial conflict, had been a major goal for two key trade unions (ITGWU and FWUI) on entering talks on the PNR. The outcome was a reduction in the working week by one hour, from 40 hours to 39, and it was applied in most employments within three years of the agreement being negotiated. But it was major problem for the employers. Then Director General of the FUE Dan McAuley encountered fierce opposition to the concession. One issue was sacrosanct from the outset: no concession on statutory union recognition. In other words, employers must continue to hold the advantage held by them under the Constitution, which gives the employer the apparent right to recognise or refuse to recognise unions for the purposes of collective bargaining.

Like the trade unions, the employers also possessed leaders whose ability impressed the other negotiators. None more so than John Dunne, who was part of the FUE negotiating team on the PNR talks and led the FUE into the PESP negotiations and beyond. Paddy Teahon, who took 'huge comfort' from Billy Attley's capacity to reach agreement on the trade union side, believes that Dunne 'was one of those people who had the capacity to take the big picture view, to situate the perspective of the employer in the wider national interest.' The employers took some persuading at the outset but, in Teahon's view, they became a 'fuller partner' in the 'John Dunne period'.

MOMENTUM BEHIND DEALS

As we have seen, the key question for the employer side in entering and sticking with a national agreement is the price individual employers have to pay. That price should not, as it had often done in the past, act as a floor for further wage demands. It was difficult to convince them that this could be achieved in 1987, given their experiences with the twin National Understandings of 1979 and 1980. With the stability of the PNR, however, getting individual employers to back centralised deals was relatively easy. For example, IBEC members backed the PCW to such an extent in early 1994 that, at eight committee meetings, members drawn from the regions gave their unanimous acceptance to the agreement. And, at the general council level of the organisation, out of the 60 delegates who attended, there were only four votes against the PCW. A further 100 were not present which indicated, at the very least, that they were unconcerned about the cost of the agreement. John Dunne says that the 100 absentees would have to be regarded as 'yes' votes, 'because people who are against things always turn up to vote. You are talking about the biggest margin in favour I have ever seen down through the years.'

Evidence of how far the employers 'travelled' was provided by the fact that the FUE moved from reluctantly agreeing to discuss pay in 1987 to being perhaps the strongest advocate of centralised bargaining when the PESP expired at the end of 1993. That said, evidence of just how easily the pay terms of a national agreement could be blown off course was provided by the currency crisis of late 1992 and early 1993, when the Federation of Irish Employers (FIE) came close to advising its member companies not to pay the final phase of the PESP. However, this in itself should not be seen as surprising, given that competitiveness and 'ability to pay' considerations were a feature of all three programmes (1987–97).

A CLOSE CALL

For the main employer organisation to come so near to advising all member firms not to pay the increase indicates how critical the often forgotten currency crisis was at the time. However, the FIE drew back from such a strong stance at the last minute, and instead put pressure on the Government to alleviate the currency crisis by seeking extra aid for business and by privately hinting that a re-alignment of the pound was needed to maintain the competitiveness of Irish firms exporting to Britain. The crisis was resolved in late January 1993 when the Government eventually bowed to market pressures and devalued the punt by 10 per cent.

IBEC had other reasons for staying with the process. Why return to the uncertainty of a 'free-for-all' system in an era of very low inflation, pay stability, industrial peace, and enhanced profitability, particularly when the Government – fiscal considerations permitting – was able to ensure that this 'virtuous circle' could be maintained with a modicum of tax concessions? A key factor in the sustained employer support for partnership was the fact that IBEC's larger members (who pay the highest membership fees) remained in favour of negotiating a central pay deal as long as the 'price is right'.

There was, however, no evidence to support the contention that these key companies supported centralised bargaining as a concept, in other words for ideological reasons. Initial scepticism in 1987 of anything which smacked of the National Understandings had been overcome by a mixture of persuasion and, perhaps, a degree of subtle pressure, particularly by the Haughey-led Fianna Fáil minority Government in 1987. Given that they were being offered a moderate pay agreement, the employers might have paid a different price had they remained opposed to a return to centralised pay bargaining. As *Business and Finance* noted in October 1987: 'The swingeing cuts in public spending since the Government took office were the kind the private sector employers have been urging for years . . . the private sector employers could not be found wanting in their endorsement.'

The changeover at director general level in the FUE was the key personnel change during the period, with John Dunne assuming the post of director general in July 1988 in place of Dan McAuley. Dr Eugene McCarthy was regarded as the somewhat more right-of-centre of the two main candidates within the FUE and was seen by many as the favourite for the post at the time.

THE DUNNE FACTOR

In John Dunne, the main employer's organisation possessed a leader who was chiefly a pragmatist, with an ability to reach an accommodation with the other side whilst remaining firmly in touch with his own constituents. As new director general, he was particularly well suited to the demands of the period. Dunne understood well the political terrain in which everyone was operating. He strongly believed that the Thatcherite approach to the trade unions was not the way to go in Ireland; moreover he did not believe it would have been possible.

One leading employer believes the FUE might have been a bit more right-of-centre had Eugene McCarthy taken over but observes that McCarthy had supported the PNR: 'The "heavyweights" would nearly always say that, if the price is right, a deal at the centre in the Irish context is better than a deal at enterprise level. The thing that would drive them [large companies] off course is whether they believe the indirect cost is too high. That is what had stopped them in 1981.'

The overall perspective outlined above also accords with the view that Ireland's very size and the close relationships between the partners, when set within a small economic and political entity, make a more extreme form of political experiment – whether of the right or left variety – difficult. Despite the fact that there were no centrally negotiated pay agreements between 1981 and 1987, relations between leading employer and trade union figures during this period were cordial at a personal level, irrespective of public differences on a variety of issues.

While the FUE and the FIE concentrated on pay in the early years of social partnership, they gradually began to see their role as a wider one. Padraig O'hUiginn said their confidence in the process was well rewarded 'by the rigid adherence of the unions, in the subsequent three years' to the terms of the PNR. O'hUiginn credited the employers for fully supporting the social provisions of the programmes (see Chubb's *Federation of Irish Employers 1942–1992*).

THE GOVERNMENT AS SOCIAL PARTNER

When the PNR was debated in the Dáil in 1987, the main opposition parties were hostile to the agreement negotiated by Charles Haughey's minority Fianna Fáil administration. This hostility was not confined to criticism of the nuts and bolts of the agreement. It was also attacked on the grounds of being either 'just a pay deal' or on the alleged basis that it was some form of 'capitulation' to interest groups.

Such attacks on any major initiative by the government of the day are not unusual. What was evident in 1987, however, and again to a more limited extent in regard to the PESP in 1990, was the fact that the agreements were seen by some to be a threat to the democratic system itself. They were regarded by a number of critics as being too corporatist, a criticism not unconnected to the personality of the Taoiseach, and were seen as somehow relegating the role of the parliamentary opposition to playing second fiddle to the social partners.

John Carroll, former ITGWU President, recalls his reaction to the attack on the PNR by Labour Party leader, Dick Spring: 'I made a fierce attack on the Labour Party and what appeared to be their negative attitude to the trade union movement.' Carroll himself was and still is a member of the Labour Party. He said that later Labour, Fine Gael and the PDs all accepted the aims and objectives of the PNR.

The perception that Charles Haughey, in particular, was soft on the unions had gained ground during his first term as Taoiseach (1979–81). The claim had considerable justification. At the time, the FUE was extremely critical of the manner in which the second National Understanding was secured in 1980 when, according to Niamh Hardiman in her book *Pay, Politics and Economic Performance in Ireland, 1970–87*, Haughey 'made it clear to private sector employers that the Government wanted an agreement to be negotiated'.

Memories of this earlier period, therefore, combined with the poor relationship between the 1983–87 Coalition Government and the trade union movement, made opposition parties suspicious of anything that resembled the National Understandings. However in 1987 the difference was that economic circumstances had changed to such an extent that the electorate was prepared to accept a tough stance on public pay and spending, and the unions also knew that they would have to give their tacit consent to harsh measures if they were to secure a place within a tripartite framework.

What is noteworthy is that, by 1990–91, opposition party criticism of the programmes which followed the PNR, namely the PESP and the PCW, tended to focus on the detail of the agreements (such as the pay arrangements) rather than on the notion of consensus per se. In fact, there was an emerging political consensus that the partnership approach was the best option for the economy. There was, therefore, little in the way of political controversy as long as the price of such programmes was regarded as affordable and if key EU-related financial targets, such as the Maastricht criteria, were adhered to. The price was generally understood to relate to keeping the public finances on an even keel and maintaining competitiveness.

Between the PNR and the termination of the PCW, five main political parties in the Dáil were involved in government: Fianna Fáil, Fine Gael, Labour, Progressive Democrats and Democratic Left. Three of them were involved in negotiations on at least one of the agreements (Fianna Fáil, Labour and PDs). Meanwhile, three of the parties, on assuming office, fully supported agreements which were already in place (Fine Gael, PDs and DL). After Haughey's departure, two other Taoisigh, Albert Reynolds

(Fianna Fáil) and John Bruton (Fine Gael) were to conclude national pro-grammes, before Bertie Ahern became Taoiseach in 1997 and became the figure most associated with the process.

POLICY CONVERGENCE

The 1987–96 period was, therefore, marked by a considerable policy convergence among the political parties, even in the case of seemingly implacable political positions from different ends of the political spec-trum, such as the PDs and DL. The PDs, characterised by most political commentators as right wing, were feared by the trade unions as the thin edge of the wedge in respect of the sort of changes seen in the UK in the 1980s and 1990s. However, the fact that this party could so easily embrace the PNR (which was in place when it joined Fianna Fáil in coalition in 1989) and was able to take part in negotiations on the PESP in 1991, sug-gests that the simple Thatcherite label is not only over simplistic, but lacks analytical rigour. Director of the NESC Rory O'Donnell, looking back over almost twenty years, during which time the PDs have been in gov-ernment with 'pro-partnership' Fianna Fáil for some considerable length of time, reflects:

> I think the position of the PDs is interesting because they are the nearest thing to a neo-liberal party. You would have to say it is one of the rea-sons that the unions were fearful that the whole Thatcherite thing, in its cruelest manifestation, would rule the roost here. That clearly influenced them, as Billy Attley has said, 'to be part of the solution rather than the problem'. But their position on partnership was interesting. The Tánaiste [Mary Harney, former PD leader] [has] often articulated the democratic critique view and she has articulated the 'embeddedness' view very strongly that partnership is the way we do our business.

Given that the party was born out of discontent within Fianna Fáil and to a lesser extent within Fine Gael, its membership and its electoral base effectively draws on a similar 'catch all' constituency as the main parties. This perspective should, perhaps, come as no surprise. While Fine Gael in particular and Labour to a lesser degree have been sceptical of certain aspects of the process, all of the mainstream parties at one time or another have negotiated at least one of the programmes.

THE FAMILY – FEELING AT HOME

Talks on the national agreements have always taken place at Government Buildings. Since the refurbishment of the Merrion Street complex when Haughey was Taoiseach, the comings and goings of large negotiating teams, particularly on the trade union side, has been a regular feature every three years or so. When it was necessary to produce 'good bottles of wine with food in the early hours of the morning', this was done, according to Paddy Teahon. He says it was not quite a family, but nor was it 'too far removed from the family in terms of the extent to which people related to each other'. A sense of belonging was important even though, as Teahon puts it, the deals could have been settled by simply bringing the key people together. According to Teahon: 'You were giving them good food, lunches, dinners and coffees through the day. So there was a level at which they saw themselves, one hundred people or so, as spending a couple of months of their life every three years in Government buildings . . . There was a whole atmosphere of people coming together.'

We have already seen that many of the objectives all sides held in common at the outset emerged largely from the NESC report of 1986, and from later reports from the same body. These helped considerably to shape the basis of the consensus approach embodied in the PNR, PESP and PCW. A broad consensus on objectives was essential to the operation of the NESC in the first place. The fact that most of the personalities engaged in the talks knew one another also aided this process, a factor that PSEU General Secretary Dan Murphy believes can never be underestimated in a small economy and society like Ireland. He says there was a considerable degree of continuity at the top of the employer and trade union bodies, as well as at a political level, and 'a succession of remarkable people in important official positions, particularly in the Department of the Taoiseach'.

It was at the NESC, as social partnership took shape, that these relationships were turned to advantage and maintained. According to John Dunne, many of the key people knew each other 'extraordinarily well' and, as the first deal (the PNR) had 'gone so well, there was a growing feeling we shouldn't let it go so easily'. In the introduction to the PNR in 1987, for example, the shared objectives of all signatories to the programmes were clearly set out. These objectives continued to act as a bedrock for the PESP and PCW. Briefly, these objectives were: creation of a fiscal, exchange rate and monetary climate conducive to economic growth; movement towards greater equity and fairness in the tax system; diminishing or removing social inequities in our society; and intensification of practical measures to generate increased job opportunities on a sectoral basis.

These objectives were to be based firmly on the achievement of macro-economic stability, involving a reduction in national indebtedness (with different targets for each programme) and a monetary policy consistent with a stable exchange rate within the European Monetary System (EMS). It was clearly understood by each of the social partners that the agreements could only be realised within the confines of such parameters. In other words, each had to be based on solid foundations. No-one was going to be allowed to return the country to the crisis that had led to the need for a coming together in the first place. This situation was in stark contrast to the national wage agreements of the 1970s, a period marked by a high level of strike activity, and the two subsequent National Understandings (1979 and 1980), both of which failed to stabilise pay.

In return for trade union support for a major overhaul of the public finances under the PNR, the Government agreed to maintain the value of welfare payments and to introduce tax changes that would benefit employees. The PESP and the PCW, which followed the PNR, also covered three-year timeframes with broadly similar commitments. The PESP, which Billy Attley recalls was negotiated against the backdrop of the first Gulf War (1991), included a local bargaining pay element (up to 3 per cent), which employers generally didn't like.

This led to consistent opposition to further local bargaining clauses in subsequent national pay arrangements. Former IBEC Divisional Director Liam Doherty explains that employers 'wanted a national or a local agreement, not a hybrid.' In IBEC's view, local bargaining also tended to encourage 'a culture of pay for change associated more with the public sector'.

PESP also saw the establishment of partnership companies, set up on a pilot basis, to tackle the problem of employment and social exclusion.

THE ECONOMIC RECOVERY

The economic recovery over the first years of the partnership agreements placed the Irish economy among the top performers in several international league charts, even before the real boom years from the mid 1990s onwards.

Sustained growth, low inflation, a strong international balance of payments and a consolidation of the fiscal position, were among the most positive features. According to a 1994 report by the Economic and Social Research Institute (ESRI), the difference between this new era of growth and previous experience was stark:

> The last period of rapid growth, ending in 1981, bequeathed a record external deficit (over 14 per cent of GNP) and inflation approaching 20 per cent. In contrast, the Irish economy in 1994 is running a large balance of payments surplus combined with a low inflation rate.

There had been a genuine fear in the early to mid-1980s that the country's indebtedness, due to the imbalance in the national finances, raised the spectre of defaulting on debts and the consequences which could flow from that. Bertie Ahern has said that when State papers from that period are revealed thirty years on (in 2017), we will see just how close the country was to a major calamity. The debt/GNP ratio had been exacerbated by the oil price induced recession of the 1970s but, according to an ESRI report in 1991, restoring a more healthy balance was assisted in the late 1980s by a 'long delayed domestic fiscal reform and a buoyant world economy'.

The bulk of the adjustment in terms of expenditure took place in the years 1988–89, during Ray McSharry's tenure in Finance. As he described it, he was 'happy' to be the one that stood firm, a stance that made it easier for other ministers to blame him. It took the pressure off everyone else. He recalls closing down plenty of 'quangos', but he didn't come under much pressure on that score. However, as McSharry tells it: 'Haughey didn't like being the bad boy. I didn't mind and my job became easier after a month, once they realised the answer was "no". I'll never forget those days in Finance; committees and ministers coming in and sitting down and saying, "We're going to the country", and I said, "What about it?! This has to be done and it's only the start." I felt it was the right thing to do.'

Few questioned that major expenditure reductions were essential for survival, even if no-one liked the cuts in their particular area. However, the Budget of 1990 relaxed this process of adjustment somewhat and kept expenditure roughly constant in real terms, providing only a modest reduction of the Exchequer Borrowing Requirement (EBR) from 2.3 to 2 per cent of GNP. Nonetheless, progress was made in reducing the debt/GNP ratio and the NESC's target of a ratio of 100 per cent was achieved by 1992, although the January 1993 devaluation of the Irish pound resulted in a once-off increase in the debt/GNP ratio.

Thus, the stated target of the PESP was achieved a year in advance. This was similar to what had happened in the PNR regarding the aim of reducing the EBR to between 5 and 7 per cent of GNP, which had been comfortably surpassed. The government deficit as a percentage of GNP declined from 8.5 per cent in 1987 to 2.3 per cent in 1994; the debt/GNP ratio also improved, falling to 91 per cent in 1994. Lower interest rates followed quickly during the PNR period, inflation declined and competitiveness improved.

'NOTHING ELSE HAPPENED'

As we have already seen, there had been a real fear that the country's indebtedness raised the spectre of the State defaulting. The adjustment that began in 1987–89 kick-started the 'virtuous circle' effect. The then Director of Economic Policy with the CII Con Power believes that, without social partnership, Ireland at that time 'was a lost cause'. Partnership was the ingredient 'which made it possible to bake the cake'. For Power this was not a fanciful view. The figures said it all. By 1987, the unemployment rate had jumped to almost 18 per cent, up from about 7 per cent in 1979, while emigration took off in the 1980s, with what seemed a whole generation bound for the UK, the US and beyond. By 1987, the debt/GNP ratio was almost 130 per cent and there were genuine fears of national bankruptcy.

The PNR helped to turn these indicators around in a very short space of time. As Bertie Ahern puts it, '*Nothing else* happened between 1987 and 1990.' This is his response to critics who suggest the PNR had nothing to do with the dramatic improvement. Going out of his way to praise the trade union leaders who backed the new approach, Con Power maintained: 'I believe that it stemmed social upheaval. I would never underestimate the leaders of ICTU. I don't think it would have been possible for the most intelligent budget speeches and the most intelligent Minister for Finance to have done something because what we were doing was trying to lead all the economic actors and that cannot be done by macro economic papers.'

John Dunne of the Chamber of Commerce was a fan of partnership in this early period and had little doubt about its immediate impact: 'When history is written, for all Charles Haughey's many warts, one of his great achievements . . . will be social partnership. I think he recognised that getting everyone into a room and getting agreement gave everyone the necessary cover to make the hard choices.' Support for this broad perspective comes from Jack O'Connor of SIPTU who, looking back, believes that Haughey and Bertie Ahern understood 'the need to bring people together'.

There was, however, one area in which the gains did not come quickly enough. Unemployment remained stubbornly high over the course of the first three programmes. However, with the pick-up in manufacturing jobs, unemployment gradually started to fall as job opportunities grew. Long-term unemployment remained a persistent problem. It would be another ten years before a dramatic reversal of what had become a seemingly endemic condition came about.

'Jobless Growth'

The so-called 'jobless growth' conundrum was undoubtedly the most disappointing feature of the PNR, PESP and PCW, particularly from the perspective of the trade unions and various governments (the employers were initially more defensive in their reaction). David Begg recalls that, during the first two agreements (PNR and PESP), the economic fundamentals had been corrected, but 'they hadn't managed to do anything for the basic agenda of the trade unions, which was to do something about unemployment and emigration'. The term 'jobless growth' – a misnomer – was coined as a result, although this phenomenon was certainly not true of the entire first ten years of partnership. More jobs were being created, but not at a fast enough rate to absorb new entrants into the labour market, as the high emigration of the 1980s began to tail off. Some of the key unions understood that there was a 'lag' factor at work. Peter Cassells puts it this way: 'If you take the 1980s, profits would have reduced significantly. This might sound strange coming from a union source – but you are not going to get investment into a company in terms of job creation and new development unless that ratio in terms of profit was improved.'

Cassells says it was part of ICTU strategy to 'hold this for another three years' to see if the jobs and reinvestment would happen. Ray McSharry believes that this was a patriotic act. The then Finance Minister, who had overseen harsh cutbacks in the 1987 Budget, suggests that the trade unions deserve great credit for sticking with centralised wage agreements as time went on, when they could clearly, in his view, have negotiated higher pay deals had they opted out of the process.

During the period of the PNR (1987–90) total employment grew by an average of 15,300 per annum; but between 1990 and 1992, the level of employment merely remained stable. Unemployment, however, rose substantially (by an average of 23,000 per annum), reflecting the very rapid growth in the labour force during 1991 and 1992. The latter, in turn, was prompted by a sudden cessation of emigration, which had previously been running at very high levels. Total employment hovered around the 1.1 million mark between 1987 and 1989, with the beginnings of a real take-off only slowly becoming clear between 1993 and 1994, by which time employment had risen to 1.22 million.

Thereafter, the rise in employment was quicker, but only really took off rapidly after 1998 during the Partnership 2000 period. While, relative to the major improvement in almost all other economic indicators, the employment performance was disappointing between 1987 and 1996, the unemployment rate did fall from almost 18 per cent in 1987 to 11.9 per cent by 1996. When combined with the fall-off in emigration, the trend was very clear.

THE INTEL EFFECT

In the IDA, they knew what was happening. Even during the dark years, its people had never lost faith. Padraig White, IDA chief executive 1981–90, recalls a time when 'everybody was writing us off.' White is adamant that the PNR was critical in turning things around: 'We were convinced about the capability and strength of Ireland. We were proven right in 1988 and 1989.' The 'millstone around our neck', as he describes it, was an environment 'which was hostile to investment'. This all changed with the PNR. The transformation between the mid-1980s and post-1987 can be summed up by reference to two actual situations concerning the key companies Intel and Wang.

White is convinced that the industrial relations climate was a crucial element in the decision of some firms not to invest in Ireland in the 1980s, and says that Intel's decision to invest here in 1989 was a major signal that Ireland was a good place to invest. The giant multinational may have been a non-union oufit, but it seems it was not immune to the influence of social partnership: '[The] IDA had been courting Intel for over a decade.

This was Intel's first plant in Europe. The PNR had unique features you would not find anywhere: predicable wage increases, industrial peace and the government commitment to use the tax system to moderate wage rises and increase after-tax income.'

White says that Intel narrowed their choice of European locations from eight to four and then to two, with the UK in the final round. He is convinced that the PNR was the critical element in the final shake-out: 'It became our calling card, because it was not just about unions but about a whole national compact which dealt with so many of the things that business was concerned about.' Kieran McGowan, next into the IDA hot seat as chief executive (1990–98), concurrs: 'In my view 1989 was the key year. We had been chasing Intel for 20 years.'

What of their non-union status? According to McGowan, the unions felt the IDA was not being helpful: 'We explained that these firms were non-union and they might not come. We said we would help them with their sub-suppliers [who] were less likely to have the same dogma.' The issue of trade union recognition was, however, to remain a difficulty on the fringe of the process for many years, before a real effort was made to resolve it in the late 1990s.

PATRIOTISM IN ACTION

Looking back, former ITGWU President John Carroll recalls that the IDA would organise meetings with employers: 'The object was for me to meet the top management [of foreign companies] and convince them that if they came to Ireland they would not face a communist onslaught.'

It was a time for taking a wider view, and a pragmatic one. This was evident in the decisions made by some union officials in the 1980s, even before the PNR was negotiated. It showed that some realised new thinking was needed. There is much validity in claims that the social partnership philosophy brought out the best in many of the participants. A case in point occurred in Limerick in the 1980s, concerning the computer multinational Wang. This case is unlikely to have been unique and mirrored the approach adopted by ITGWU President John Carroll towards Intel. The outcome set the tone for what was to happen more and more in the 1990s and up to the present day.

Chairman of Forfás Eoin O'Driscoll, who worked in several multinational firms in Ireland and abroad over the past twenty years, recalls that

Wang, with which he was involved at the time, had insisted on a non-union set-up. Local ITGWU branch official Frank Prendergast, who was also a prominent local Labour Party leader, had come to O'Driscoll and told him the union was going to organise in Wang. O'Driscoll recalls: 'I remember sitting across the table from him and saying, "Frank, if you want to unionise us, you probably can do it. All I can say is the growth planned here probably won't take place if that happens."' As O'Driscoll puts it, 'Limerick had a negative cloud hanging over it.' Prendergast asked O'Driscoll if he was being serious and was assured he was. O'Driscoll describes what happened:

> When he was convinced we were going to run a progressive operation, he said, 'I will let you progress it here, but if there is a need for union representation, I'll be there. But if there isn't, I won't make a big issue.' He said he wanted me likewise not to join the FUE [the employers' union]. He asked me that, because I told him my philosophy was one of independence, sorting out our own arrangements; we didn't want third parties. I probably got more pressure from FUE for being a non-member! They were quite nervous that these companies were coming in and weren't joining.

O'Driscoll describes Prendergast as a very experienced union official who could easily have organised in Wang 'because I was totally inexperienced and had a young team'. Looking back, he says that Prendergast realized that the 'realities' of job creation were far bigger than the smaller goals he might have had.

Raising the Bar

O'Driscoll describes a new breed of company in the decades that followed – some unionised, more non-union – whose culture allowed people to work in partnership, and 'not have to go outside to get third party people to communicate between those of us who work here'. In other words, most of them didn't want trade unions. He said, however, that some of the firms that did this well were unionised, 'but the union would have recognised that this was progressive and would have supported it.'

McSharry credits trade unions for this 'let's make it happen' attitude to tackling the crisis of the 1980s, and credits the partnership agreements as helping to establish a positive business environment: 'If you are talking to a chief executive who picks up the impression that there's a pro-business environment, it's a huge thing. There are other countries that are less pro-business.' Many of the FDI successes boosted national self-confidence, he says. 'They were trophy projects. They made us feel good about ourselves.' That was hugely beneficial as 'people are interested in raising the standard of Ireland. Partnership was the first thing to capture that.'

Former General President of SIPTU Des Geraghty's view of modernisation and inward investment is not entirely dissimilar. On modernisation, SIPTU had seen that the highly unionised areas were declining, while the unions were weak in the growth areas. Were they actually 'going to beat up on these companies where we are organised so they couldn't bring in new machines, couldn't be competitive, couldn't give productivity?' The most successful aspect of the national agreements, according to Geraghty, was the security it gave investors, employers and government 'who actually did some planning for the first time'. He said the three-year pay deals meant that government had to look at three-year budgets and employers had to look at three-year investments. This all helped to foster a longer term perspective and was 'one of the big driving forces that changed the Irish economy'.

Patricia King, currently SIPTU Dublin regional secretary, and who was something of a self-confessed 'firebrand' in the 1970s, believes that trade union leaders, locally and at higher levels, took some brave decisions: 'The easiest thing is to stay running with the members. The hardest thing is to lead them into the big picture.' She recalls representing workers in the engineering company Airmotive, the management of which wanted to facilitate the upskilling of general workers. It was a move viewed with suspicion by the craft unions, but it was the sort of modernisation initiative and new thinking for which leaders at that time took risks. Billy Attley and others, she said, realised by 1987 that to attract new investment into Ireland they had to change: 'There was a lot of change and pain, yet the trade union leadership was prepared to stand up and say, "This is where we have to go to get to the next place."'

IDA Chief Executive Kieran McGowan considered that the social partnership agreements were 'a huge help when selling Ireland to companies against the UK'. The British 'could not offer the same sort of assurances about the stability of the environment'. Having the 'national benchmark' set by partnership was a big help for non-union firms. 'It allowed them to say back to HQ, "we have made a settlement of X and it is in line with the national agreement." I know it was extremely helpful.' In a way, he said, the national agreements were as influential with these FDI companies 'as if they had been part of it. It had the same beneficial affects for them.'

Domestic firms also began to sense the change. Billy Attley recalls that, by the time they went into the PESP agreement, there was a 'positive feel'. Stability and industrial peace were being delivered: 'I recall the guy who owns Glenn Dimplex. He said to me, "Just before you did the PNR, I was about to make a major investment in Northern Ireland; but, as a result of the PNR, we took our time and we waited and said we'd give it a year. And when it looked good we invested down South. But up until that the board had decided to put the plant in the North." '

Paddy Teahon, who was to become secretary general in the Department of the Taoiseach, suggested that such investment decisions and a new wave of key FDI companies were critical in reinforcing the benefits of the partnership approach: 'That was hugely important because if that hadn't happened I think inevitably people would start saying, "What's this about? We have all this growth and what the hell good is it if we can't employ our people at home." I think it was that turnaround that underpinned the success of social partnership.' The patience referred to by Ray McSharry would not, it seemed, be wasted. Meanwhile, those in work, starting with the PNR, had quickly begun to benefit from real increases in living standards as inflation fell and their tax burden began to fall.

Looking back on the ten years that followed the PNR, Taoiseach Bertie Ahern says that he still worries today about getting research and development (R&D) into the country, 'but last year we had 25 announcements of major world-wide companies opening up R&D in Ireland. I think that on the question of foreign direct investment . . . it is because of the conditions the country created [between] 1987 up to 1997.'

THE PAY-TAX TRADE-OFF

A key element in the improvement of the trend in real take-home pay was the series of tax concessions made by the government, starting with the PNR in 1987. This mainly involved a gradual move from three to two tax bands, as well as providing relief on the bands. In the first Budget, after the negotiation of the PNR (1988), tax concessions cost the Exchequer £150 m in a full year – twice as much as had been forecast in the context of the overall commitment in the PNR to grant £225 million in reliefs over the entire three year period of the programme. However, despite this impressive first step in reducing personal income tax levels, reductions in subsequent years were modest, with those who benefited most from the early agreements on above-average earnings.

Overall, however, by 1996 all employees – whether single or married – were better off in real terms than they had been at the outset of the PNR in 1987 (see Table 3.1). This was also due to falling inflation in the same period, ensuring significant reversal of the real income declines during the pay free-for-all of the 1980s. According to economist Paul Tansey, in his book *Ireland at Work*, while low income households made meagre gains between 1987 and 1992, a re-direction of policy in subsequent years helped their relative position. The biggest gains in real purchasing power over the years 1992–97 were made by single people on half the average manufacturing earnings (see Table 3.1).

TABLE 3.1 CHANGES IN REAL PURCHASING POWER BY
HOUSEHOLD TYPE 1987–97

Household Type	1987–92	1992–97	1987–97
Single people On twice av. Pay	+19.2	+11.2	+32.3
Single people on av. Pay	+12.9	+13.6	+28.2
One-income Married couples on twice av. Pay	+13.0	+13.3	+27.9
Single people on half av. Pay	+6.6	+14.9	+22.6
One-income Married couples on av. Pay	+8.2	+11.6	+20.7
One-income Married couples on half av. Pay	+5.1	+13.3	+20.7

Source: Tansey, Paul (1998), *Ireland at Work*, Dublin: Oaktree Press.

WAGES AND COMPETITIVENESS

By 1989, the economy had been growing rapidly for some time and the NESC believed the associated revival of labour demand and fall in unemployment could have been expected to increase the rate of wage settlements. However, according to a 1993 NESC report, adherence to the wage growth elements of the PNR 'right to the end of the three years arrested the decline in wage competitiveness and this was a major factor in enabling Irish employment to expand rapidly in response to favourable international conditions between 1987 and 1990.'

Pay rises tended to mirror inflation rather than chase it although, in some years over the 1987–96 period, they slipped below the inflation rate. Despite this, the trade unions by and large did not press for compensatory pay rises, largely due to the fact that government provided modest income tax relief to boost real disposable incomes, and social welfare and other social spending was generally maintained at a level that matched the basic commitments in the programmes. This is where the stability of the agreements was critical, as referred to by all shades of opinion.

Dermot McCarthy believes that the early agreements benefited people not just in creating the conditions for employment growth but, after a decade of falling living standards, 'The transformation of the real incomes position of those at work was dramatic.' The NESC suggested that what appears to have happened during this period is that Ireland experienced gains in cost competitiveness against the UK which offset losses against our other main trading partners, 'leaving the overall position for the PNR virtually unchanged.'

These gains against the UK mainly reflected lower cost inflation in Ireland than in Britain. However, a subsequent decline in competitiveness with the UK in the 1990s was apparently due to a combination of the lowering of the differential between Irish and UK wage inflation and the depreciation of Sterling. This overall assessment was supported by the CRC in its 1994 report, which also addressed the impact on competitiveness of the 1993 currency crisis and suggested that exporters secured a competitive boost due to the 10 per cent devaluation of the Irish pound. That decision boosted competitiveness, and ultimately enhanced economic and employment growth.

The three wage agreements (PNR, PESP and PCW) certainly did not hinder competitiveness but, perhaps more importantly, they allowed employers in all sectors to plan on the basis of certainty in regard to wage increases over an extended period. This was not the case under previous experiments with centralised bargaining, in particular during the two National Understandings. Stability and certainty were bywords used during those years. Looking back, former IBEC Director General John Dunne points to the remarkably strong backing the pay deals got from his members, despite annoyance about local bargaining (PESP) and the one hour reduction in the working week (PNR). Kevin Duffy puts it this way:

> It was important, particularly for employers in the multinational sector, to have some idea of what wage rates were going to be, and some assurance that supplies weren't going to be cut off by industrial disputes. A lot of these companies would have been somewhere in the supply chain and, if they were knocked out of business, the whole thing's kaput.

HR Director of Penneys Breege O'Donoghue, looking back over the entire social partnership period, says that for multinational companies 'it must be very comforting to ring head office and say we have an agreement and this is what it is going to cost us.' Partnership created conditions where the tax burden went down, where real incomes increased and where industrial peace was largely achieved. It has even suited those foreign firms 'who were not part of the partnership process at all', she says.

INDUSTRIAL DISPUTES AND STABILITY

If the earlier national agreements of the 1970s failed to deliver industrial peace, the first three programmes (1987–96) certainly coincided with a new era of relative stability. Economist Jim O'Leary believes, 'the decline in industrial activity pre-dated 1987. You had a big rump of days lost in the 1960s and 1970s and then they were falling.' While it is clear that all of the credit for this reduction cannot be attributed to national agreements, the fall in the level of strike activity was still highly impressive (see Table 3.2). It is plausible at least to argue that the agreements enhanced the likelihood of industrial peace, certainly in relation to pay and other issues covered in the pay and industrial relations aspects of the deals.

Factors such as the high level of unemployment and ever-increasing competitive pressures – with a consequential threat to jobs – were also seen as important elements in explaining the dramatic decline in industrial

TABLE 3.2: No. OF STRIKES AND WORK DAYS LOST 1969–94

Year	Strikes	Days Lost (to nearest 100)
1969	134	935,900
1979	152	1,427,000
1988	65	143,000
1989	38	41,000
1990	49	223,000
1991	54	86,000
1992	38	191,000
1993	48	65,000
1994	32	24,000

Source: adapted from Central Statistics Office data.

disruption. Companies continued to restructure their labour practices to meet competitive pressures during the period.

What happened in high profile disputes is that the 'wagons were circled' once a big dispute threatened major disruption or was seen as a real challenge to the integrity of any of the agreements. IBEC's Turlough O'Sullivan and ICTU's Kevin Duffy formed a sort of special firefighting double act to counteract these headline cases. Duffy describes their duet as an informal one, but their role was clear: 'Ensuring the process wasn't damaged by either unions or individual employers going offside.' Disputes emerging that might damage the process: 'they were managed effectively. And that often involved a level of co-operation between government, employers and ICTU. [Disputes were] [n]ot policed as such, in that you couldn't stop things happening, but you could manage the fall-out.'

In Chapter 5, we will see how IBEC and ICTU moved to protect the PESP pay agreement in two key cases – the ESB strike of 1991 and the nationwide bank strike of 1992. In the private and public sectors there were disputes where either major restructuring or the introduction of some far-reaching technological change sparked potential trouble. For example, unofficial action occurred in TEAM, the Aer Lingus subsidiary, during the summer of 1994, although no official strike ever took place. Likewise, a dispute in An Post (public sector) in 1992 over the company's recovery plan involved no formal industrial action at all, but severely affected postal services for five to six weeks.

'DON'T SQUEEZE THE PESP'

Public service pay was a particular problem for the social partners, and one that tested the ingenuity of government and the relevant ICTU unions. It was also a sore point for the employer and farming bodies. A key aim of the public service unions entering the PNR was to retain intact their conciliation and arbitration pay system. Charlie McCreevy believes that the 'leapfrogging' nature of that system was rooted in Irish history: 'The unions were negotiating all the time, doctors following nurses, following firemen, following county council employees. It never ended.'

Leaders such as Dan Murphy, Phil Flynn and Kieran Mulvey understood the value of the system for their members but they also knew that pay had, at the very least, to be held in check until such time as the public finances were revived. The C&A scheme linked private sector pay movements to analogous grades in the public sector, but it had become increasingly irrational, triggering a plethora of 'special' pay rises. As Charlie McGreevy suggested, 'if one group got less than another group it would set the whole thing off again.' Reform would come much later but, in the early days of the PNR and PESP, the trade unions showed they were prepared to be patient, as long as their pay system was essentially retained. As Dan Murphy puts it, 'action had to be taken to get us into growth mode.'

In late 1991, a year into the PESP, the public service unions faced what was perhaps their most difficult crisis in the first decade of social partnership. The Government had decided that, for fiscal reasons, it had no option but to alter its commitment to honour deferred 'special' pay awards in 1992 and 1993. After initially announcing a decision in this regard, the Government entered talks with the unions and concluded an accommodation after a major 'Don't Squeeze the PESP' billboard campaign by the unions concerned. In effect, what happened was that the unions made a 'loan' to the Government which was paid back at a later date with full retrospection when budgetary conditions allowed, which of course they did. The principle of negotiated change was thus maintained, an important principle for the union side and one that was understood by Haughey, McSharry and Ahern on the Government side.

The second strand in the Government's efforts to curb public expenditure in 1987 and beyond was to reduce numbers in the civil service through the first ever public sector Voluntary Early Retirement (VER)

TABLE 3.3: PUBLIC SERVICE EMPLOYMENT 1987–96

Year	Total	Change
1987	215,135	–
1988*	207,806	−7329
1989*	195,792	−12014
1990	195,386	−406
1991	198,599	+3213
1992	202,049	+3450
1993	205,357	+3308
1994	208,183	+2826
1995	212,393	+4210
1996	215,833	+3440

* Voluntary Early Retirement scheme in operation
Source: *Industrial Relations News*

scheme (see Table 3.3). While the VER scheme was initially successful in its aim of reducing numbers – it was an attractive scheme as Ray McSharry has acknowledged – the level of public service employment soon began to rise again.

The potential for longer-term savings was eventually eroded due to the renewed growth in numbers because the 20,000 public servants who left under the scheme at a cost of £130 m were replaced within seven to eight years. It did not matter as much by then, however, as the State's finances had turned the corner.

Essentially, what the Government had succeeded in doing in 1987 was to push forward the payment of 'special' pay awards, whilst maintaining the pay machinery in place. This was a key issue for the public service unions. According to a 1987 issue of *Industrial Relations News*, 'While the pay increases negotiated by ICTU are beyond what public service unions could have hoped to achieve outside an agreement, undoubtedly the icing on the cake is the preservation of the arbitration system.' Attempts to reform the system were to follow at the outset of the second ten years of social partnership, firstly in the form of the so-called PCW restructuring clause. This was such a failure that it, in turn, gave rise to a fresh impetus to find a new solution. The result was the benchmarking system that remains in place today and which is discussed in Chapter 6.

A FESTERING SORE

One festering sore did remain, however, between employers and the government on the one hand and the trade unions on the other. The conundrum that surrounds trade union recognition for the purposes of collective bargaining remains a problem up to the present day. A number of serious and well publicised strikes after 1987, such as the lengthy and controversial disputes involving Nolan Transport and SIPTU and Pat the Baker and SIPTU, highlighted the issue. These disputes helped to keep the spotlight on this thorny problem and just what could be done about it at social partnership level. The first move was to refer it to the Employer Labour Conference as part of the PESP, but nothing concrete emerged from the Conference in this regard; perhaps it was not meant to. The ELC, which played a role in the negotiation of centralised pay agreements during the 1970s, was almost dormant at this stage anyway.

Union recognition was not something desired by the Government or its employment agencies, such as the IDA. There was outright opposition from employer bodies to any suggestions that unions should secure any formal rights in this area, a position that rankled with the trade unions who constantly asked how a partnership system could oppose their right to recognition. It was an issue that was to continually raise its head during national talks in the years that followed, before exploding in 1998 with the infamous dispute at Dublin Airport, which was sparked by the refusal of Ryanair to recognise SIPTU. In turn, that row would give rise to far-reaching legislation, which will be covered in the next chapter. Suffice to say, that the recognition question was one that had begun to crystallise by the time the PCW expired in 1996.

PREPARING FOR TAKE-OFF

The task of securing a fourth programme had fallen to the 'Rainbow' Coalition Government, made up of Fine Gael, Labour and Democratic Left (DL). As the Fine Gael Taoiseach John Bruton said, the DL component of the coalition helped to anchor the three-party Government, providing this unexpected coalition with a cohesiveness few had anticipated. Bruton himself had made the conversion to social partnership by then too. But getting the new agreement, Partnership 2000, ratified by the trade unions in early

1997 was difficult. The economy was taking off and the PCW restructuring debacle in the public service had been gaining momentum, factors which led to some jockeying for position among the trade unions. Nonetheless, the pro-partnership side won the day again, with the employers following suit.

In the run up to the general election of June 1997, all of the mainstream political parties issued statements backing Partnership 2000 (P2000), with commitments to honour its terms should they form part of the next government. It was a remarkable convergence, almost ten years after the PNR had been roundly attacked in the Dáil by Fine Gael and Labour. Perhaps that hostility was as much directed at the then Taoiseach Charles Haughey as at the deal itself.

In the fullness of time, not even the most vociferous opponents of social partnership in the wider 'commentariart' would have a bad word to say about the PNR. The agreements that followed and social partnership per se would be criticised, and Fine Gael in particular would blow hot and cold on the concept. But in what were the beginnings of the real take-off in Ireland's economy from 1997 onwards, the degree of convergence at political level was a testimony to the political buy-in for social partnership, even if that was based on a very loose understanding of what social partnership actually was.

The difficulty that ICTU leaders had in securing acceptance for P2000 was also an indication that the process wasn't set in stone. It did not have the solid bedrock of the legalistic systems that peppered the European mainland. It remained to be seen if it would acquire this permanence in the ten years up to 2007. Social partnership in Ireland between 1987 and 1996 had to be managed carefully by the players; it was almost policed, to ensure it stayed the course. Any of the parties to it could have walked way at any time, as there was no element of legal compulsion forcing them to stay.

What was about to happen, however, was that the social partners would put in place more sophisticated monitoring mechanisms, in tandem with the increasing encroachment of the law into industrial relations. The debate about whether social partnership was enhancing democracy or diminishing it would also continue on the fringes. What it certainly had become by the end of 1996 was a uniquely Irish thing, born out of crisis and now set to play a role in managing success.

CHAPTER 4

In the Eye of the Tiger: 1997–2006

It's hard to explain to outsiders. If you try to explain it as just social partnership, it doesn't add up. If you look at all the ingredients – the tax changes, Europe, inward investment, public service change and the young, educated population – they were there before and it didn't work. What social partnership did was make all those ingredients work by bringing it all together.

Peter Cassells, former general secretary, ICTU

At the start of 1997, the Irish economic miracle known as the 'Celtic Tiger' was already well under way. A decade earlier, as the PSEU General Secretary Dan Murphy puts it, 'We were fast approaching the abyss. We looked over the edge and didn't like the stuff at the bottom.' Now Ireland was poised for a massive increase in employment, so huge that the number of people in work would almost double over two decades.

The period since 1987, when the PNR was agreed, had seen a major recovery in the State's finances, rising living standards, gradually increasing social provision and the beginnings of employment growth as foreign direct investment firms began to increase in number. The first ten years under the partnership process that was born out of the PNR, and the two agreements that followed it (PESP and PCW), had seen a major reversal of the decline and depression that had marked much of the 1980s. What was to follow over the course of four further national programmes was nothing short of a national transformation.

Within that bigger picture there runs a parallel story involving the social partners and the role they played 'in the eye of the tiger'. The ten years since 1997 witnessed the transformation and modernisation of industry as globalisation intensified. Massive labour market demand was partially met by burgeoning inward migration. There was wealth creation on a scale hitherto unimaginable. Steps were taken to reform the public sector, while deregulation in the formerly protected semi-State sector continued. These changes were more profound and deeper than those which marked the 1987–96 period, and the role the social partners played and the way they interacted was, in itself, a major part of the Irish success story.

Taking the three main social partners – government, trade unions and employer bodies – there is little doubt that, over the last 21 years, the industrial muscle of trade unions has diminished due to a range of external factors. In 1987, the trade union movement had been accepted by other interest groups – and commentators generally – as a central player in the drama and an influential partner in the combined effort to avert calamity. By 2007, some economic commentators and media pundits were questioning the right of the trade union movement, or even IBEC on the employer side, to be inside the tent at all. Moreover, they believed social partnership of itself had run its course and was hindering necessary change.

But this was not how successive governments saw it, nor of course did the main social partners believe that partnership had outlived its usefulness. Those at the centre of the process, including most key trade union leaders and influential employers, believed that the process had not only played a pivotal role up to that point, but that it was worth embedding as a way of doing business long into the future.

Senior union leaders were able to argue with considerable legitimacy that, while their penetration of the private sector was down to historically low levels by 2007, their ability to influence government was higher than it would have been 'outside the tent'. Of course, overall membership was at a record high due to the massive rise in employment and, while they may not have had a 'seat at the cabinet table', the union leadership believed they were playing the only game in town.

For the employers, the terms of the pay agreement remained paramount, while the role they played alongside senior trade leaders in managing difficult industrial relations issues and major crises, and securing consensus on legislative change, made the process worthwhile. For the government side, the benefits of partnership had a self-evident ring. All political parties supported the concept, although some had harsh criticisms to make of elements of the deals, such as the public service benchmarking system that emerged in the new millennium.

Many of the primary issues that marked the 1987–96 period were again central to the concerns of the social partners between 1997 and 2006. These included employment creation, the State's finances, living standards, the pay/tax trade-off, social spending, employment legislation and so forth. Added to the list in the later period, however, was a host of new concerns, such as infrastructure spending, skills training, deregulation and privatisation. Thorny issues emerged such as demands for a statutory minimum wage and labour standards, public service benchmarking, trade union recognition in the workplace and the very nature of the industrial relations system itself. Meanwhile, the emergent labour force from other EU (and non-EU) countries met the urgent labour market demands of the 'Tiger', a phenomenon that posed serious questions for the social partners and the political system, and about the ability of society to absorb the newcomers. And, at the top of the social partner organisations, there were leadership and personnel changes of some significance in relation to the continuity, style and *modus operandi* of the partnership system. These changes tended to alter the manner in which the various crises that sprang up were handled.

In this chapter we will survey the landscape which the social partners traversed over the 1997–2006 period, tracing the key themes that emerged during these ten or eleven years, mostly through the eyes of important players who have been at the centre of the process itself. This period and the first decade of social partnership (1987–96) are directly linked. Yet they also have their own distinctive features. Some of these, for example the surge in inward migration, tend to reflect the extent of the economic and social changes that occurred in the second half of this 21 year process. It is a story that is best told by weaving in and out of the various agreements, touching on important events and delving into the central themes that emerged, and those that may soon appear.

MANAGING THE CONSTITUENCY

Four agreements cover the 1997–2006 period: Partnership 2000 (1997–99); The Programme for Prosperity and Fairness (2000–02); Sustaining Progress (2003–05); and Towards 2016 (2006–07).

By 2006, the choreography around the talks had changed little from 1987. Large delegations still gathered in Government Buildings – on and off over several months – before the Government and perhaps the Taoiseach of the day made what might be a decisive intervention. On the trade union side, the agreements took progressively longer to negotiate, despite broadly increasing levels of support, while IBEC, whose decision-making process is far simpler, appeared to have strong support for all of the agreements, although this diminished somewhat for Towards 2016.

A joint survey conducted by the Irish Productivity Centre and IRN in 1999, in the midst of the Celtic Tiger boom period, gives a clear picture of employer and trade union opinion at that time. It coincided with the final year of Sustaining Progress, a time when pay had started to drift from the solid moorings of the first decade or so of partnership. Almost 60 per cent of the respondent companies were Irish owned operations, the balance were from the US, Europe or the UK. Some 70 per cent were private sector companies, evenly balanced between manufacturing and services. Most were in existence for more than fifteen years (80 per cent), with 76 per cent employing over 150 people.

Starting with overall perceptions of what the achievements of partnership were at the time, both management and unions placed pay moderation as 'the single most significant achievement' of the P2000 agreement, with 'industrial relations stability' next, followed by 'tax reform' and the achievement of 'constructive trade union-employer' relations. 'Social reform' came last of the five rankings used.

A large proportion of management respondents (42 per cent) reported pay rises outside the terms of P2000, which was above the proportion of cases where the terms of P2000 were breached in three separate analyses by IRN, IBEC and SIPTU. Nevertheless, the vast majority of all respondents (management and unions) considered that the continuation of pay bargaining and partnership at national level was important to the success and competitiveness of the organisation in which they operated. Some 92 per cent of management and trade union respondents wanted a successor to P2000 to be agreed at the end of 1999.

TAPPING INTO THE MEMBERS

The employers' decision-making process on the partnership agreements has always appeared to be straightforward. Despite some leaks to the media, such as concern over the prospect of a local bargaining clause, the support of employers has remained fairly constant over the period. However, more companies have recently begun to question the value of the process in the wake of Towards 2016. IBEC had a tougher job selling this deal, as many employers regarded its pay terms as being on the high side, while concerns over trade union recognition, the need for flexibility and public sector reform have also been evident in recent times.

Nonetheless, one employer close to the process says there would also be a concern that, without a national pay agreement, private sector unions could succeed in targeting sectors, or particular firms, and use these as a benchmark as they had in the past. But under social partnership even the FDI sector is, by and large, expected to apply the agreements; 'Not to do so could attract the presence of unions.'

Over the two decades of partnership, IBEC has had to manage competing interests. According to former Director General John Dunne: 'From banks to manufacturing, from retailers to people running hospitals, from people who run private schools, to people in research institutions. Any person who employed people had a pretty good chance of being a member. They could employ two people or 10,000.' Dunne said it was a basic tenet that they had to have a cohesive position that 'everyone could bind around'. This entailed a considerable communications effort across the organisation. 'I don't think we would have got to where we got to, and we wouldn't have had agreement after agreement, if the communications process wasn't very significantly developed. People were brought along at each stage.'

According to Dunne, IBEC had a whole series of mechanisms, from very frequent meetings of the National Executive Council, with 60 to 70 people representing members from all over the country, to regional meetings where members were briefed: 'All of that was undertaken in great detail and at the same time of course you were negotiating in confidence, so you couldn't reveal all of your hand at all of these meetings.' IBEC had to get a sense of what was achievable and 'test the water all the time'. The negotiators had to be comfortable and make sure 'you weren't going to be too far ahead of the troops at the end of the day. But it was a torturous and complex process on our side.'

The regions where strongest opposition to the pay deals was found were usually the mid-west and north-west, the former associated with manufacturing industry, the latter an area of traditionally high unemployment. But the deals all passed. Opinion was judged simply by a show of hands at the regional meetings and, until recently when IBEC did away with its General Council, this had been the final decision-making body. Now the National Executive Council makes the final decisions.

There was the added difficulty of IBEC's link to the government side in their mutual role as employers. According to John Dunne, 'government had the pressure of the public finances and the pressure of what might be achieved within that, and the effect of the pay increases in the context of the public purse.' One employer close to the process said that it also gives IBEC a degree of influence over the public sector, the benchmarking exercise being the obvious example. While access to State agencies would be available anyway, under social partnership 'the extent of this access might not be as great.'

IBEC had the pragmatic view of securing pay terms that would not upset competitiveness in the private sector but, better still, would enhance it, 'but being also aware that if we did X, it could have Y effect on the Government's position.' This led to a considerable degree of trust between senior people on the Government and business sides of the table.

Dunne, from his observations and interactions with the trade union side of the negotiations, believes their problems were similar: 'Various groups felt they were being constrained within this process. The overall position, which I think the trade unions adopted, was that at the end of the day some people would do less well and some would do better than if "individual bargaining" were the order of the day.' But, as he saw it, tensions would come from those who felt corralled by this approach. 'Those tensions would become clear from time to time and you could see that across the table, as I'm sure they saw our tensions.'

MAINTAINING A UNITED FRONT

It was on the trade union side that the real drama was often to be found, either in the talks phase or in the run-up to the formal votes on the various agreements. Fears of a dramatic upset were common, but never quite realized. The pro- and anti-partnership arguments had become overly familiar and somewhat jaded by the mid 1990s. But other differences between unions – often between public and private sector unions – would open up from time to time, generally to be closed in the name of solidarity. But the public-private divide, which the union movement tends to deny, was not the only difficulty. There were, of course, the traditional differences between Irish and UK trade unions over centralised pay bargaining, and sometimes tensions erupted between unions in situations where members of one union wished to transfer to another. All in all, however, an impressive degree of unity was maintained.

The P2000 agreement in early 1997 was a classic case where some of this internal tension emerged in the public domain. There were real fears that P2000 would be thrown out when ICTU unions met in what the *Irish Times* reported was a smoke-filled Liberty Hall – despite the 'no smoking' signs. They eventually voted in favour, by the relatively healthy margin of 217 to 134. The critical SIPTU membership vote registered 65,000 for and 49,000 against, one of the tightest margins ever within the country's largest union. It was not to be repeated, as the margin in favour within SIPTU has increased in subsequent agreements, averaging a two-thirds majority for both the SP and Towards 2016 agreements. (From 1997 onwards, the union decided to undertake a more extensive consultation process than was already in place.) Meanwhile, due to rapid membership growth, IMPACT – also a solid supporter of the agreements – increased the 'yes' vote, due to the fact that the union's delegate count at special ICTU conferences jumped from 19 to 35.

Smaller yet influential unions tended to switch sides from time to time or, after strategic re-evaluation, to move from what were once entrenched positions. A one-time traditional supporter of social partnership, the secondary teachers' union (ASTI) voted against P2000, but this opposition was countered by a 'yes' vote from former opponent, Manufacturing Science Finance (later Amicus), which then became a fairly staunch advocate of the process. This was an indication that some unions shifted positions over time, while others would vote tactically, agreement by agreement. There were also signs that, where the members were given a formal vote on their pay deal for the first time (as happened in the MSF and, eventually, in the NUJ), they backed the deals, overthrowing hitherto ideological stances adopted by activists and officials. The latest union to do so was the ASTI.

SIPTU, with one-third of its members in the public sector (larger in fact than any of the exclusively public service unions) perceived that other unions could strike militant poses, while leaving it to 'carry the can' for partnership. There were concerns too, however, that some smaller unions felt sidelined by the 'pro-' partnership unions. One senior ICTU figure described how, over time, an element of wish fulfillment would enter the process, whereby influential negotiators would not bother seeking concessions for consistent opponents of the agreements. As he put it, 'If there were particular concerns that were realistic, you would address them. [But] if they came from a union that was going to vote against the agreement, no matter what you did for them, you'd direct your efforts elsewhere.'

The run-up to the ICTU delegate vote on the various agreements could be a time for wheeling and dealing. Former teacher union leader Joe O'Toole (INTO) had risen to speak at the P2000 special conference to mingled boos and sniggers. What prompted this minor outburst was a last minute decision by O'Toole's union to back the deal after the Government had sanctioned 3,000 new promotional posts for primary teachers. The other teacher unions were furious and his counterpart in the TUI, Jim Dorney, openly attacked such 'side deals', to which O'Toole replied: 'We took nothing belonging to anyone else and we didn't eat anyone's dinner along the way.'

CHASING THE TIGER

By the time Towards 2016 was negotiated in mid-2006, almost ten years after P2000, the margin of acceptance on the trade union side was the highest ever (242 votes to 84). This was despite the fact that the deal had taken almost nine months to negotiate due to the fall-out from the 2005 Irish Ferries dispute and a major bust up over non-payment of national wage rises in An Post. By 2006, trade union unity was on show, although ICTU delegates at the September 2006 delegate conference may also have been worn out with 'talks fatigue'. There was certainly none of the colour and acrimony that had marked the ratification of P2000.

Such public spats were fairly unusual. ICTU was always anxious to prevent a public sector versus private sector row from building around the talks. But in the run-up to talks on the PPF (the successor to P2000), another public disagreement revealed real tension between private sector and public sector unions within ICTU. Delegates at the special conference to decide whether to enter talks (November 1999) heard the then SIPTU president-designate Des Geraghty get stuck into teachers' union leaders over public service pay. Geraghty was speaking immediately after the General Secretary of the TUI Jim Dorney had warned delegates that there was 'unfinished business' arising from the PCW, a reference to a so-called 'catch up' claim after the nurses' dispute that year: 'We want that gap bridged, there is no question about it, and we want it bridged as a priority outside the agreement. If that isn't done, and I say it with the firm support of my executive, we will not support the continuation of talks.'

In what became a much publicised remark, providing plenty of meat and drink for radio phone-in programmes, Dorney added that there were 'young computer graduates' who were earning as much after two years in private industry as their lecturers at colleges of technology.

Referring to the catch-up claims, Geraghty replied: 'You can chase pay for a long time – and I want to say this to public service representatives here – but you don't live on the moon. Don't expect that private sector workers are going to sit back and see you going in for your special, and your other special, plus the other national pay agreements and say, "That's grand. We don't notice.' " Geraghty added:

> And I'd say to Jim Dorney, don't be surprised that some young person who left the education system came back with more money after two years because the level of productivity, the level of commitment to change, the development of the economy in the private sector are leading the world. We are not doing it in the public sector, and there is a challenge to all of us to do it.

ASTI delegate Irene Irish from Wexford said she was appalled at Mr Geraghty's remarks, and said that teachers would be better off outside ICTU. It was a comment that presaged the ASTI's almost immediate departure from ICTU. The episode lifted the veil on tensions within ICTU unions, which the trade unions themselves were usually so careful not to reveal in public.

Tension between private and public sector unions was again evident in the lead-in to talks on Sustaining Progress, as the ICTU negotiating team was restricted to its General Purposes Committee, which has often been dominated by influential public sector union figures. Given the prominence of public service benchmarking on the talks agenda, private sector unions felt excluded. Dan Murphy says it was a mistake and would not be repeated. Some people, he says, did feel excluded from the negotiations 'simply by not being physically present in Government Buildings, even through they might not be very involved if they had been there.' While the trade unions were good at covering up these differences, there was little doubt that social partnership did pose questions regarding relations between different unions and wider questions about the role of unions into the future.

With almost 560,000 members, ICTU is the largest civil society organisation in the Republic. The days when general secretaries or union presidents could direct members on how to vote on issues were long past by 2007. Twenty years ago, all thirteen unions listed as voting for the PNR at the Special Delegate Conference to approve the terms in 1987 held some sort of ballot among their members. Of the fifteen unions listed as voting against the PNR, the decision was made by the executives in seven cases, by some form of ballot in six cases and by a show of hands at branch meetings in the Union of Construction Allied Trades and Technicians (UCATT). Today, almost all unions provide for a secret ballot of the membership.

In the debate on the Programme for Prosperity and Fairness, then SIPTU vice-president Jack O'Connor warned the unions that economic growth was not an end in itself and that 'The key to good agreements, partnership or otherwise, is good trade union organisation.' He called on the movement to learn lessons about the way 'in which we have entered these agreements, the way we consult in advance, the way we campaign for greater understanding of them and the way we exploit them.' O'Connor was not an entirely new voice on the national stage by then, but he was soon to emerge as the main voice of SIPTU, which would place him centre stage at a time when a new set of challenges – epitomised by the Irish Ferries dispute – would severely test the unions and the partnership process.

EMERGING DISTRUST ON PAY AND CHANGE

The pay agreement in P2000 (1997–99) was the first since the PESP (1991–93) to allow for a local bargaining element. There were verbal clashes early on over the notion of 'pay for change' deals at local level and whether these could be justified under the special 'partnership chapter' (Chapter 9) of P2000. Later in the year, SIPTU caused something of a storm by announcing that it was targeting profitable companies for increases above the 2 per cent local bargaining limit. IBEC responded by suggesting that such claims would represent a serious breach of faith, and said the claim raised doubts about entering further agreements with SIPTU.

The row was an early indication of trouble ahead in the private sector. This was to burst out more openly in the final year of P2000, and dramatically under the PPF agreement that followed. This triggered the creation of the National Implementation Body (NIB) in early 2001, the social partners' own informal body which continues to oversee implementation and act in a troubleshooting capacity to protect the integrity of the agreements. In Sustaining Progress (2003) a further 'enforcement tool' was added by the establishment of a group of special assessors under the wing of the Labour Relations Commission to oversee 'inability to pay' claims. As IBEC Director General Turlough O'Sullivan succinctly puts it, by 2003 the 'pitch was more clearly marked out'.

The strong adherence in the private sector to the pay terms in the early programmes (PNR, PESP and PCW) had started to gradually decline in the latter half of the P2000 agreement. A survey published in *Industrial Relations News* in 1998, year two of P2000, showed that, while adherence to the deal was still high, significant 'fringe benefits' were starting to feature strongly as part of local deals. Meanwhile, in the public sector, government pay policy had started to seriously unravel, with the so-called 'early starter' groups waiting to pounce on concessions the Government might make to the nurses who had launched another major pay campaign. Therefore, in both the private and public sectors, the success of the economy had put inevitable pressure on the pay deal. The job of the social partners was to manage these pressures in such a way that partnership could survive in the successful economy that everyone had set out to achieve in the first place.

During the PPF (2000–02), which coincided with the epicentre of the Celtic Tiger boom, pay drift in the private sector reached what Turlough O'Sullivan calls 'crisis proportions'. IBEC blamed the trade unions, while the unions pointed to labour shortages, both skilled and unskilled. In reality, trade unions were exploiting a tight labour market in traditional ways, while employers were fighting a war for talent and a general shortage of labour, both at the same time.

Pay leakage was inevitable, although there is evidence that the PPF held up stronger than some critics suggested. It was certainly upheld by the State's dispute resolution agencies. According to a survey by IRN, the adherence rate in the unionised private sector was still around the 70 per cent mark (compared to 95 per cent in the earlier agreements), which was impressive in the context of economic growth rates of around 10 per cent and an unemployment rate that actually went below 4 per cent in 2001. IBEC and SIPTU surveys came to broadly similar conclusions, but there was evidence of a higher level of leakage behind these figures. A joint Institute of Personnel Administration (IPA)-IRN survey found an adherence rate of just short of 60 per cent, with just over 40 per cent of management respondents saying that they had paid more than the strict terms of P2000. But this did not stop the vast majority saying they wanted a follow-on national pay deal, an indication that many by that stage saw the deals 'as a valuable floor, even in cases where the deal is breached'. There was no reverting to the pay bargaining trends before 1981. The Irish labour market 'had become less dysfunctional, thus more responsive, to external forces' (see Brian Sheehan's chapter in the 2002 book *The John Lovett Lectures*).

TIGHTENING THE LID

The pay instability generated by the very success of the economy and occasional inflationary 'wobbles' was also reflected in the structure of the pay deals over time. The P2000 pay agreement was the last simple three-year deal and even it had a local bargaining element. Within a year of its ratification, the PPF had to be 'adjusted' due to rising inflation and expectations. As a result, neither IBEC nor ICTU were prepared for a full three-year agreement under the next programme, Sustaining Progress (SP). So they 'split the difference' and came up with two phases of eighteen months each, set within a three-year timeframe. In the current programme, Towards 2016, the pay deal is worth 10.4 per cent, on a cumulative basis over 27 months.

For all of the 'above the norm' pay deals generated by the success of the economy between 1998 and 2001, the fact is that pay stability more or less returned during the SP agreement and continues up to the present day. The international slowdown after the events of 11 September 2001 and the entry of workers from new EU accession states after 2004 dampened pay demands and meant that the pay stability of the first decade of partnership had more or less resumed by the end of the second decade of the process.

The story of the pay agreements in the public sector was quite different, although the emergence of one overall coherent system in the form of the benchmarking exercise undertaken by the Public Service Benchmarking Body was a major improvement, compared with the discredited and confusing system that been allowed to develop prior to 2001–2002. On the enforcement side, the same skills that were evident in managing private sector pay problems were called into play in the public sector. The social partners had to manage disputes like the ASTI's 'go it alone' pay campaign and the more recent challenge by two nursing unions, the INO and the

PNA, to seek concessions outside the benchmarking process. In both cases, the partnership system, through some of its key actors, worked to ensure that the respective agreements were ringfenced and protected. The social partners had perhaps learned the lessons of the nurses' dispute of 1999 and the 'pay restructuring' debacle at that time, which had led to the infamous 'blue flu' campaign by the gardaí and a whole range of pay leakages.

THE TROUBLESHOOTERS

It is inevitable that once there is an industrial relations crisis or dispute, the National Implementation Body (NIB) intervenes to help guide those involved towards a resolution. Established in 2001, it has become an almost seamless part of the Irish industrial relations landscape. It is a 'virtual' body, having no offices, secretariat or paid employees. It may also represent the best value for money of any State or non-State entity. Operating out of the Department of the Taoiseach, the Secretary General Dermot McCarthy is one of three permanent members. The other two are the General Secretary of ICTU David Begg and the Director General of IBEC Turlough O'Sullivan. These three key players can be joined or replaced at any given time by experienced players from any of the three 'arms' of the NIB.

A notable feature of recent national agreements has been the range of monitoring mechanisms and policing measures that they contain. These innovations indicate a desire on the part of the social partners to exercise a greater degree of monitoring and control over outcomes. The NIB is per-haps the central cockpit of an evolving system of regulation within the IR arena. The new role for the LRC and the Labour Court in assessing 'inability to pay' claims since the start of Sustaining Progress amounts to a more streamlined and far stronger enforcement 'system' compared to previous national agreements. Anyone attempting to undermine the agree-ments, even inadvertently, are kept in check by agreed procedures and, ultimately, may face the experienced players in the NIB. As has been shown, while the social partners have acted this way for decades now any-way, the difference today is that the rules and the mechanisms that the NIB oversee represent a far more structured approach than has been seen at any time in the past.

The NIB is seen as a critical part of the certainty that the former IBEC leader John Dunne saw as crucial for employers. Referring to the NIB and mechanisms that protect the integrity of the agreements, Dunne says, 'I'm quite sure there would have been a mechanism developed of some description. The fact is, these types of organisations have worked.'

THE LIMITS OF THE STATE

By 2003, it appeared that ICTU policy on privatisation had moved full circle, all the way back to its pre-1987 position. At that time, then General Secretary of ICTU Peter Cassells secured an assurance on the public ownership of semi-State companies from the former Taoiseach Charles Haughey in the context of negotiations on the Programme for National Recovery (1987).

However ICTU's traditional stance was later to change, as the political system succumbed to a number of influences and imperatives: the UK privatisation splurge; the knock-on effects of the drawing down of the Iron Curtain on Soviet-dominated Eastern Europe; and the impact of EU-driven deregulation. In essence, by 1990, ICTU's position came to gradually mirror the Fianna Fáil one – to take each case on its merits. The employer position was influenced by developments in Britain, although IBEC generally left it up to government to make the running on privatisation, placing the emphasis on the primary need for competition.

The biggest asset sale, involving Telecom Éireann, came to represent both the apex of the privatisation drive and, ultimately, the start of a growing disillusionment with the experience, not just by shareholders but also within the trade union movement. A union that wasn't complaining was one whose members benefited from the deal – the Communications Workers' Union (CWU), whose one-time General Secretary David Begg was later to spearhead a major re-think (other such unions included IMPACT, the PSEU and the Civil, Public and Services Union – CPSU). David Begg drove the Employee Share Ownership Plan (ESOP) strategy that gave rise to the Telecom ESOP, a scheme that, from a worker perspective, was a major success. But the experience ultimately sparked off Begg's own disenchantment with privatisation. Essentially, Begg believes that the Eircom privatisation fell short because, firstly, the company failed to invest in a serious broadband roll-out, which the country needs, and secondly, because of the delay in updating telecom services generally. In Begg's view, Eircom switched from being a public sector monopoly to being a private sector one, and he does not want this to happen in other areas of the 'public realm'.

Commentators have suggested there is an irony here, in that the union leader associated with the country's most spectacular privatisation is now looking to prevent others from taking a similar route. But that view fails to grasp fully the context in which Begg backed the Telecom ESOP. Simply put, he was faced with the inevitability of privatisation and, instead of a futile campaign of resistance, he adopted a strategy aimed at maximising his members' advantage.

The result was a 2005 ICTU document, under the Begg's stewardship, which proposed a new governance structure for State companies. This would allow them easier access to capital and greater commercial independence. It urged the establishment of a holding company that would allow State companies to operate free of political interference. The proposal suggested that the new structure would separate State ownership from policy formulation, allowing those companies that seek to expand to have ready access to capital if their investment proposals are robust enough. Where they were required to fulfill non-commercial roles, they would be transparently compensated by the State.

In Towards 2016 the Government responded by stating its commitment to 'active engagement with the social partners on the future of the commercial, semi-State sector on the basis of the Government's commitment to its role in providing services of world-class quality at a competitive price to the consumer, with a viable long-term future for individual companies based on the most appropriate form of ownership or structure for its particular needs.'

This rather bland pronouncement was based on a number of equally bland principles that emphasised the need for sharing information and what's best for the public interest, which could include a 'good business case' for further investment. In other words, this was the original 'case by case' approach re-stated and updated in response to the ICTU demand for a new approach. By 2007, it was significant that the sale of a majority shareholding in Aer Lingus, and the almost immediate swoop by rival airline Ryanair to buy a major stake in the former State-owned company, meant that privatisation policy, such as it was, was thrown into confusion. Shortly after, the Government angered the ESB unions by proposing in an energy White Paper to transfer the transmission arm of the company to a separate entity, EirGrid. But the fact that EirGrid was also a fully fledged State company signaled a halt to any further plans for privatisation. The Government's appetite for further divestment had been diminished.

MODERNISATION AND THE NON-UNION CHALLENGE

The challenge of modernisation in an economy exposed to both the benefits and challenges of globalisation was a critical one for the partnership system, and one that the major players were acutely aware of. We have already seen that many trade unions realised that Irish industry had to modernise.

Des Geraghty, former SIPTU president, believes that the unions helped to modernise Irish industry in ways the employers themselves hadn't done. He puts it like this: 'If you were going to live up to the standards of national agreements, you had to address things like work reorganisation, productivity and competitiveness. The agenda we had created was ripe for that and a lot of good firms in Ireland got on top of their act, and the ones that did have survived to become world leaders.' Geraghty admitted that some trade unions had sometimes 'in the old days' been reactionary, stopping technology and machinery. He says that 'Irish trade unions were at their best when they were leading change and saying "this is the way Irish industry must go."'

Much of industry knew it had to adapt and did so, also learning from the new FDI firms. But this meant a gradual shift away from traditional industrial relations to more human resource management techniques, some of which were marked by best international practice, others that were not. It was a shift that had been happening for some time, starting in the 1980s and working its way through industry during the 1990s and into the new millennium. IBEC's Turlough O'Sullivan observes that the entry of foreign non-union companies 'had a dramatic effect on trade union attitudes and the trade union leadership' even as early as the mid to late 1980s. Before this, he said, it was assumed they would simply 'go down the unionised road and interview a number of unions that were appropriate to the operation they were about to set up and do a deal with one union for general workers and one or two unions for craft workers.' According to O'Sullivan:

> That was the pattern. Pre-production, closed shop type agreements were kind of the norm. But because of the fact that the whole unionised system had come into some disrepute, particularly about the ability to get change, firms began to say, 'Well, this is not really working. What are the prospects of coming in here and setting up a non-union shop, paying people better and investing substantially in the leadership and management of the employees in a much more sophisticated and professional way.'

90

The trade union movement had played a major part in setting the country to rights but, by the mid 1990s, it looked like there would be no substantial union membership dividend. In fact, as employment began to really accelerate in the 1990s, unions scored numerical gains in overall numbers but the crucial density level, which measures the proportion of union members to the number of employees in the work-force, came down inexorably. Billy Attley, former SIPTU president, agrees this was a 'massive annoyance in that the longer you stay in the process, institutionally, you are damaging your own ability. The basic marketing strategy of a union is to drive pay up!' He says the recruiting field was made up of those who were 'disenchanted' with 'bad employ-ers'. But Attley says this level of discontent 'doesn't happen in the big American companies, because they have sophisticated IR systems which effectively are far greater than the traditional Irish systems, so it is a huge drawback.'

A survey of new job announcements in 2001–03 showed that new unionised jobs in the multinational sector had become scarcer and scarcer, 'especially as many are now in services rather than manufacturing' (*Industrial Relations News* 2004). Just one of the seventeen major new international companies setting up in Ireland for the first time over that three-year period had recognised a trade union, while only four of 22 com-panies announcing expansions considered that the new jobs would be unionised. An earlier 1996 survey – which looked at 51 new job announce-ments in 1994 and 1995 – had found that two out of 32 new companies recognised unions, while ten out of eighteen announcing expansions pro-vided for recognition (*Industrial Relations News* 1996).

A CLASSIC IRISH 'FUDGE'?

What had been happening since the late 1980s was something of an Irish 'fudge' as the IDA, which in earlier times had advised incoming firms how to unionise, now informed them they didn't have to if they didn't want to. In essence, as social partnership developed, so too did at least two parallel systems of employee relations. One was founded on the old sys-tem of collective bargaining: the recognition of trade unions by employ-ers. The other was a growing non-union sector, made up largely of US multinationals, who simply wanted to operate non-union human resource management (HRM) methods.

There were variants of these models, as some of the non-union firms had more sophisticated 'people' policies than others, while there existed a growing number of smaller indigenous companies in sectors that unions had always found hard to organise. There was also an emerging group in the first years of the new century that started to take a more aggressively anti-union stance, not relying on sophisticated HR standards and sometimes operating outside the voluntary boundaries of the State's dispute resolution agencies.

These changes exposed a fundamental dichotomy at the heart of social partnership. In the 1980s and early 1990s, there was a pragmatic understanding that, without this duality (or, more correctly, a multiplicity of practices around two core positions), FDI firms might not locate in Ireland and the shining new industries that signalled an economic breakthrough might not come in sufficient numbers. For some, however, it was a contradiction that could not be ignored indefinitely. This shift away from traditional industrial relations created a separate challenge for the trade unions and the social partnership system. It raised the problem of trade union recognition in the workplace and placed it centre stage by the mid-1990s. It was an issue that had been handled pragmatically up to that point, but was becoming increasingly awkward as the decade wore on. It was a potential tinderbox within the partnership process, a fuse waiting to be lit by a number of emergent companies. These were exhibiting a more old-fashioned hostility to unions. Ryanair, the budget airline, represented the epitome of that approach.

Employers in Ireland have the right to refuse to recognise trade unions, based on comments in Supreme Court judgments. This can cancel out the aspirations of any individual who joins a trade union with a view to securing the right of that union to engage in collective bargaining on their behalf. In other words, individuals have the right to freedom of association, but this is of little use in a collective bargaining context if the employer refuses to recognise the union concerned. Put simply, one right cancels out the other, leaving trade unions with a problematic situation: they have a partnership agreement at national level, but have no statutory right to recognition in the workplace.

THE RECOGNITION CONUNDRUM

This problem had been left in abeyance during the earlier partnership agreements, merely being referred to what was, by then, a dormant Employer Labour Conference under the PESP in 1991. As we have seen, the IDA and successive governments realized that many incoming multinationals, particularly from the US, were hostile to trade unions, while bringing in sophisticated HR techniques. Nonetheless, union recognition was a problem that could no longer be avoided by the mid- to late 1990s. It was the proverbial elephant in the room that gradually began to sour the relationship between the trade unions, the Government and IBEC. Essentially, the trade unions knew that, while the sophisticated multinationals were, in a practical sense, off limits, this still left a growing swath of domestic companies that were able to simply ignore them unless they could mount an effective campaign of industrial action.

The task of finding a suitable compromise eventually fell to what was called the High Level Group, made up of the social partners under P2000 in 1997. The Group's first report was knocked off course by the infamous Dublin Airport dispute in 1998. Industrial action by SIPTU members in Ryanair, who had been denied recognition, led indirectly to sympathetic protests, closing the whole of the airport. The Group's second report, which took account of that dispute, led directly to the Industrial Relations Act 2001 and the Miscellaneous Provisions Act (2004), the combined effect of which allowed unions to represent workers in non-union companies (where there is no collective bargaining) in the Labour Court and to secure legally binding decisions on legitimate claims.

The High Level Group opted not to go down the route of giving workers a statutory right of recognition as applies in the UK, USA and other European countries. There was still a fear at government and IBEC levels that this might put off FDI firms, while the trade unions preferred to stick with a voluntary system as opposed to overly legalistic solutions in traditional IR areas.

The 2001 and 2004 Acts resulted in a series of cases in the Labour Court, which generally involved employees in smaller indigenous non-union firms securing advances, if they could show that their pay and conditions were below the collective bargaining norm for their particular industry or sector. This meant that non-union workers could achieve parity in the Labour Court if they were not matching their counterparts in unionised jobs. These decisions are binding and enforceable in the Circuit Court. The winners were workers in smaller local firms, as foreign multinationals in the FDI sector already tended to pay at or above the going rate. It was never contemplated that such firms would be caught by it. However, a ground-breaking Supreme Court ruling in early 2007 in a case involving Ryanair, the Labour Court and the pilots' branch of the IMPACT trade union, placed a real question mark over the future operability of the Acts from the trade union perspective.

The Supreme Court found that the Labour Court hearing in the case had been procedurally flawed, as it had not adopted sufficiently stringent judicial standards, for example, by not calling any trade union pilot to give evidence. To the surprise of trade union leaders, the Supreme Court also disagreed with the Labour Court's basis for concluding that collective bargaining did not exist in Ryanair. Ryanair had operated an in-house employee representative committee (ERC) for years until it collapsed in 2004. The Supreme Court concluded that the pilots could not collapse such a body and then claim they didn't have collective bargaining. Such a body, it would seem, has the status of an 'excepted' body under the 1941 Trade Union Act and, as long as the employer agrees, may be regarded as a collective bargaining unit. It must also be demonstrated that the body concerned operates as an internal unit.

Such a unit does not have to have trade union status. Indeed, it may be set up by an employer and need only apply 'fair and reasonable' standards of representation. The case was to be re-heard, the Supreme Court ruled.

The outcome gave the social partners plenty to think about. It was welcomed by IBEC and raised by union leaders inside the social partnership process. The fall-out from the case, which was still only being digested at the start of 2007, was sure to be an issue in the following round of national talks.

A question posed by some observers was whether the Supreme Court findings would have arisen at all if IMPACT had simply not pursued grievances on behalf of its pilots under the 2001–04 Acts. In other words, why take on Ryanair given that its Chief Executive Michael O'Leary is not only hostile to trade unions, but had gone on record as warning he would go all the way to the Supreme Court? One employer source close to the union recognition debate doesn't agree with this argument. He believes that there are enough anti-union employers with deep pockets and who are ideologically motivated. It was only a matter of time before someone would take a challenge all the way, 'They just don't want a trade union.'

KEEPING A SECRET?

As a result of the ruling confusion surrounded the 2001–04 Acts, presenting the social partners with a twin challenge. Employers, particularly those in the FDI sector, had already been growing increasingly wary of the potential impact of Labour Court decisions under the 2001–04 Acts, even though the legislation was not expected to affect them. Trade union hopes were seriously dampened in the aftermath of the judgment.

Secretary of the Department of the Taoiseach Dermot McCarthy agrees that, not only are more FDI companies now 'less comfortable with partnership' than they used to be, but the 2001–04 Acts created unease: 'For those who are passionately non-union, if not anti-union, the very real prospect that they might be required to engage at the Labour Court with what they would see as disaffected employees is something which literally terrifies some of them.' Somewhat startlingly, McCarthy says some of these local operations are nervous that their head office 'would ever find out about this because they see it as creating instability in what was perceived to be a very stable and settled labour market. I wouldn't want to exaggerate it but there are some companies who do have an exaggerated sense of what has happened.'

Eoin O'Driscoll, who has also been involved with the influential US Chamber of Commerce in Ireland, explains the FDI perspective on the Acts. He says that pay in the (non-union) sector has always been influenced by the national agreements, but there has been freedom to innovate at local level, 'But now you have the ability [through the 2001–04 Acts] to invoke the Labour Court, even if you are not unionised.' There is a 'general concern that a smaller and smaller section of the economy, the non-traded sector, is actually deciding upon issues like pensions and wages,' according to O'Driscoll.

Former IBEC Divisional Director Liam Doherty believes that the solution to this vexed issue may ultimately be handed down from Brussels. He says that a constitutional referendum, which is likely to be necessary to allow for a statutory right to union recognition, might be a 'bridge too far' for the IDA and the Government, not to mention IBEC. In the past, solutions to local problems have come down via the European route, and eventually this could happen in the area of collective bargaining rights. Doherty also believes that, from a trade union point of view, 'the prospect of an unsuccessful constitutional referendum campaign on the issue could be disastrous.'

OUT OF THE BLUE

'I didn't see it coming I must admit,' said Dermot McCarthy of the Irish Ferries dispute in 2005. It appeared to emerge out of the blue. But this dispute and a number of other high profile cases – where foreign workers had been short-changed – gave the private sector unions a real cause. A huge rumpus over labour standards was triggered. Much of the problem seemed to lie in the construction industry and on major infrastructural projects where work was contracted out to companies bringing in workers from new EU accession states or countries outside the Union.

SIPTU Regional Secretary Patricia King has always believed in a pragmatic approach to social partnership but, while she had met 'some employers who have a good ethos', she 'never got to a place where, ultimately, I would trust them'. So the climate generated around the Irish Ferries controversy came as no real surprise to her. She did not accept it was an aberration, as some employers had told her. IBEC Director General Turlough O'Sullivan does not agree with her assessment. While admitting that there were a 'very, very small number of incidents in recent times', he insisted these had been 'latched onto by the trade unions and maximum embarrassment heaped upon IBEC [whose] overall record is so good'.

Patricia King does not even like the description 'partnership', a distaste she shares with SIPTU President Jack O'Connor. The two were to form a formidable partnership themselves during the exhausting talks process, which would eventually give birth to Towards 2016. In the year immediately before the agreement, a series of disputes and problems had emerged in the area of labour standards, the most significant of which was the Irish Ferries dispute. This followed the major furore generated by the failure of Turkish construction firm Gama to fully pay its Turkish workers in Ireland, after initially strenuously denying such claims. The case kicked up a political storm in the Dáil, raised by Socialist Party TD Joe Higgins. The unions then made effective representations on behalf of the workers.

Ironically, in talks on the mid-term review of Sustaining Progress, former Minister for Finance Charlie McCreevy had agreed to fund more labour inspectors in the Labour Inspectorate, after SIPTU raised the issue. McCreevy says that years later when the Gama controversy arose, it was reported in SIPTU's magazine that former Minister McCreevy had agreed new inspectors should be appointed. Looking back, McCreevy says the Department of Enterprise and Employment simply wouldn't give in because there was a recruitment embargo in force.

ICTU had, of course, secured a national minimum wage by 2001, introduced by then Minster for Enterprise Trade and Employment Mary Harney. Although not welcomed by IBEC, it initially proved to be something of a damp squib for both sides as it came at a time when there was already strong upward pressure on pay. Ultimately, it was to provide a real safety net for the growing number of EU (and non-EU) workers that would enter the country, particularly after the entry of new accession states like Poland, Latvia and Lithuania.

THE NEW ARRIVALS

From 2004 onwards, the new wave of migrants created both a problem and an opportunity for the trade unions. On the one hand, it helped to dampen wage expectations as employers took advantage of the much-needed new pool of labour. On the other, thousands were recruited into trade unions. By 2007, immigrant workers made up 10 per cent of the Irish workforce, a similar proportion to that which applies in other advanced EU countries. Indirectly, this was to trigger the crises that surrounded the negotiations on Towards 2016, including the Irish Ferries dispute, and raise doubts about the future of social partnership on both sides.

Inward migration had provided an employment pool that posed a challenge for the relevant authorities in a society that already found the enforcement of labour laws difficult. SIPTU President Jack O'Connor says his union did not oppose the opening of borders after the new states joined the EU but, in a formal review of Sustaining Progress, they had told the Government that it required action on enforcement legislation, 'But we did not persuade them.' Policy, he claims, was 'dictated' by the Department of Enterprise, Trade and Employment, a department that Patricia King describes as 'not being at the races' when it came to protecting existing employee rights.

In the end, the social partnership process proved its robustness in the face of the seemingly sudden appearance of employment standards and the 'job displacement' issue. The impact of the crisis was central in setting out much of the core agenda for ICTU in the talks. This meant a nine-month talks process rather than the usual two to three months, although Dermot McCarthy believes the extent of the delay was unnecessary: 'We had several months of talks about talks, whereas if we had actually talked about the problem we might have got there earlier. Hindsight is easy but I do think the partnership process did manage the problem, which was virtually a crisis, given the emotive character of the particular dispute that triggered it.'

The dispute between Irish Ferries, with its brusque Chief Executive Eamon Rothwell, and SIPTU harked back to a harsher era. The company's plan to replace most of its Irish workforce with staff from Eastern Europe was described by Taoiseach Bertie Ahern as 'unacceptable, deplorable and against the spirit of social partnership'. SIPTU had a minority of the workers in the company; the rest were members of the relatively pliant Seamen's Union of Ireland. The company wanted to replace 543 directly employed seafarers (mostly SUI members) with lower paid agency crews. The SUI had little problem with that, as a relatively attractive redundancy package was on offer. Redundancy payouts varied according to length of service; the average was roughly €60,000. Irish Ferries would also 'reflag' its vessels to Cyprus.

Provoked by management's move, which was backed by a security presence, to place agency crews aboard Irish Ferries vessels, SIPTU officers reacted (they had already balloted for industrial action). Irish Ferries ships were laid up in Welsh and Irish ports for close on three weeks. Meanwhile, a national day of protest prompted by the union official at the heart of the dispute, SIPTU's Paul Smyth, was backed by SIPTU Dublin Regional Secretary Patricia King and SIPTU President Jack O'Connor. The subsequent march, organised and strongly backed by ICTU, attracted a surprisingly large turn-out and considerable public support.

During the dispute, Taoiseach Bertie Ahern said there was little the Government could do to stop Irish Ferries as the company was not acting outside the law. But Mr Ahern raised no overt objections to the union adopting a robust approach on the ground. In effect, he was saying that once Irish Ferries acted in a way that was out of sympathy with the social partnership process, then so be it. The NIB also implicitly endorsed the view that Irish Ferries' management had adopted a course that took the company outside the bounds of social partnership. It conveyed its concern that the 'situation which has now evolved has the potential to damage significantly the climate of trust and stability which has developed over the years in the context of social partnership'.

Jack O'Connor is certain that the labour standards protection mechanisms could not have been achieved through any other process – 'But I also don't believe that they would have been achieved were it not for the campaign that we ran.' He also praises the insistence of a number of people in the trade union movement, such as ICTU's David Begg and IMPACT's Peter McLoone: 'The result would not have been achieved were it not for all of them.'

IBEC was just as concerned as the Government. A senior employer who observed the dispute at close hand puts it this way: 'SIPTU had to achieve something tangible in the circumstances if social partnership was not to be destabilised.' By deciding to delay talks on Towards 2016, SIPTU President Jack O'Connor took a risk, but it was one that was strongly endorsed by his members. The aforementioned senior employer believes that the SIPTU leader's strategy was fully vindicated, and that it also gave private sector workers something to fight for: 'Jack was dead right, they had rolled over in the past. Himself and Patricia King also put a huge amount into it personally.'

IBEC members were concerned that the row could unleash forces, which most of them would prefer to see kept under wraps. Many among the wider population also saw in the Irish Ferries approach something of a harbinger of a more uncertain future, raising all sorts of issues in regard to attitudes towards migrant workers. Simply put, the genie raised by the dispute had to be put back in the bottle. This is where the NIB, and the subsequent social partnership talks on the issue of employment standards at the heart of the row, came to the fore.

STICKING WITH THE PROCESS

The Irish Ferries deadlock was broken in the Labour Relations Commission following the prior intervention of the NIB just fresh from a major inter-vention to resolve an equally difficult problem in State-owned An Post. There was something for everyone in the outcome. Irish Ferries achieved its main aims, securing a green light to outsource crews and reflag its vessels to Cyprus, with all vessels to be managed on a contract basis by a shipping agency based in that country. The wages of the new agency seafarers would be significantly lower than those that had applied, while the company also secured a three-year industrial peace (no-strike) clause, with any issues of dispute going to binding arbitration. SIPTU had achieved a negotiated settlement on the application of Irish minimum wage standards, while the pay and conditions of those who chose to remain with the company were maintained.

The Irish Ferries row handed the wider trade union movement a big issue to play for on the national stage. It also showed how the partnership process could absorb and handle a real crisis. It could not have done so, however, had IBEC not stayed the course, despite the problems the dispute caused the organisation. The employers' body could sympathise with much of the company's cost-driven plan, but it took a strategic decision that it would quietly distance itself from company's overall strategy and tactics.

The signal that IBEC would stay the course had already been given in a quite separate dispute in State-owned An Post, also in late 2005, and which carried a threat to the talks process perhaps equal to that of Irish Ferries. The postal service had refused to budge on back money due under a previous national wage deal, a move that sparked a threat of action by the CWU, the union that ICTU General Secretary David Begg used to lead before he departed for the charity Concern.

IMPACT's Peter McLoone recalls the problem in An Post as he saw it:

> Here was a State company pleading inability to pay and seeking co-operation with change that the workforce thought was not just way out of proportion to what was necessary, but was missing the point in terms of the challenges that faced that company. It was almost bringing us back to the 1980s and we looked at the way the key union, the CWU and the management were engaging with each other. It was based on absolute hostility, total mistrust, boiling raw hatred.

Efforts to introduce change in An Post had always provoked major conflict, and industrial relations there harked back to a pre-partnership era.

The NIB however, faced a problem inherent in its very make-up. Two of its three 'arms', ICTU and IBEC, were in direct opposition, given that they also represented the two protagonists in the dispute. However, with the help of its Chairman Dermot McCarthy, the NIB showed its adroitness and vast experience by calling in an outside firm of accountants to assess the issues behind the company's 'inability to pay' claim. That move helped unlock the dispute by, as he put it, 'creating a space' that enabled management to make good the back pay.

But more importantly, the way the NIB resolved these very difficult disputes showed how the social partners were able to protect the process, as they had done for almost twenty years. Peter McLoone, who also sits on the board of the NIB, suggests that the decision by NIB employer member (and IBEC director general) Turlough O'Sullivan to work through that difficult dispute enabled him and his organisation to move on to the Irish Ferries row. It showed that, by sticking with social partnership through those two disputes, ICTU, IBEC and the Government were not going to be easily blown off course.

The negotiations on Towards 2016 finally got moving in the aftermath of the Irish Ferries dispute after the unions received assurances that the issues raised by the episode would be taken seriously by the Government and employers. The fact that IBEC had maintained its faith in the process during the two disputes, allied with the determination of Taoiseach Bertie Ahern to show his continued allegiance to partnership as a core belief, set the scene for a breakthrough.

EMPLOYMENT STANDARDS AND ENFORCEMENT

The groundwork was agreed prior to the negotiations on Towards 2016 by a new NESC strategy report (*Strategy 2006: People, Productivity and Purpose*). The NESC played its usual scene-setting role as it had done since 1986–87, with the social partners reaching a consensus on policy in a range of social, economic and fiscal areas. The pay element of the agreement – 10 per cent increase over 27 months – and its attendant industrial relations provisions were set within the ambit of an overall ten-year approach to social partnership, which is reflected in the title of the pact. This suggests that similar deals on pay and related issues will be negotiated every two or three years during the ten years of the framework.

Towards 2016 includes a general package of measures dealing with employment standards. As Dermot McCarthy explains it, the major part of the package is 'increased enforcement to ensure better compliance with pre-existing requirements'. The new elements are 'modest enough' and 'I think were designed to give effective reassurance about the more extreme forms of behaviour which certainly underpin the fears of a lot of workers, which in reality are probably very rare.'

Essentially, there are two distinct elements within this strand of Towards 2016: the first concerning the enforcement of existing laws and the second involving the more complex area of acceptable behavioural norms or standards. There was to be a 'major enhancement and expansion of the existing Labour Inspectorate' to increase its effectiveness in the form of a new statutory National Employment Rights Authority (NERA). The number of labour inspectors was set to be increased from 31 to 90 by the end of 2007. The changes would allow authorised officers of the Department of Enterprise, Trade and Employment and NERA to join with the Department of Social Welfare and Family Affairs and the Revenue Commissioners to work together in Joint Investigation Units 'involving staff of both organisations in joint investigations in appropriate cases'. Every employee must have an identifiable employer within the State who has a legal responsibility for compliance with all aspects of the applicable employment rights legislation. Better payroll records are to be enforced and, if they are not, fines of up to €250,000 may be applied.

The unions insisted on new measures to prevent an 'Irish Ferries on land' scenario, fearing that any company could offer voluntary redundancy to existing unionised workers on good pay and conditions and simply replace them with workers on minimum legal rates. IBEC said these fears were exaggerated but agreed to a limited range of new measures, which could act as a disincentive to any employer that might consider this route.

The agreement states that the 'possibility of the collective compulsory replacement of workers' by lower paid workers from new EU member states has, 'in certain circumstances', the potential to be harmful to the maintenance of good industrial relations. A special Redundancy Panel was to be established to advise the Minister on whether a particular case should be referred to the Labour Court for a 'binding opinion'. This opinion could be appealed by either party to the existing Employment Appeals Tribunal. Specific criteria were to be applied to identify such cases. 'Normal and legitimate' business activity could not be affected, which indicated that employers were concerned that trade unions could use the new rules to stymie normal business restructuring.

'SOCIAL PARTNERSHIP PURGATORY'

David Begg says that the unintended consequence of the Irish Ferries plan was to impose on the whole business community 'a regime of labour market regulation which will be quite significant'. It showed the value of partnership for the trade unions. Begg says he is aware that, if trade union strength 'dwindled away', there would be no point being in social partnership 'because we couldn't make it stick'. IMPACT Deputy General Secretary Shay Cody says the unions had been 'blessed in its enemies' and thanked Irish Ferries – and Ryanair – for putting the focus on the need for labour standards and galvanising the movement.

The sheer length of the talks leading up to Towards 2016 came as something of a surprise to someone just cutting his teeth in industrial relations – IBEC Director of Economic Policy Danny McCoy. McCoy referred to the length of the negotiations as akin to 'social partnership purgatory'. When the issue of outsourcing and displacement blew up, McCoy suggests there was an agenda 'driven by an ideological push to the Left. Social partnership was delayed around straw men created as a result of ideological zeal.' The company (Irish Ferries) had 'a good case which was not effectively communicated'.

But as we have seen, this did not mean that IBEC was prepared to jettison partnership. The organisation distanced itself enough from the company to enable the State's dispute resolution agencies to get involved and, in so doing, also ensured the social partnership process could move on. On the employment standards measures, however, McCoy believes what was actually achieved by the trade unions was much narrower than what they were looking for. Nonetheless, he warned: 'It is clear that some firms – multinationals in particular – would feel that the legislative thrust in the direction of employment standards is already too much.'

NOT MUCH APPETITE BELOW

Progress in building partnership in the workplace has been disappointing, almost the mirror opposite of what has been achieved at national level. As Professor Bill Roche of UCD wrote in a recent ESRI report: 'A decade on from the emergence of partnership at the workplace as a core issue, it is hard to avoid the conclusion that progress in this area remains patchy and the momentum has dropped.'

Social partnership at national level would seem to have been the ideal vehicle to promote and create a favourable climate for the growth of local partnership in enterprises, private and public. It was for this reason that the social partners agreed to the establishment of the National Centre for Partnership (NCP) during P2000 (1997–99) and then established its replacement, the current and more substantially funded National Centre for Partnership and Performance (NCPP) during the PPF (2000–02).

However, such agreements remain relatively rare. Former IMPACT General Secretary Phil Flynn says that the hopes for such arrangements have fallen flat and that everyone has to bear responsibility for this failure. Most local arrangements tend to be consultative, often involving only a very limited degree of joint decision making. Perhaps the most significant public sector partnership arrangement has been in the ESB, starting with the 1996 Cost and Competitiveness Review (CCR). The CCR was a three-way agreement between the (former) Department of Public

Enterprise, the ESB and the ESB group of unions on all aspects of change driven by EU regulations. There was a consensus that change would have to be introduced at all levels of the business, although the underlying industrial relations climate remained intact. Traditional pay for change agreements were still accommodated. A subsequent agreement in 2000, known as PACT, also demonstrated that the traditional collective bargaining processes, particularly within the power generation stations, remained unscathed by the partnership process. A new agreement, this time between the ESB and the unions without the Department being directly involved, was agreed at the tail-end of 2005.

By contrast, the Telecom Eireann partnership agreement between the former State-owned telecommunications company and its unions appeared to be more far reaching. Management and unions were more successful at grafting partnership onto the pre-existing industrial relations model under pressure from a fully opened telecoms market. Negotiated in parallel with the agreement was an Employee Share Ownership Plan (ESOP) under which staff received 14.9 per cent of the company, in accordance with policy guidelines drawn up by the Fianna Fáil party prior to its entry into coalition government in 1997. The ESOP was seen as a vital tool in helping to secure the partnership agreement, the aim of which was to create 'a new relationship between staff, unions and management, making co-operation in transformation a positive benefit for the whole community of Telecom Eireann and its customers.' Floated in 1999, Telecom changed its name to Eircom and went through a number of ownership changes. A key element in these moves was the insistence by the unions that the partnership agreement be adhered to. And in the case of the ESOP, the employees had increased their shareholding to 35 per cent by 2006.

Developments on enterprise level generally have been limited and often disappointing, despite official endorsements of co-operative involvement or participation initiatives in recent social partnership agreements. In the private sector, partnership arrangements at companies such as Waterford Crystal, Aughinish Alumina, Bausch & Lomb and Galtee Meats have been cited as examples of progressive and practical private sector agreements. While these sorts of agreements did exhibit some innovative features, they were the exception rather than the norm across private industry.

One significant exception is AIB, one of Ireland's two largest banks. In April 2003, 6,000 members of the Irish Bank Officials Association (IBOA) voted to accept a three-year industrial relations agreement, concluded with the assistance of an independent consultant, Phil Flynn, a former general secretary of IMPACT. Flynn describes the AIB/IBOA model as one of the 'best of its kind in operation in these islands'. The agreement was one of very few developments in this area, but it did signal the completion of a successful healing process between the union and the bank after a very bitter strike in 1992.

A major disappointment occurred at the former semi-State airport management company, Aer Rianta. Management and unions agreed a well funded 'compact for constructive participation' in the mid-1990s, viewed in many quarters as the most radical and wide-ranging exemplar of enterprise partnership in Ireland. By 2003 it was defunct. One of the central principles of this inelegantly titled agreement was that no one party would seek to impose change. The agreement was overly reliant on key senior management and trade union champions and, once this inner circle disbanded, there was little to prevent the process from withering on the vine.

In the public service, the Strategic Management Initiative (SMI), launched in 1994, set the agenda for change in the Irish Civil Service, focusing as it did on developing strategic capability in government departments and offices. The objectives of the SMI, to be implemented on a partnership basis, were contained in the policy document *Delivering Better Government* (DBG), published in May 1996. Critics of SMI have observed that the history of public service reform pre-SMI has shown how well public servants can side-step change, while at the same time advocating support and commitment.

Bill Roche says that the public service partnership 'has been treading water', and has generally has been confined to softer, albeit worthy, issues like communications, the climate of relationships and so forth. There has been little evidence of agreement on harder issues such as work practice change, career progression and pay and conditions. However, a recent partnership agreement involving over 6,000 workers in Dublin City Council, which aims to facilitate change and incentivise workers, may point the way forward. It has certainly been welcomed by advocates of local partnership who will doubtless hope that it helps to kick-start a new effort in this area.

Essentially, employers tend to regard local partnership arrangements as suitable as long as they are confined to areas such as information and consultation, but they are generally wary or even hostile about more concrete involvement in decision-making, which they see as a central management prerogative. But wariness of local partnership initiatives is not confined to management. In unionised employments, there remains suspicion at shop-floor level of some partnership-style initiatives. In most cases, where part-nership arrangements have been formally agreed, traditional collective bargaining issues are specifically excluded. In a sense both employers and unions remain reluctant to move from traditional preserves at local level, despite the national partnership agreements and despite a formal commit-ment to extend the idea downwards.

Phil Flynn, who is now an industrial relations consultant, agrees with this assessment: 'You can see that by definition the employer wouldn't be automatically disposed towards empowerment but what I find, as a practi-tioner, is that partnership at local level has become a dirty word. On the union side it is often used as a veto on change and on the management side it's frequently used as a stick by which to beat or threaten workers.' Flynn concludes that, while the national macro-level partnership has achieved its potential, this has not percolated down to local level, although 'funny enough, some of the better models are in the non-union sector.'

Bill Roche asks how the momentum for workplace partnership might be regained and ponders the likely impact of the transposition of the EU Directive on Information and Consultation. This introduces a set of arrangements for keeping employees informed of a company's plans, but it requires 10 per cent of the workforce in a company to trigger local infor-mation and consultation arrangements. Roche is not optimistic, suggest-ing that in many firms the provisions are unlikely to institute anything more than 'rudimentary arrangements for information and consultation, or for partnership more generally.'

LOOKING BACK, LOOKING FORWARD

It is hardly surprising that the achievements of social partnership since 1997 are harder to quantify than for the first ten years of the process. After all, Ireland was on its knees in 1987, with high unemployment, inflation and interest rates, falling living standards, fiscal meltdown, falling profits and rising emigration. Ten years on from that first agreement, the PNR, it was not difficult to conclude that social partnership had, at the very least, helped to provide a stable backdrop for improving business confidence, attracting new industry, raising living standards and increasing job creation.

In the eleven years since 1996, which have been the focus of this chapter, we have had far more than more of the same. The success of the so-called Celtic Tiger is accepted, although aspects of the wider social benefits of this success story are a matter of some debate. Nonetheless, it would be churlish in the extreme to do anything other than applaud the massive rise in job creation and the transformation of the economy. Truly, at least in that sense, Ireland has come of age, finally experiencing our own version of the 'long boom' that helped to build the economies and societies of our Western European neighbours between 1945 and the first oil shock in 1973.

While it is relatively easy to give social partnership a large share of the credit for the first ten years of this Irish boom-time story, how much credit to give it for what followed from P2000 onwards is hard to assess. Critics of the process have emerged in recent years and they often make the case that social partnership has had little to do with the success of the Celtic Tiger; instead they point to factors like the labour market, tax cuts, foreign direct investment, government policies, EU money and so on. The proponents of social partnership agree that all of these factors were important in creating the Celtic Tiger. However they believe that buy-in by major forces in the economy and society still provides an underlying stability which makes Ireland an attractive place to do business in a global economy.

Other opponents argue forcibly that a malign dynamic has been increasingly at play, namely that social partnership tends towards a negation of our democracy, by reducing the sovereignty of parliament and increasing social partner regulation in areas hitherto the preserve of independent decision making. Supporters of partnership argue, however, that the involvement by a greater range of groups within social partnership enhances its accountability to the wider society, and helps society arrive at consensus based solutions and strategies. These arguments have emerged over the past decade without really getting the sort of sustained or considered airing they deserve in the media or in the Oireachtas.

Looking back over the last two decades, the eminent Professor Bill Roche of UCD commented in a recent ESRI article (Spring 2007): 'Much that had seemed fixed and immutable is now changed or in the melting pot, especially in the areas of the alignment of employment relations with business imperatives, the role of the State, the conduct of collective bargaining, the circumstances of trade unions and the implications of the increased openness of the Irish labour market.'

Roche goes on to suggest that areas of continuity with past practice should be given due weight, particularly the limited emphasis on competition through investment in 'human assets' and 'the faltering progress' of partnership at the level of the workplace. He also highlights some of the contradictions raised in this chapter by many of the key players. Roche says the trade unions have been 'invited to become social partners' but they increasingly appear unwelcome in the workplace. Meanwhile, on the ground, the emphasis on the public policy of investment in the development of skills and associated work practices as a primary driver of competitive advantage 'falls well short of such a vision'.

Our increasingly open labour market, Roche observes, opens up avenues for employers to compete on the basis of lower labour costs. Roche touches directly on some of the central issues that emerged around the negotiation of Towards 2016: 'Whether Ireland develops a model of work and employment consistent with the aspiration of moving up the value chain and promoting economic and social inclusion remains an open question.'

It certainly remains open to any of the partners to walk away if they find the process no longer answers their needs. No-one really knows what would happen if they did. Jack O'Connor probably best sums up this sort of speculation by suggesting it is a bit like 'the debate about God'. Everyone's contribution to that debate is 'equally valid and undoubtedly some of them are correct but in order to find out you have to die'. He adds, 'There are people on both sides of the equation – and there are increasing numbers on the employer side – who never experienced things as they were. They may not be in favour of [social partnership]. I don't know, when it comes right down to facing the consequences, whether people will opt to leap into the abyss.'

Many of the themes covered in this chapter continue to loom large, from the urgent need for greater efficiency and effectiveness in the public sector, to Ireland's ability to continue to attract investment. Can these challenges be met in a fashion that meets the growing social agenda of ICTU, but in such a fashion that keeps business competitive and drives the reform of our public sector? After twenty-one years, issues like this are left unanswered, forcing the social partners to reassess the relevance of the process, and to sharpen and prepare it to meet today's challenges.

CHAPTER 5

From Failure to Success – Pay in the Private Sector and the Semi-States

It was about two in the morning and I was taking a stroll around the old Department of Finance building, killing time. Suddenly I saw a bunch of employers who were not part of the talks. Haughey had sent for the 'big boys'. 'Look', he had told them, 'you have been telling me you want to restore confidence in the economy and here I am trying to put a deal together with this crowd [the unions] who, in my judgement, will deliver a very moderate pay deal. And I have your organisation doing nothing but puting the boot through everything.'

Senior trade union leader at the PNR talks, 1987

The above quote may be somewhat apocryphal in the details it describes, but it sums up neatly the central importance, for the employer side, of ensuring trade union adherence to the terms of national pay agreements. It also illustrates that the unions had apparently given then Taoiseach Charles Haughey sufficient assurances that they would stick to the prospective new national pay agreement – the PNR – if others kept their part of the overall bargain.

The history of pay bargaining in the private sector (and the commercial semi-State companies) in the decades leading up the negotiation of the first of the partnership programmes, the PNR, had largely been one of failure for employers and trade unions. In the period from the end of the Second World War in 1945 up to the negotiation of the first National Understanding in 1979, pay bargaining shifted alternatively from relatively simple national level pay agreements to local or decentralised agreements negotiated on a sectoral or company-by-company basis. Over time, the Government gradually become more involved in pay settlement, through the establishment of a number of enabling institutions, such as the Employer Labour Conference and the National Industrial and Economic Council (later to become the NESC). In other words, there was a gradual drift towards mapping out the background or context for centralised agreements, a journey that tended to reflect the economic, political and social development of Ireland since the War.

This trend culminated in 1979 and 1980, when the Fianna Fáil Government, the FUE and ICTU agreed two successive National Understandings (NUs). These were prototypes for what was to follow in 1987. Both agreements were more than just pay deals. For the first time, they included commitments in areas such as employment, tax and social welfare. One of the chief failures of both agreements, however, was that the pay terms tended to be regarded as a floor by private and public sector trade unions, which were powerful enough to be able to build on this floor to secure higher pay rises. This did not bode well for future employer support for national deals.

The weakness of the NUs was that, quite simply, they failed to achieve any of the objectives of the parties involved. The pay deals were broken, with the Government often the side to cave in to pressure, initiating a pay spiral that set in a train a vicious circle of higher inflation and lower real living standards. Neither was there a peace dividend. In fact, the level of industrial disputes, which had risen during the 1970s, did not abate during the National Understandings. For example, in 1979 a six month postal strike led to the destabilisation of the then Fianna Fáil Government under Taoiseach Jack Lynch. The result of all of this disruption and breaches of the NUs was that talks on a new centralised agreement collapsed in 1981, triggering a so-called 'free-for-all' in the private sector until 1987.

In the book *Industrial Relations in Practice* (1997), Professor Bill Roche, a keen analyst of the industrial relations scene at the time, noted that this return to free collective bargaining between 1981 and 1987 proved to be 'no panacea for employers, while unions feared marginalisation and their members suffered declining real incomes'. In other words, for both of these prospective social partners, the overall outlook was even more dismal by 1987 than it had been in 1980. This was because the economy was struggling, company profitability was down, living standards were in decline and the national finances were a mess. By 1987, the verdict was that neither centralised nor de-centralised bargaining had been able to produce a cohesive or rational pay system. But getting the employers to sign up to a new centralised deal might prove to be problematic, given their earlier experiences under centralised agreements.

PATTERN BARGAINING

Looking back on the 'free-for-all' period (1981–87), Billy Attley, who was then FWUI General Secretary, says the simple fact was that 'people were 7 per cent worse off [in real terms] than when we had started.' Dan Murphy, general secretary of the PSEU and a key negotiator in the Congress team entering the PNR talks, says the unions may have secured pay rises that matched the high levels of inflation in the 1980s, 'but there was a recognition among a certain strand of the trade union movement that some things were incapable of being achieved by mere negotiations with employers.' Murphy and others like him believed that only the State could deliver on their other concerns, specifically tax reductions and the 'big issue' of the time: tackling mass unemployment, which stood close to a crushing 18 per cent.

One union that had been able to successfully target headline companies was the MSF, which engaged in the phenomenon known as 'leapfrogging'. As one of its senior officials explained, it would select key companies and conclude agreements, thus setting a benchmark for others to follow. This pattern bargaining was engaged in by all of the major unions. Billy Attley recalls how they used to be able, in his words, to 'hit the fat cats and then try and make it stick with the lower fat cats'.

However successful it was in the short-term, this tactic failed in its ultimate objective of improving, or even sustaining, living standards for trade union members. Moreover, as we have seen, unemployment and increasing emigration worsened in parallel with declining incomes. It was this combination of factors that forced a major trade union re-think, not just on pay but on the need for pay stability. Peter Cassells says that it could be debated whether stability was there before the PNR or not, 'but it [the PNR] meant that you had to deliver. Part of that was keeping your own house in order.'

PHONEY PRODUCTIVITY

For then FUE Director Turlough O'Sullivan the agreements of the 1970s had been nothing short of a disaster for employers. The era was marked by what he describes as 'phoney productivity' deals. The same productivity was 'sold time after time'. Many of the productivity deals had been tested by the Labour Court. If they had actually been delivered then things would have been different, O'Sullivan believes. But management also gets some of the blame from O'Sullivan for being, as he puts it, 'unprofessional and lacking in awareness of managing human resources'. In his view, the business of managing people was ground that had been ceded to the trade unions.

As a result of their experience in the 1970s, the FUE appointed a group of experts labeled the 'three wise men' to assess the pay scene. Their report found there was no connection between the money paid by firms and their performance in the marketplace. It was, O'Sullivan says, 'almost as if the money was coming from the Government or the EU'. The result was that the employers pulled out of centralised national pay talks in 1981, opting instead for free collective bargaining, known colloquially as a 'free-for-all'.

Six years into this 'free-for-all', the private sector employers were able to report some success in securing their agenda for competitiveness. Rising unemployemt helped them in gradually getting pay rises down. But they were unable to get wage increases down below the rate of inflation. The unions were still partially successful in targeting key companies and piggybacking on these local deals. So, while the employers were close to where they wanted to be, they were still not there and the overall economic situation was dire. Still, given their experience of the 1970s, it would be difficult to get them to re-engage with national level bargaining. Why go back and lose the limited gains of the 'free-for-all period?' As Turlough O'Sullivan puts it: 'We were sceptical. Pay levels had started to reduce and firms began to connect performance with pay and get staff to understand that. The thought of going back into national agreements and giving that up really rankled.'

Nonetheless, even during the 'free-for-all', the FUE was unable to force member firms to adhere to its suggested pay norms. Like ICTU on the trade union side, the employer body had no power to compel members to do anything in Ireland's voluntarist based industrial relations system. When selling the PNR to its member firms, the executive council of the FUE was also motivated by an increasing concern with the size of settlements arising from Labour Court recommendations. But, most of all, it took government action on the national finances, already evident since the extremely stringent March 1987 Budget – and the prospect of a very moderate national pay deal – to force a major employer re-think in the PNR talks.

THE GREAT PERSUADER

The employers simply didn't want to return to the 1970s. To get them back into national pay bargaining, the Taoiseach Charles Haughey of the new minority Fianna Fáil Government visited FUE headquarters in Baggot Street with the goal of getting them on board. Turlough O'Sullivan, who was at the meeting, said the new Taoiseach listened to the scepticism and heard the fact that most of them were relatively happy with free collective bargaining compared to the alternative. It was only when they saw how modest the pay levels were going to be over three years that they were tempted to give it a try. O'Sullivan says they were also affected by the 'national interest' and what he describes as the 'persuasiveness' of Haughey at the time. Haughey assured them the unions would deliver.

Billy Attley's more colourful description has the former Taoiseach telling influential FUE members, this time in Government Buildings in the midst of the actual talks, 'You have been out there shouting and roaring, "do this, do that", and I'm trying to do exactly what you want. You are going to have to make some contribution. Now is the time.' Given the scale of the economic crisis, plus the fact that the Government was already well on the way to addressing the State's fiscal mess, what could the employers do? They could not simply walk away when the Government were making the hard decisions many had demanded for years. And they were being offered what IBEC leaders at the time agreed was a 'no brainer' pay deal. It had been negotiated behind closed doors by an influential group of trade union leaders and Padraig O'hUiginn, the secretary of the Taoiseach's Department. In reality, they had little option but to sign up (interview with Haughey, early 2001). Kevin Murphy, secretary for Public Service Management and Development in the Department of Finance, said the Department agreed figures with O'hUiginn and Paddy Teahon from the Taoiseach's Department. Murphy says, 'IBEC were brought in, just invited in [and] told this was it.'

Dan McAuley, then director general of the FUE, says that, in the course of discussions with the Government, they were told the unions were prepared to sign off on a three-year deal with annual rises of just 2.5 per cent a year. However, according to McAuley, 'That didn't cause us any great problem, because I remember our anticipation was that, although prices were falling, and pay increases had been falling, we were expecting pay increases in the region of 4–4.5 per cent at local bargaining at the time.' With the Government already delivering on commitments to curb spending, the Minister for Finance Ray McSharry realised that the critical issue for the employers was whether the unions would comply with the pay deal. They had seen how the Government meant business on the national finances, McSharry said. Now they had to be persuaded that the trade unions would keep the pay deal.

But there was one more serious hurdle to be overcome. It arose, as one employer remembers, 'out of left field. Totally out of the blue'. Apart from the crucial issue of ensuring trade union compliance with the deal, the FUE was extremely reluctant to concede a trade union demand for a reduction in the working week from 40 to 39 hours. One employer insider recalls very strong resentment was expressed by FUE members that the Government was prepared to agree to this concession, given that it would mostly fall on the private sector to implement.

For the trade union side, however, the 39-hour week was hugely symbolic. It was regarded as a major achievement, one that lay on the social side of the social partnership ledger. It is recalled as one of those demands that came from the top down, not from the trade union membership. After all, given the economic backdrop of falling living standards, punitive personal taxes and rising unemployment, there was little expectation of such a concession. Reduced working hours were regarded by trade unions in Europe at the time as having the potential to create jobs, but the evidence for this was scanty. By getting the Government to persuade the FUE to concede it, however, the union leadership in Ireland was able to point to the potential of such agreements; in other words, they could move beyond pay and tax and into the social arena. It was a totem of sorts, pointing the way to a wider agenda in subsequent agreements.

FAVOURABLE CLIMATE

For their part, the trade unions could deliver their members if they could show them that a modest pay deal, combined with personal tax cuts, would see real incomes gradually start to rise after years of declining living standards. Employers, of course, had no problem with the tax reductions. For both sides, the result would be positive. Real incomes did start to rise for workers. And employers, after years of declining profitability, began to experience a real boost in their ability to compete and in their confidence to do so.

In the private sector, including the commercial semi-State companies, the result of the PNR and the six agreements that followed suggests that, compared to previous attempts at national wage deals in earlier decades, the compliance issue was largely resolved. This happened through a combination of factors: pressure from government; voluntary observance; external economic and labour market pressures; compliance efforts on the part of the social partners; and the role the State's dispute resolution agencies (the Labour Relations Commission and the Labour Court) played in maintaining the integrity of the agreements.

KEEPING THE BARGAIN

Backing for social partnership and advocating pay discipline is easy enough for ICTU 'because it is one step away from the membership', as Peter Cassells explains. 'But the individual unions had to manage it. They had to rigorously implement it.'

Right from the outset of the PNR, the importance of adherence to the terms of the pay agreement was seen as the critical factor needed to bind the first programme together. The evidence is clear that the PNR was honoured by the vast majority on both sides of industry, thereby setting a pattern that was largely repeated over the six agreements that followed throughout a remarkable period of almost twenty years. There is no evidence to suggest that the pattern is not being maintained during the current agreement, Towards 2016.

For the trade unions and their members, a key objective was the goal of improved living standards through rising real disposable income. This objective was already met during the period of the first two agreements (1987–92). Real take-home pay increased considerably, especially when compared to the 'free-for-all' which preceded the PNR. A key element in this improvement in the trend in real take-home pay was the tax concessions made by government, starting with the PNR in 1987. (See Table 5.1 for an overview of changes in take-home pay, 1980–92.)

The PNR was particularly important in that it helped to set a trend for the programmes which followed. Where companies or unions did breach the national terms, they did so voluntarily and without any knock-on implications.

TABLE 5.1: CHANGES IN REAL TAKE-HOME PAY 1980–92

Period	Average Manuf. Earnings		Average Male Manuf. Earnings Earnings		Average Building & Construction	
	Single	Married	Single	Married	Single	Married
1980–87	−7.0	−5.2	−10.8	−4.8	−16.0	−15.9
1987–90	+8.1	+4.9	+9.2	+5.7	+8.9	+4.9
1990–92	+4.4	+3.3	+4.3	+3.4	+9.8	+10.0
(Cumulative in each case)						

Source: Central Review Committee (CRC) (1994), *Progress Achieved Under the Programme for Economic and Social Progress.*

STATEMENT OF INTENT

The first significant step in the cementing of the private sector pay agreement in the PNR came immediately after the new pact was ratified in the form of a brief but unambiguous statement from then Labour Court Chairman John Horgan: 'The Court regards the ratification of the agreements as a major stimulus to industrial harmony for the next three years of economic recovery and its policy will be to support the implementation of those agreements.' That set the positive tone, which has remained unchanged in respect of both the Labour Court and the Labour Relations Commission.

A detailed analysis by then SIPTU Research Officer Barbara Kelly, just after the termination of the PNR (1990), found there were just 39 private sector settlements that her department regarded as being above the basic terms of the agreement. Given that over the course of a normal wage 'round' she would have monitored anywhere between 700 to 900 pay agreements, this is evidence of the 'stickability' of the PNR. The importance of this compliance rate was not lost on the NESC, the body that provided the theoretical bedrock for the agreements:

By 1989, the economy had been growing rapidly for some time and the associated revival of labour demand and fall in unemployment could have been expected to increase the rate of wage settlements. In this context, adherence to the wage growth elements of the PNR right to the end of the three years arrested the decline in wage competitiveness and this was a major factor in enabling Irish employment to expand rapidly in response to favourable international conditions between 1987 and 1990.

The evidence on the ground that the deal was being honoured by the trade unions meant that the employers were now on board for a follow-on deal, according to Paddy Teahon, then secretary general of the Department of the Taoiseach. When the PNR was seen to hold in place they 'really started to believe in it'. Teahon describes them as being 'of the St Thomas Aquinas persuasion' since '[u]nless they put their finger into the wound, or heal up some of the wounds they had from the past, they weren't going to believe it.'

The next pact, the Programme for Economic and Social Progress (PESP), followed a similar pattern. By November 1991, almost a year into that agreement, *Industrial Relations News* was able to show that the compliance rate under the PESP mirrored the level of adherence that had occurred during the PNR. The IRN study of 550 pay deals showed that the strict terms of the PESP were rigidly observed in over 90 per cent of cases.

LOCAL BARGAINING HIATUS

The PNR also stipulated that no further cost increasing claims were to be allowed over the course of the deal. Due regard was to be had for the 'economic and commercial circumstances of the particular firm or industry'. In reality, this amounted to an inability to pay clause, which the Labour Court would take on board in cases where a company or industry could show that to pay the agreed increases would be detrimental to survival. These provisions remained broadly intact in subsequent agreements, allowing a degree of flexibility for employers who were in difficulties as long as they could convince the trade union(s) involved, or the Labour Court, of their case.

The trade unions succeeded in negotiating a local bargaining clause in the PESP in a bid to make up for the modest pay rises in the PNR. This was controversial and opinion remains divided on its impact. Negotiations were to take full account of the implications of competitiveness, the need for flexibility and so on. For Billy Attley (by then SIPTU joint president), 'any trade union official worth their salt' would ensure payment of the extra 3 per cent.

For Turlough O'Sullivan and the employers, the local bargaining clause was something of a nightmare, providing a window back into the 1970s: 'That was a bad experience for the employers because the unions did not deliver. It was sold to the employers on the basis that it was limited and tight. The ink was not dry on it when senior trade union leaders were telling their branch officials to go and get it and any union official worth his salt should get it.'

The application of the local bargaining payment was by no means uniform, with IRN showing that in just over half the cases where it was conceded, workers agreed 'significant concessions' or 'radical concessions'. The agreements also allowed for a degree of flexibility to cater for some of the difficult and genuine anomalies that arose from time to time. Billy Attley recalls how a number of the construction and craft unions supported the agreements at various times for this reason: 'They realized they were better off inside the tent than looking in from the outside.'

The pattern of adherence to the next two national agreements, the PCW and Partnership 2000, was broadly similar to that witnessed under the PNR and PESP, although P2000 did start to leak around the edges in its final year when the labour market was starting to tighten considerably due to burgeoning employment growth and a shortage of workers.

NEW TIMES, NEW MEASURES

During the fifth agreement, the Progamme for Prosperity and Fairness (PPF), the hitherto strict adherence to the pay terms started to alter dramatically. The booming economy and the almost full employment it brought meant that a whole range of industries and services were crying out for labour. This was the trigger for either employers or unions to push beyond the boundaries of the PPF. It was a labour market-driven breach in the agreement, the sort of breach that economists could understand. As long as those who needed the coverage of the basic agreement could get comfort in the Labour Court or the LRC, the national wage bargain could still be seen to work. But the employers had to get a new method to enforce compliance in those firms that wanted to maintain adherence to the strict terms of the deal.

Turlough O'Sullivan says, 'it got to crisis proportions and we were not prepared to have a national agreement to follow the PPF unless it differed very substantially on compliance. We took the view – what's the point in having a national agreement if it is just being ignored.' For IBEC, however, it was the ability of the unions to, in their view, use the national agreement as a floor that gave rise to this renewed concern about the compliance issue. An IBEC report in April 2002 warned that there could be no follow-on agreement after the PPF expired 'unless there is a substantial improvement in the delivery of national agreements'. For Turlough O'Sullivan it raised 'echoes of the 1970s'.

In 2001, the IBEC campaign for a new compliance initiative paid dividends midway through the PPF, with the establishment of the social partner operated National Implementation Body (NIB) to oversee the agreements. The NIB was made up of key players from ICTU and IBEC and the secretary general of the Taoiseach's Department. It remains in place today, playing an ever increasing role in not just monitoring the pay deals, but in micro-managing major disputes that have the potential to upset the partnership edifice. Two years later, in the Sustaining Progress agreement, IBEC and ICTU reached agreement that a group of independent pay assessors, under the auspices of the LRC, would be established to handle 'inability to pay cases'. Taken together, the pay assessment system and, where necessary, the NIB would establish the veracity of inability to pay claims. The cases could then be passed on to the Labour Court, which could make binding industrial relations decisions in such cases in the context of the agreement, although they were not enforceable by law.

Turlough O'Sullivan says that what resulted 'was very beneficial, very welcome, and has proved to be very effective ever since'. On the trade union side, there was some uncertainty initially around the measures, but, looking back, ICTU General Secretary David Begg believes that the new system helped to ensure greater fairness and transparency.

MAJOR DISPUTES AND PAY STABILITY

Major disputes in previous decades had often undermined national agreements, but the social partners were clearly determined not to allow this to happen in the post-1987 era. Big rows that had the potential to unhinge the pay agreements had to be settled without damaging their integrity. As Kevin Duffy recalls: 'You found a solution, but one that was within the concept of social partnership, that didn't damage the process.'

ICTU's Kevin Duffy and IBEC's Turlough O'Sullivan worked together on many tough disputes in those days, with the same goal in mind – keeping the lid on the deals. Peter Cassells describes the duo as an 'institution'. At the same time, the process had to be seen to get results and deliver solutions, 'while not leaving a situation where the union felt it had been defeated'.

Turlough O'Sullivan recalls: 'Duffy and I worked with each other on the biggest disputes in the country and we worked on the basis that both of us were committed to compliance with the national agreement. That was the key issue for us, to get these disputes sorted in a way that protected the agreement.' It has been suggested that this relationship formed a sort of prototype for the eventual creation of the NIB, a view shared by O'Sullivan.

Two major disputes – one in the ESB, the other in the 'big four' banks – illustrate just how the partners acted to protect the agreements. A five-day strike by electricians in ESB in 1991 was seen by the Government of the day as a threat to the pay terms of the PESP. Maintaining adherence to the PESP in the commercial semi-State sector was crucial, as any breach could have damaged the national agreement. This had happened in the bad old days of the 1960s and 1970s. From the Government's perspective, the strike had to end with a virtual climbdown by the electricians' union, the ETU. The ETU (part of the TEEU today) may have genuinely felt that the PESP had nothing to do with its claim, but that was not the perception of the Government, nor indeed of ICTU, the FIE or the ESB itself. The odds against the union were considerable, even though it possessed some of the most powerful industrial muscle in the country with its members in various power plants. When the deal was done on terms that involved juggling a lump sum payment already due to them, the then Minister for Labour Bertie Ahern insisted that the PESP remained intact. No-one disputed his assessment. The proof was in the outcome: the settlement meant no knock-on claims by other groups.

A second, albeit inadvertent, attempt to unhinge the PESP was made by the Irish Bank Officials Association (IBOA) the following year. The white collar banking union had traditionally been hostile to national agreements and was at that time outside the ICTU. The IBOA argued that the four main banks could justify a 6 per cent increase on 'self financing' grounds, quoting a separate productivity related agreement negotiated within the ESB. Even though a non-ICTU union was involved, both it – and the FIE – played a role in helping to pave the way for a settlement. The degree of co-operation between the social partners in bringing the dispute to an end also showed how cohesive they could be in defence of a national agreement. According to *Business and Finance* in April 1992, the lesson was not lost on commentators: 'The outcome probably confirms the view that any group taking on government pay policy will generally come off worst – the last ESB strike twelve months ago is another case in point.'

LEGITIMACY ENHANCED

The story of the conformity of the majority of employers and trade unionists to the terms of the pay deals in each of the programmes cannot be told without showing how the agreements were legitimised within ICTU and the FUE. However, there are a few important points to make in the context of the compliance and stability issues that lie at the heart of this chapter.

The employers' bottom line was fairly straightforward: was the deal affordable and could it be enforced? Over twenty-one years the answer has been 'yes' with some qualifications, particularly during the PPF. However, the deals brought more than pay moderation, according to HR Director of Penneys Breege O'Donoghue. They also meant increased productivity and stability, 'and were associated with the introduction of new technologies and work practices, competitiveness, and an improved industrial relations climate.'

For the trade unions, the legitimisation of the agreements was a more complex issue, and required considerable effort and ingenuity. Over time, the deals have tended to garner support the more they have been opened up to membership ballots, in comparison to when they were simply accepted or rejected by union executives. Of course, the picture is not uniform as many unions adopt tactical positions, agreement by agreement. SIPTU President Jack O'Connor, who heads the union without whom no agreement would be practicable, observes that the voting trend for private sector members of his union, which make up around two-thirds of the SIPTU membership, has tended to increase in favour of the deals over time. He suggests that this is hardly surprising as 'the pay rises have cumulatively increased pay substantially above the rate of inflation.' The union has also extended its consultation process since the late 1990s, in a move intended to add to democratic accountability, while at the same time enhancing the stability of the programmes.

A BROAD CONSENSUS

Pay discipline has largely been maintained in the private sector and in the semi-State companies over the course of the six already completed centralised agreements since 1987, despite there being some significant exceptions in the private sector during the PPF, which were driven by a very tight labour market. There is every indication that Towards 2016 is following the overall pattern. Such widespread adherence over such an extended period of time is unprecedented in the Irish context. The main employer and trade union federations have actively supported the programmes. They have also generally been more effective in helping to maintain adherence to the agreements than they were in the past.

Their efforts have been reinforced by economic circumstances, the role played by the State's dispute resolution agencies and by new enforcement mechanisms established by the partners themselves. Underlying all of these factors, however, is the fact that the individual trade union members and the employers affected by the agreements have endorsed what they consider to have been the most achievable compromise in the circumstances in which they found themselves.

CHAPTER 6

Changing the Public Sector Pay System

It was like a circle that would never end. It was crazy, ridiculous. It was a mad system because you could not finish anything.
    Charlie McCreevy, Minister for Finance 1997–2004

By 2000, public service pay policy was in chaos. Twenty years of difficulties, and the failure of well-orchestrated attempts at pay reform, had resulted in three years of highly disruptive industrial unrest involving nurses, health professionals, the gardaí and others. The disputes starkly exposed the pay system's inability to respond to substantial changes in responsibilities and working practices within certain grades and professions, and an abject failure to reward them without setting off a chain of expensive pay awards through the prevailing system of cross-sectoral pay links. In 1998, the then Taoiseach Bertie Ahern, in a letter to ICTU, made it clear that the public pay system had to be radically reformed and that this reform must include an end to separate pay mechanisms for different parts of the public service. The introduction of the benchmarking process into the Irish public service in summer 2000 finally drew a line under some two decades of upheaval and encapsulated such reform.

Since the late 1980s, serious thought and effort had been devoted to ending the system of pay relativities which saw key groups of public servants 'chasing each other' for special grade claims. These payments were additional to basic cost of living rises and were designed to compensate public servants for falling behind comparable private sector pay rates.

Many of these claims and disputes were fuelled by the prevailing system of public service pay determination, which consisted of a complex pattern of pay links. For example, pay increases for executive officers and higher executive officers in the civil service led to increases for administrative grades in the local authorities and the health boards which in turn led to increases for nurses, and led to increases for prison officers and the gardaí, soldiers, firefighters and others, creating the perception of public service pay 'leap-frogging'.

Throughout the 1990s there was growing dissatisfaction with the system, which was increasingly seen by government, economists and commentators as the main obstacle to public service reform. Three problems stood out and were well-articulated by ICTU at the time as:

- Firstly, grade pay increases were tied in theory to public service modernisation, but the pay links system struggled to accommodate this. In reality, there was little incentive for grade 'B' to accept change when its pay rise was automatically linked to that of grade 'A'. All the focus was on internal pay relationships, rather than the needs of specific public services or the wider economy.
- Secondly, it was impossible to implement effective modernisation and change against the background of industrial action that increasingly arose from grade claims, particularly in the second half of the 1990s.
- Thirdly, public servants whose jobs, responsibilities and qualification requirements had grown substantially could not be rewarded for their increased effort and productivity because of the constraints of the pay link system. This exacerbated recruitment and retention bottlenecks, which were fuelled by substantial pay rises in the private sector during the economic boom at the end of the 1990s. Public service quality improvements were stifled as a result.

In the end, major reform in a new benchmarking process, enshrined in the Sustaining Progress (SP) agreement, delivered something similar to productivity bargaining in the private sector whereby workers and managers agreed additional pay settlements in return for additional performance and verification.

The road to reform was both complicated and bumpy. But, ultimately, it was the determination of former Finance Minister Charlie McCreevy and the then Taoiseach Bertie Ahern that drove the change through Cabinet with little support from other ministers.

The two major requirements, which always had to be addressed and included in any reform package, were firstly the need for pay certainty for government, and secondly the necessity of having all groups included in the process and not letting one group lodge or process a claim in a 'solo run'. For the unions, fairness in terms of process and outcomes was to be the key to acceptance. Effectively, this meant having all the groups at the 'starting gate' at once and having different claims dealt with simultaneously to prevent groups following each other in a spiral of increasing pay claims.

Public service pay was a topic that never seemed to be far from the top of the Government's agenda. Charlie McCreevy recalls a story often retold in the Department of Finance which he maintains is 'absolutely true'. The story goes that in the early 1950s the Department of Finance was told to prepare a 'war book', which earmarked key actions for each department in the event of a nuclear war or some other hostility breaking out. Top of the Department of Finance's list of planned activities was 'suspend the conciliation and arbitration scheme', the centerpiece of the government's public service pay machinery.

THE LONG ROAD TO REFORM

The story begins with attempts by government to reform the public service pay machinery in the 1980s, when it proposed an overhaul of the various conciliation and arbitration schemes covering civil servants, teachers, local authority and health workers, as well as the army and the gardaí. Major government concerns centred on controlling the cost of the process, and creating stability and predictability in the process, while at the same time being seen to treat groups fairly.

Years of fruitless negotiation ended up with a Government decision not to appoint the public service pay arbitrator in 1985 – a central figure in the pay process – in an effort to control costs and force some re-assessment of the way business was done.

It was clear that the Department of Finance wanted a greater level of influence and control over the pay process. The argument was that it was wrong that the public service arbitrator should supervise a pay system which effectively soaked up almost half of day-to-day spending without coming under greater government control.

Postponing payment of special pay awards as a means of trying to control public expenditure was nothing new. Such delays had been sought by government and conceded in the mid-1980s. But the real ongoing concern of government was that any pay award for a so-called 'marker grade', like the civil service executive officers, would end up being claimed by groups who had no direct pay linkages, and who did very different types of work in different sectors of the public service.

The Public Service Executive Union (PSEU), which represented executive officers (EOs) and higher executive's officers (HEOs), had a shared interest in seeing reform. For years its General Secretary Dan Murphy, one of the most influential public service union leaders, had sought to 'get the monkey' of pay relativity off his back.

His union felt the fact that these EO and HEO grades were so pivotal in determining payments (which eventually knocked-on to so many other groups) meant that they were penalised in terms of having the changes in their own work patterns and burden of responsibility recognised. However solid the union's case for pay increases, claims would be judged on their implications for the wider pay bill, rather than on their merits. As Murphy recalls:

> Eventually the pay of executive officers determined the pay of firemen which always struck me as a bit odd. And we had a significant influence on the pay of academics at a certain level and there were connections with the nurses, paramedics, prison officers through the psychiatric nurses and from guards to firemen. It meant, as far as we were concerned, that when we went to negotiate, we were not just negotiating for us but we were carrying all this other weight. It was just intolerable from our point of view.

The Department of Finance tried – and failed – to deal with the problem under the Programme for National Recovery. The public service pay deal contained in the PNR only committed the Government to pay 40 per cent of outstanding pay awards, which had been deferred in the mid-1980s, from July 1989. It was subsequently agreed to pay the balance in two phases, 30 per cent from April 1990 and 30 per cent from October 1990.

Under an additional clause, clause 3.4, the PNR agreement allowed grades that had not received deferred awards in the mid-1980s to process claims through the Conciliation and Arbitration scheme. Awards arising from this would be paid in three phases: 40 per cent from 1 July 1989, 30 per cent from 1 March 1992 and 30 per cent from 1 September 1992.

IMPACT General Secretary Peter McLoone recalls that Kevin Murphy, the then secretary for Public Service Management and Development attached to the Department of Finance, believed this mechanism would exhaust all the pay specials in the system and that Finance had finally got a handle on what was coming down the line in terms of further pay claims. It then emerged that, despite the determination to restrict special claims to the period of the PNR, later carrying into the next agreement – the PESP, a number of additional claims had 'slipped through the net' through the utilisation of the conciliation and arbitration schemes.

THE CAMPAIGN TO DEFEND PESP

A Government decision to withhold and delay some of the rises (specials and general rounds) due under the second agreement, the PESP, produced considerable friction with public servants in 1992. The Public Services Committee of ICTU mounted a major campaign to 'Defend the PESP' when, in that year's Budget speech, the Minister for Finance Bertie Ahern declared that he was not making any commitment to additional pay rises other than those already committed to within the current year.

Ahern told the Dáil that 'true consensus requires that problems of significance now faced by the Government should be discussed frankly with the parties concerned.' He assured the parties at the same time that in these discussions the Government would try and find solutions which were 'fair and equitable' and which he hoped would not prejudice discussions on a further national agreement following the expiry of the PESP.

Mr Ahern also criticised what he saw as 'the air of unreality' in the expectations being voiced by some public service unions at the time. It was, he argued, 'totally unrealistic' that further claims should be pressed in a year in which the general increases being paid to public servants was subject to a ceiling of £6.50 a week under the terms of the PESP. He pointed out that many private sector employers were having to refuse increases provided for in the pay agreement. And in a show of further determination he said that taking such additional demands on board 'would require offsetting action by government' to prevent the budgetary strategy going off course.

Following a meeting with the Government preceded by a meeting of the ICTU General Purposes Committee (GPC), the Vice President of Congress Phil Flynn said that they were responsive to the difficult economic climate and were particularly mindful of the frightening level of unemployment.

However he added that public service unions absolutely rejected any suggestion of blame or guilt, however indirect, attaching to public servants. On top of the need to pay the full awards due under the PESP, Phil Flynn pointed out that the agreement contained a guarantee that the arbitrator would be appointed and he suggested that the unions had been 'receiving mixed messages' on this issue.

The arbitrator issue needed to be put beyond doubt, he argued. In advance of calling off the 'Defend the PESP' campaign due to commence in early 1992, a guarantee had been received that the limits imposed on the general round increases from 1 January 1993 would be removed from 1 December in the same year. They also received a commitment that the arrears due from the capping in 1992 and 1993 would be paid in early 1994.

At a meeting on 10 March 1993, the Secretary for Public Service Management and Development Kevin Murphy re-stated the serious position of the public finances. And he re-iterated that there could be no increase in the Pay and Pensions Bill in 1993 over and above the £4.035 million provided for in the Budget. There was already concern about the carry-over into 1994.

Following negotiations with the Department of Finance, a meeting of the IMPACT delegate conference in April 1993 adopted an emergency motion, noting with 'anger and deep concern' the procrastination over the appointment of an arbitrator, growing uncertainty in relation to the removal of the 'cap' and the absence of meaningful discussions which were due on the various arbitration and agreements.

A programme of escalating industrial action was planned commencing with a one-day strike in June followed by a two-day strike the following week. Public service unions demanded the early appointment of the arbitrator, an end to the cap on general round increases, payment of arrears from deferred pay awards, freedom to pursue claims under Clause 3 of the PESP, implementation of outstanding arbitration findings, and speedy access to third party arbitration where disagreements remained.

The Government moved quickly to heal this significant rift with the unions. It renewed its commitment of 17 January 1992 to restore aspects of the PESP general ground increases which were deferred in 1992 and 1993.

It also confirmed its intent to remove the ceiling of £6.50 a week which had applied to the 1 January 1992 PESP general increase and agreed to pay the losses arising from the imposition of the cap in the first place.

ATTEMPTS AT REFORM

The second national agreement, the PESP, also contained a provision for local bargaining in the private and public sectors worth 3 per cent. But the application of this award to the public service was to take some time and be the subject of intense discussion. It effectively set the parameters for the next agreement (the PCW) and eventually exposed fundamental weaknesses in the process of pay linkages which existed between the key public sector groups.

The so-called 'marker grades' had always argued that their pay awards were artificially depressed because of the costly repercussive effects. They felt that they did all the work in processing the claims, while the related groups followed automatically behind simply because they held a traditional pay link. Additionally, sometimes the linked grades used the increases secured by the 'marker grade' as a 'floor' and in some cases sought to achieve a higher level of increase through the conciliation and arbitration machinery and were successful. This prompted Dan Murphy of the PSEU, which represents the key marker grade of executive officer, to remark on the need to 'get the monkeys off my back'.

Accordingly, while Finance was pushing for change at one end, some of the main public sector unions were pushing at the other end – a force which would in time make change inevitable. But the solution in the mid-90s, the PCW restructuring clause, was also a costly failure. Under restructuring, each group was offered the option of going for a straight 3 per cent increase, as conceded to most private sector workers under the PCW, or do a deal which would concede grade-specific productivities which would allow increases of up to 5.5 per cent of the total payroll costs of the grade, group or category.

On the one hand, Finance felt this would introduce the notion of concession bargaining in the public sector with a carrot approach, i.e. enticing groups to concede flexibilities by offering a bit more than 3 per cent. More importantly, though, the real intent was to sever the pay links. A linked group could no longer expect to get the same deal, unless they were willing to concede the same value of flexibilities. Pay increases of the linked grades were no longer to be rubber stamped or passed on automatically as in the past.

The agreement outlined that if the 5.5 per cent restructuring route was taken, then there was no rigid limit on the cost increase which would arise and the agreement would also provide a timetable for implementation which, in any event, was meant to be no less favourable than that applying to people taking the 'straight' 3 per cent route. Whichever route was taken, employees were expected to 'make a contribution to change and flexibility which must result in savings and improve the quality of the public service'.

The PSEU, as one of the first groups to make a restructuring agreement under PCW, had tried to play the modified pay system by the rules with their claim being processed early in the pay cycle, something they were to suffer for later. In the end they were to pay a price for this approach in terms of seeing other groups, who went through the process later, securing much higher settlements partly due to challenging the political system and pay militancy.

The PCW agreement also re-stated the commitment made by ICTU and the Government to agreeing changes in the way public service pay was determined. Significantly, ICTU also said that any new machinery should include periodic comparisons of public and private sector pay to ensure that civil servants did not fall behind private sector workers doing similar jobs. Without making a firm commitment, the Government indicated a willingness to discuss this approach in the context of new pay determination machinery. The first blocks of a new system of public pay determination were being laid.

This agreement included the appointment of a facilitator to aid the negotiations process between the parties and provisions for a four yearly review of grades and pay conditions as well as the creation of a unit of the Labour Relations Commission to verify information advanced by either side in pursuit of a claim.

Early deals with teachers, civil servants, and local government and health administrative grades hovered just below the 6 per cent mark but later deals with nurses, the gardaí and prison officers broke through the 15 per cent barrier. This caused resentment and eventually unrest and led to problems for those who settled early in the pay cycle.

Opening the talks with the Health Service Employers Agency (HSEA) in late 1995, the Irish Nurses Organisation set itself a target of £20,500 for staff nurses. The initial HSEA offer was worth £10 million but this rose to £37.7 million by April 1996 and, ultimately, to £50 million by November 1996. The cost of final settlement was five times the level of the initial offer, indicating the enormity of the challenge the nurses' claim represented to the system.

The nurses' pay row came in two phases: in 1997, after earlier direct discussions with the Department of Health in February 1996 failed, and in October 1999. The nurses pay settlement that emerged in 1997, brokered by the Labour Court which averted a major dispute, worked out at up to a 20 per cent pay increase for some senior grades. The Court also recommended the creation of the Commission on Nursing to look at wider staffing and grading issues within the profession.

Following the publication of the *Report of the Commission on Nursing,* 1999 began with the nurses airing their pay case again at the Labour Court, following their 'round one' pay settlement in February 1997. The core issue, in fact the dominant issue right up to the nurses taking to the streets for nine days in October 1999, was the demand for three long service increments of 6 per cent, a demand that, if conceded, would have cost £200 million and caused a pay stampede among other groups.

The Labour Court proposed the creation of a new senior staff nurse grade worth a 5 per cent increase of salary and broke the logjam following a nine day dispute which saw a two-stage resolution process. The settlement was designed to discourage knock-on claims by other key groups. Nurses who had started their campaign in 1996 with a salary target of £20,500 ended up with a basic salary for a staff nurse of £21,500, which was higher than the target set by the INO. Between 1996 and 1999, staff nurses secured increases worth 26 per cent, ward sisters got 37.4 per cent and directors of nursing received a 46.6 per cent increase.

Gardaí put in a claim for a 15 per cent increase and, on a refusal, marched on the Dáil on 21 April 1997. The 'blue flu' day followed on May Day 1998 and the GRA threatened a second day of unofficial action on 11 July. In the end they accepted 4.5 per cent, backdated to July 1996, and a further 4.5 per cent, backdated to July 1997; but not before there was widespread concern at the sight of gardaí marching on the Dáil and public comments on the breaches of discipline that the event represented.

By the end of the 1999 nurses' strike, it was clear to everyone, including the more astute trade union leaders like Dan Murphy and Peter McLoone, that the situation was completely untenable. Public sector pay policy had all but collapsed. A pay clause originally worth 3 per cent had delivered 20 per cent for many and the Government's credibility on the issue of public sector pay had been undermined.

Meanwhile, any notion that such increases were supposed to be tied to modernised working practices or improved services had largely been ignored or forgotten. And, despite the disruption and the cost of the debacle, many large groups of public servants (especially those in white collar marker grades) were incensed that they had been penalised for playing by the rules – so much so that the Government found itself in the extraordinary position of agreeing an additional increase for the 'early settlers' who had kept the terms of the national agreement by settling in a range of between 3 and 5.5 per cent of payroll costs.

The public was by now totally puzzled at the bizarre and expensive pay determination system that had developed and was growing increasingly unwilling to accept a continuation of this approach in the public services. Ministers and senior officials in the Department of Finance were bent on change. Public service leaders like McLoone and Murphy, together with Blair Horan (CPSU) and Joe O'Toole (INTO), realised that unless a new way was found to handle public service pay, the Government would simply force change because of the high cost of public service pay and the slow pace of reform, a situation which was becoming increasingly untenable.

OFF THE STREETS

By the end of the 1990s, when the nurses were concluding their deal, Ireland was right in the middle of the 'boom' and the purse strings had loosened considerably. The so-called 'early settlers' felt hard done by and talk of top-up claims left public service pay in a worse state than it was prior to restructuring. The growing unrest in the public sector also came just as the same economic growth led to demands on the public service from business and a public who were demanding a more flexible, efficient and cost effective public service.

The unrest now threatened the continuation of the national pay agreements. The public sector unions too were starting to lose control of the members and, like Finance, they needed the reassertion of some discipline and control that would take public sector pay negotiations off the streets and back into procedure.

In addition, the Government was attracted by the prospect of reintroducing certainty over its pay costs. Peter McLoone recalls a discussion with then Finance Minister Charlie McCreevy when benchmarking was subsequently attracting criticism in the media: 'He predicted that history would record that a Minister for Finance who stood up in the Dáil between 1990 and 2000 could not say what they were going to provide for public service pay costs with confidence and credibility because nobody knew what was going to happen in a given year.' But under the new benchmarking system, he was confident that a minister who stood up in the Dáil in the period 2000 to 2010 could credibly predict public sector pay costs. And that is how it has turned out.

In terms of creating a reformed pay system, it was widely recognised that the key elements (later enshrined in the pay Benchmarking Body) should include:

- Maintaining the traditional Priestly principle that public service pay should not lead private sector pay developments but that those doing similar work in both sectors should be similarly rewarded.
- That the practice of cross sectoral links at the heart of 'leap-frogging' should be ended.
- That all groups be assessed by any system at the same time.
- That any new pay system be linked to modernisation and industrial peace.
- That the implementation arrangements for any changes in pay would be negotiated as part of the next pay deal.

This would give the Government certainty each Budget day when making provision for the next year's public sector pay bill.

The dawning reality was that, unless change was implemented, a situation would emerge where public service pay would develop a life of its own. As Dan Murphy recalls:

> The danger was that you were going to have nurses chasing guards, chasing prison officers and going around in a circle and at some point I knew very well, and I did not know and what point it was going to be that [we would say], 'Stop, we are not going to do this anymore.'

So maintaining some sort of order in the pay system, including pay predictability, was something that the unions themselves had a stake in, despite public perceptions to the contrary.

In terms of desirability of change, whatever about the appetite among union leaders who generally recognised that some new model was urgently necessary, the mood among public sector workers on the ground was slightly less positive. It is probably fair to say that there was suspicion rather than opposition to the idea of change. PSEU members, the group at the heart of the pay system and the group on which other groupings had usually based their claim, were very positive about it. People were essentially being asked to move away from a system where they got additional pay awards for little or no additional work or responsibilities, to one where there was a direct linkage between pay and the way in which work was carried out.

Looking back, former Minister for Finance and now EU Commissioner Charlie Mc McCreevy says that the inherited system was 'mad because you could not finish anything'. The parties were in negotiations the whole time; it was 'doctors, followed by nurses, following firemen and country council employees. It never ended.'As he colourfully put it, 'if the doorman in the Department of Finance got a rise, within no time at all, the head surgeon in the Mater Hospital would be entitled to the same thing.' To McCreevy it was 'like the circle that would never end'. You would never finish negotiations on anything.'

SHAPING A NEW FRAMEWORK

Unions themselves had come to the conclusion that change was necessary. This arose out of the breakout from the terms of the PCW and the chaotic experience of the distribution of the so-called 3 per cent bargaining clause, the roots and aftershocks of which effectively dominated pay for the entire decade.

Initial discussions with the Department of Finance had exposed some tensions between Finance and the Department of the Taoiseach over performance pay. The Taoiseach was seen to be a supporter of performance pay but Finance reportedly had a lot of misgivings about whether the mechanisms were in place to make it happen.

In a letter to the General Secretary of ICTU Peter Cassells in November 1998, the Taoiseach Bertie Ahern referred to his earlier comments at the Plenary Meeting in Dublin Castle the previous July in which he suggested the need to take a 'fundamental look' at how pay bargaining and pay management were approached in the Public Service after Partnership 2000. He outlined his belief in the need for a public pay policy, 'which, by more closely relating pay to performance, meets the aspirations of public servants while maintaining the unavoidable limits of public spending'.

The Taoiseach suggested that events since the summer had 'made this task more urgent' and that the difficult nature of many of the issues which needed to be tackled reinforced the need to begin work at 'an early date'. He formally invited the Public Services Committee to commence discussions on these issues. In responding, the Public Services Committee said that they had already conveyed that there were existing problems for trade unions representing groups who had made settlements under the PCW restructuring arrangements, 'which had been shown to be worth considerably less than settlements with other groups'.

Addressing the problem at the heart of the 'early settlers' issue and how groups who had lost out in the pay round would be handled, the Committee had already warned that there would be a reaction 'if certain groups fared better than others in pay deals'. In this context, in a clear reference to settlements with the nurses and the gardaí, the response was that 'it was simply not credible to believe that some groups can be dealt with in isolation.' The unions pointed out that pay constraints were 'rigidly applied' to those who settled in the early stages of the PCW but that the parameters had been 'extended considerably' for those who settled later. Having made clear that they were disappointed with the lack of response to these concerns by the Government to date, they agreed to enter talks.

The Public Service Committee's priority was to get the Government to address 'the early settlers' issue, while the official or Government objective was to get discussions under way on a new system for pay determination. In time, the members of this influential ICTU committee were to become major champions for the new system.

A firm of consultants was engaged to come up with a report arising out of discussions between the Department of Finance and the Public Service Unions. In the meantime, the parties themselves had been 'batting around' some key concepts and ideas which in time were to prove to be the skeleton of what emerged as benchmarking.

The ultimate plan amounted to the creation of what was essentially a pay review body which sought to implement productivity measures in return for additional pay rises based on private sector comparisons. The crucial element was with reference to what was actually happening in the private sector. The big challenge for the unions was to avoid the process being blown off course by the action of one union in particular.

Writing in *IMPACT News* in December 1999 the Taoiseach Mr Ahern ruled out 'separate or free standing' pay mechanisms for different parts of the public service. More importantly, from the point of view of the trade unions, he stressed that any change would come about through negotiation.

In an article in the *Irish Times*, Peter McLoone, the general secretary of IMPACT, warned that the talks would not simply be about controlling pay costs. His argument was that public sector pay was about investment in services that are highly valued by Irish people. In effect, he argued pay policy had to help ensure that the level and quality of public services were maintained and improved.

But the key in McCreevy's eyes was not giving in to people who wanted to be outside of the process. He remembers the 'fierce battle' and pressure on the Government side not to have a strike with the ASTI: 'The big thing I used to say to Joe O'Toole and Peter McLoone when we used to meet privately for talks over breakfast was to agree the trick that everyone would stick by this and then we would set up the next one.' His belief was that if they had the system up and running for a couple of years it would sustain itself into the longer term and effectively lay the foundation for the new system.

As General Secretary of the Irish National Teachers' Organisation, Joe O'Toole (INTO) got himself into considerable hot water for his comments and encouragement to his own members to join the benchmarking process. O'Toole, advising his own members against the background of firm opposition from the secondary teachers' union, the ASTI, said that going into benchmarking 'was like going to an ATM'. The INTO's vote on Partnership 2000 was only narrowly carried by 51 per cent to 49 per cent and O'Toole's persuasive comments have to be seen in the context of trying to engage his members in a new system at a time of considerable instability in the pay climate.

Blair Horan, general secretary of the Civil, Public and Services Union (CPSU), said that, while they recognised that the restructuring provisions had helped them address the problem of low pay with their clerical assistant grade, they realised that a more stable and long-term pay determination system was necessary 'if the Government was not going to set its face against what was there'. And the concept of pay reviews to assess developments relative to the private sector made it worthwhile.

THE BENCHMARKING REPORT

The Public Service Benchmarking Body (PSBB) was established in July 2000 under the Programme for Prosperity and Fairness (PPF) and was charged with comparing overall public service pay with the private sector pay. Its creation marked the end of a decade-long path to successful reform which ultimately resulted in agreement by all parties to a new approach to setting public pay.

The newly formed PSBB was also directed to compare the rates of particular occupational groups in the public and private sectors and studied job content, including the roles, responsibilities and duties of particular grades. As was stated at the time, it did not simply compare the pay of public and private sector jobs with the same or similar titles. It also took account of pension arrangements, which are often but not always better in the public sector and are something of a bone of public contention, as well as other factors like job security. Its terms of reference took account of:

- the need to ensure equity between public and private sector employees;
- the need to ensure ongoing modernisation and change in the public services;
- the need to sustain Ireland's competitiveness and to develop economic prosperity on a sustainable basis; and
- recruitment and retention problems in the public service.

The first PSBB report was published on 30 June 2002 to much expectation. It recommended average increases of 8.9 per cent but inevitably some groups fared better than others. The spread of rises ranged from zero to 25 per cent but it was widely recognised that the body, in trying to lay the foundations for a 'new pay order', had attempted to clear up some of the anomalies which arose out of the long-running restructuring saga element of PCW referred to earlier.

BENCHMARKING METHODOLOGY

The work and research carried out by the Benchmarking Body to determine how public pay should move was one of the most intensive and in-depth studies ever carried out into the public pay system. The PSBB found that there was so single source of data available on pay which met its requirements. And in general it also found the data held by the Central Statistics Office (CSO) to be 'too highly aggregated' for the purposes of their work and this data could be open to widely differing interpretations. The report noted that the CSO material on the public service was incomplete and that there was a specific lack of data on the health service in particular.

As a result five Irish and International consultancy companies were selected by the PSBB to undertake the research. They were Alpha Consulting, TBR International, Hay Management Consultants, and Mercer and Watson Wyatt Partners, all internationally recognised companies with special expertise in the area of reward and pay. This group of consultants visited 202 companies covering 46,351 employees and evaluated 3,563 jobs.

To compare jobs in the public and private sector, the PSBB evaluated private sector jobs using its own evaluation scheme. To do this, the body identified '276 core job capsules', encompassing and mirroring the full range of work, including the professions found in the private sector. These were then grouped into 'job families', representing different levels of responsibility in similar functions at particular levels of the organisation. In addition to collecting data for job evaluation purposes, the consultants also collected information on a full range of pay, benefits and conditions attaching in the private sector.

Having issued its recommendations, the PSBB decided to make no further comment on its findings or on the deliberations which led to the report itself. The PSBB made the decision not to publish the detailed data gathered together for the report by consultants. This material was provided on a confidential basis to the consultants hired by the PSBB and publishing it would have represented a breach of the commitments given. However, there was criticism from unions and others that the report should have been more transparent.

The Benchmarking Body's methodology was similar to the methodologies used by the Review Body on Higher Remuneration in the Public Sector. Yet this body's work has never attracted the types of commentaries and criticism generated by the PSBB report. But, as Charlie Mc McCreevy has pointed out, publishing the in-depth research and logic behind particular decisions would only have generated more heat than light and could in fact have destabilised the benchmarking process, given peoples' affinity for comparing their outcome with those of other grades.

Peter McLoone of IMPACT said that presenting the details of the research to an audience brought up in the culture of relativity claims would inevitably result in people saying, 'What did I get, what did someone else get and why did I not get the same as them?'

Some of the public service unions were initially cautious in their response to the report while some private sector employers feared that the levels of award could spark demands for increases in their sector. Generally, the report was seen to have broken with tradition and recommended larger increases for senior managerial and supervisory jobs which reflected the realities of the private sector.

One hiccup for the new Benchmarking Body, just before publication, was the departure of Jim O'Leary. O'Leary, an economist with NUI Maynooth and a former advisor to Garret FitzGerald, was regarded as a highly competent and clear-headed thinker on policy issues. Charlie McCreevy says that he liked O'Leary because he was a 'very independent fella'. In McCreevy's view: 'When it reported my friend Jim O'Leary walked off the pitch, [O'Leary] felt that conceptually you could not do it. Our job was political . . . . The benchmarking was a far better methodology than what had gone before which there was neither rhyme nor reason to.' Looking back, he recalls: 'Jim, from day one, had difficulty with the concept about weighting the increases. He had written many papers that said it was not possible but that was not the purpose of this. The purpose was to get out of the other [older] system and have some rational system to deal with the thing.'

The implementation of the Benchmarking Report was negotiated as part of the talks on the follow-on agreement, Sustaining Progress (SP), which included a detailed outline of the modernisation agenda required as a condition of receiving the benchmarking increases. Both the PSBB and the SP agreements required that the modernisation and change agenda be independently verified before the bulk of the benchmarking payments were paid. Six-person Performance Verification Groups (PVGs) were established with two representatives for management, two union nominations and two external experts, and an independent chairperson from outside the public service.

At the time of the publication of the report, Professor Bill Roche of UCD noted that benchmarking was itself 'problematic' but remarked on the 'careful and diplomatic' approach taken by the main trade union leaders and ICTU to the report and the challenges that lay ahead. Roche added that, however problematic the various parties regarded the process, 'it is not apparent that a viable alternative to benchmarking is to be found.'

Opposition to the PSBB

Even before the Benchmarking Report had hit the streets, strong opposition had been expressed by the ASTI about the benchmarking process itself. The process had come under serious attack the month before it was launched at the ASTI's annual convention in Donegal where the then Minister for Education Michael Woods was shouted down by delegates. However, the ASTI never made a submission.

Strong opposition also emerged from the CPSU, representing clerical officers, which was the first union to formally reject it, despite the fact that their award at 8.5 per cent was close to the average awarded. Many unions postponed a reaction to the outcome, pending a vote on opening talks on a new agreement with the Government.

What emerged from the other unions, particularly IMPACT and the Public Service Executive Union and their General Secretaries Peter McLoone and Dan Murphy respectively, was a determination to 'sell the deal' and highlight its long-term benefits for public service workers, balanced against its advantages to the wider public. IMPACT has remained the organisation most likely to defend and explain the benchmarking process and has expressed frustration at the unwillingness of other unions, public service employers and politicians to do so.

The core arguments made by the unions to their own members and to taxpayers in general was that benchmarking represented industrial stability, facilitating the ongoing modernisation of the public service while, at the same time, delivering rises to their own members, which took account of changes in the structure of public service pay. And they pointed out that the rises under the first benchmarking process were being spread over four budgets (2002–05), taking account of the current budgetary and economic situation.

The Aftermath and 'Sticking it Out'

Summing up developments at the time, Charlie McCreevy believes: 'We stuck it out, the unions stuck it out and they were under fierce pressure.' Despite the attacks, McCreevy never wavered on supporting the process and ultimately the payments attached to it. 'Colleagues were not out selling it,' he feels and he believes this was because of the negative media coverage and 'everything else'. But people had simply forgotten 'what a crazy system we had before'.

Looking back, McCreevy feels that the Government got totally 'rolled over' on the 'blue flu', the unofficial strike by gardaí that followed the nurses' settlement in the late 1990s: 'Let's call a spade a spade. It was an absolute disgrace – the law enforcers of the country decided to break the law themselves and that is what they did.' The teachers were the big test, given their ratio of members in Leinster House, and this was felt 'inside and outside Leinster House', he added. If they gave in to the teachers, they could have torn up the benchmarking process, McCreevy feels.

Fundamentally he believes that benchmarking could not have been created without social partnership. He also defends the decision not to publish the research carried out by the Benchmarking Body. Had they done so, the whole process would have unravelled and whatever was proposed would never have stuck.

One member of the Benchmarking Body did have concern about how its findings were handled by management and, ultimately, what they got in return. John Dunne, former Director General of IBEC, says that he does not believe that public service management got what they should have got from the process. But you cannot blame benchmarking for that, Dunne adds. Fundamentally Dunne believes that the management of the public service did not get what the agreement 'enabled them to get'. Here he appears to be criticising the management for not defending the system and securing the levels of change they might have been expected to get.

Also responding to the debate about change, Peter McLoone says that it seemed to him that management's modernisation proposals 'seldom had much to do with customers or service users'. Instead there had been a tendency to 'focus exclusively' on work practices and industrial relations issues. Sometimes this approach could be characterised as 'change for change's sake' and, at worst, according to McLoone, it appeared that many public service managers were driven by the question: 'How can we inflict maximum pain on staff?'

In 2005, Peter McLoone told a Local Government Management Services Board (LGMSB) HR conference that, if the Irish public was bewildered by the outcome of benchmarking, then it was 'at least partly due to the reluctance of political leaders and senior public service managers to explain and defend the process'. Charlie McCreevy accepts that the benefits of the process were not sold and accepts some responsibility for it but says that others, including unions, did not sell it either.

Early in 2003, speaking at the launch of *Benchmarking and Better Services: What Taxpayers and Service Users get for their Money* (a report issued by the unions explaining the benchmarking process), Peter McLoone responded to critics of benchmarking, arguing that the process had already delivered radical reforms and public servants were committed to further productivity and service improvements in exchange for benchmarking money. Describing the detailed reforms required under benchmarking, IMPACT's leader refuted claims that taxpayers were getting nothing in return for their money: 'Benchmarking has already brought an end to the much criticised system of public sector pay links and has delivered industrial peace in the public services. These are absolute pre-requisites for the other modernisation measures that public servants must give in exchange for benchmarking payments.'

Mr McLoone pointed out that further benchmarking payments were dependent on independent verification of co-operation with the changes. The changes included:

- longer opening hours and the extension of lunchtime opening;
- a standardised school year and more parent-teacher meetings outside school hours;
- the publication of service standards across the public services;
- staff co-operation with modernisation and change in all areas of the public service;
- cross-functional working and new flexible work patterns;
- the introduction of performance management systems and new measures for dealing with under-performance;
- more open recruitment and merit-based promotions; and
- the introduction of new financial systems, leading to better value for money.

While the Benchmarking Body recommended increases, in reality the awards were presented as a fait accompli and there was no question of coming back for clarification or top-ups. By linking acceptance into a follow-on national pay deal, it really gave unions no option but to accept. This is as close to binding arbitration as you can get.

The continuing importance of modernisation was highlighted in the Labour Relations Commission's 2006 report by the Chief Executive Kieran Mulvey. He said that a critical public policy concern of government was the extent of public service modernisation, particularly in the health service. In this context, value for money remained a key driver in the Government's efforts to secure as much progress as possible under the ongoing change process of Towards 2016.

CONCLUSION

It took almost two decades to successfully introduce root and branch reform to the system of public pay determination in Ireland, a system which had remained largely intact since the 1950s. The second programme, the PESP, held out the prospect of reform in terms of creating a structure to 'corral' the then existing outstanding special pay rises and end the system of relativity between key groups. The second attempt, based on the 3 per cent local bargaining rise under the PCW, which later stretched to 5.5 per cent, turned out to be a disaster because of the number of groups who 'broke through', following the nurses' settlement. The Government caved in to industrial muscle and the whole system risked collapse as a result. After much soul searching the Government, as employer, and the unions agreed to set up an objective pay measurement mechanism in benchmarking. Benchmarking sought to reward people based on the principle of fair comparison and, in the process, create conditions for the modernisation of the public service in a meaningful way, which included verification, including verification by those outside of the service. The arrival of benchmarking brought an end to the system whereby one group used another group's pay settlement as a floor for further increases and as something to build on and better in their own claim.

The benchmarking system has been criticised at different times on the issues of lack of transparency and openness. It is fair to say that the process has received a bad press and its workings are seriously misunderstood. And, as we have seen, there has been reluctance on the part of the management side to defend it.

In terms of support, once the Public Services Committee of ICTU 'bit the bullet' on changing the system, they, along with the former Finance Minister Charlie McCreevy, took ownership of the process of introducing the benchmarking process and stuck to it despite the opposition.

In early summer 2007, the system came under pressure following the strategy of the nurses' union, the INO, to 'go it alone' and prosecute a claim for a 10.5 per cent increase and a reduction in hours outside of the benchmarking process. In the end, following the intervention of the National Implementation Body (NIB), a basis was found for handling a reduction of hours on a cost-neutral basis and for handling pay via benchmarking in a fashion which preserved the integrity of the Towards 2016 aggrement.

CHAPTER 7

The Social Pillar – the Long March through the Institutions

There's negotiation and there's policy. And you had to walk out of the negotiations with some totems as well as with a policy.
    Mike Allen on the INOU walkout from the Partnership 2000 talks

Social partnership is a unique version of corporatism in Europe for many reasons, not least the involvement of the community and voluntary sectors in national agreements. One reason for this is probably the comparatively large role that such organisations play in Irish society, providing services normally supplied by the State in other countries.

Not surprisingly, in a country where the official rate of unemployment was approaching 20 per cent in the late-1980s, and the real figure was much higher (see Chapter 1), the Irish National Organisation of the Unemployed (INOU) was the first and most persistent suitor of the existing partners. Founded on an initiative of the Dublin Council of Trade Unions, the INOU was a natural coming together of local unemployment groups that had sprung up as factories closed. Its longest serving General Secretary Mike Allen was laid off in 1983 by a Galway computer company and spent the next year trying to salvage something from the wreckage by seeking new investors or forming a co-operative. The publicity campaign that shop stewards like Allen launched to highlight their effort to save jobs had the unforeseen consequence of alerting the employment exchange that they were not really 'available for work', and therefore not entitled to the dole.

It was the same in Dublin. 'Wall-to-wall children and no jobs' was how one Kilbarrack resident described the local scene. The system was keeping the lid on things, just about. The rent office had security hatches, wired windows and reinforced glass: 'It looks as though it was designed to keep all the information on one side and us on the other', said a local (see Cathleen O'Neill's 1992 book, *Telling it like it is*). In fairness it was intended to keep out armed robbers as well, although many experienced criminals were moving into the drugs market, which was safer and more profitable.

It was 1987 when groups such as Mike Allen's came together and formed the INOU. That, in itself, was a remarkable achievement. The very loss of a workplace where they could meet every day, combined with a shortage of funds, made it difficult for unemployed activists to avoid the social isolation that traditionally beset redundant workers. But, like many unemployed activists, Allen had been a shop steward and that experience provided a template of sorts for organising and campaigning. In fact, the INOU looked on the trade union movement as a natural ally in its fight for jobs.

Traditionally the unions had assumed the role of championing the most vulnerable elements in Irish society and the Irish Congress of Trade Unions had sold the Programme for National Recovery to affiliates partly on the basis that the recommendations of the 1986 Commission on Social Welfare would be met. The Commission had been set up by the FitzGerald Coalition and its proposals, including a commitment to raise social welfare rates to 30 per cent of the average gross industrial wage, would set the bar by which successive governments would be judged for the next two decades. In fact the financial situation in 1987 was so bleak that trade union leaders knew Haughey would have to introduce drastic cuts in public spending. Their priority was to ensure the worst off, those on social welfare, were not targeted to bear the brunt of the cuts. As ICTU General Secretary Peter Cassells puts it, the trade unions 'did not so much accept cuts as look the other way. The situation was so critical that the trade union movement would not pull down the house of cards – so long as social welfare was maintained.' Haughey accepted the need to spare welfare rates, but achieving increases in basic income on the scale proposed by the Commission was not within the realm of practical politics.

For unemployed activists, the failure of Congress to deliver more in this area during the PNR and its successor the PESP, convinced them that they must rely on their own resources, meagre as these were. Their first campaign was against the Jobsearch programme, which the Government intended as a means of training and motivating unemployed people to find jobs. Fears that it was simply a way to drive people off the Live Register and into the black economy were not helped by the speed at which it was introduced. Stories that people being summoned to AnCo job centres to train for telephone interviews with employers were given bananas to practise with because there were not enough telephones, may or may not have been true but quickly entered INOU folklore. AnCo centres were picketed and so was the headquarters of the Department of Social Welfare in Dublin.

Much to their surprise, the INOU leaders were invited inside, where well-briefed department officials demolished most of their arguments. It was a lesson well learnt. The INOU decided it had to know what it was talking about if it wanted to establish its credibility with civil servants and politicians. Leading future experts on social policy, such as Mary Murphy and Larry Bond, would cut their academic teeth as INOU activists looking for arguments to fight their corner.

Ironically Jobsearch was one of the early initiatives undertaken by the Department of Social Welfare that marked an end to the tradition of relative passivity that had characterised it in the past. One senior official recalls the 1980s as 'a difficult time. Our main function was to pay the punters. There was little time or resources for frills.' Assistant Secretary at the Department of Social Welfare Tom Mulherin says, 'There wasn't a huge amount of hope . . . but the Minister Michael Woods came up with this notion of re-jigging the payments system to try and get people back to work.'

Other initiatives included targeting the long-term unemployed for second chance education. The first steps were somewhat faltering. One of those involved, Brian Flynn, remembers valuable lessons being learnt from pilot schemes such as one in Letterkenny, where the local VEC provided a classroom but local unemployed people failed to turn up. They were too embarrassed to attend in normal school time, when they would be seen by their own children. Classes had to be moved outside normal school hours. Eventually some 30,000 long-term unemployed people would avail of second chance education.

By 1992, when the INOU was ready to embark on a serious, well-researched campaign to bring its concerns onto the streets, lack of funding was still limiting the amount the Department of Social Welfare could do. But valuable links had been developed, not alone with the INOU but with a wide range of other voluntary and community groups, that would bear fruit in the future. Meanwhile the INOU campaign culminated in a day of action in October. Despite months of organising, only 3,000 turned up out of an estimated 300,000 out-of-work people. Nevertheless, it was the largest unemployed protest since the 1950s and the INOU was not going to go away.

One of its most successful initiatives was to call for a Forum on Unemployment. The original idea came from economist Anto Kerins and was inspired by the Northern Ireland Forum, which had been meeting in Dublin Castle to seek a basis for ending the conflict there. This quickly gained support across the political spectrum, from the Progressive Democrats to the Workers Party. The INOU followed through with a 'Sign on to End Unemployment' petition. Among the high profile signatories were Seamus Heaney, Christy Moore, Fintan O'Toole and the then Bishop of Galway Eamon Casey. A lot of the INOU's scarce finances went on a glossy leaflet featuring Bishop Casey. It was printed just in time for Casey's 'outing' as the father of an unacknowledged son in America. As Mike Allen recalls in his book, *The Bitter Word*, 'the rest of the country was wondering about the effects on the church; we were wondering what to do with several thousand colour leaflets.'

But the Forum idea had been taken up by many others, who were now likely to be better assets in the campaign than Bishop Casey. One was SIPTU Vice-President Ed Browne, who had called for a National Forum on Unemployment as far back as the ICTU annual conference of 1990. He saw it as a means of broadening social partnership by involving public representatives and opposition political parties in the debate on economic policy. His motion was something of a new departure in that it was proposing a specific mechanism from the floor of Congress to address one of the main strategic problems of centralised bargaining – how to end the so-called 'jobless growth' that characterised the early years of partnership.

The proposal provoked a robust response from one of the main opponents of centralised bargaining, Mick O'Reilly of the ATGWU. At the ICTU annual conference in 1990, O'Reilly argued that such a forum was 'contrary to the best interests of this movement' because it 'asks us to accept that unemployment can be solved by experts, by committees, by social partners working together' when 'these very forces we are asked to sit down with are the forces who have contributed . . . to the unemployment that confronts us.' He said the trade union movement had a different philosophy from the PDs, Fine Gael and Fianna Fáil, who championed private enterprise. 'While it is legitimate for us to lobby any government, it is quite a different thing for us to subscribe to the idea that we can have a consensus with our enemies.'

O'Reilly's views at the time were shared by many activists within the INOU. One of the ironies of the debate was that some of the people most opposed to using social partnership as a mechanism for tackling unemployment were trade union activists, in a job, who were members of local unemployed action groups and would represent those local groups at INOU meetings.

By the early 1990s the debate was beginning to clarify the strategic options for the INOU. They could either stay outside the process, and criticise it, or seek to join it and find a solution to the phenomenon of jobless growth from within. After all, if partnership had delivered growth, it might be able to deliver jobs as well. Mike Allen's main concern was that the organisation might not be allowed into the partnership process and, if it was, it might not have the expertise to achieve its objectives.

A major boost to the campaign for a forum on unemployment was the endorsement of the new Fine Gael leader John Bruton, who now made unemployment a major plank in the party's programme. As it happened, despite a strong electoral performance in 1992, power remained beyond Fine Gael's grasp at this stage. Negotiations on a rainbow coalition government broke down when Labour refused to enter government without Democratic Left, a condition which was unacceptable to Bruton's other potential rainbow coalition partner, the Progressive Democrats. Instead, Fianna Fáil and Labour formed an administration.

The new Government established a Joint Oireachtas Committee on unemployment, which was succeeded by the National Economic and Social Forum (NESF). The NESF was set up to provide advice to the Government on policies to achieve greater equality and social inclusion in the context of social partnership. When the Rainbow Coalition (incorporating Labour, Fine Gael and Democratic Left) came to power in 1994, it continued funding for the NESF, on which the INOU was given representation. The INOU saw the NESF as very much the outcome of their sustained campaign on unemployment and an anteroom to social partnership. 'If social partnership were heaven, then the National Economic and Social Forum was purgatory', is how Allen describes it. 'The Government was doing a whole range of things. The National Economic and Social Forum was a space where they could find out for themselves . . . if this was something that was actually going to work.' Eventually, he believes, the Government and the other social partners decided 'these people are problematic but they have something to offer. They are not just messers.'

The key to opening the partnership door was the Irish Congress of Trade Unions. Relations between the INOU and ICTU had become quite strained. 'At one level the leadership of the INOU always . . . retained the political viewpoint that our ally was the trade union movement, in a platonic political sense', Allen says. But at the same time the INOU 'had come to the conclusion that we weren't going to get any actual assistance. There were deliberate and direct attempts by the trade union movement to close us down. I mean on two or three very specific occasions we had to fight for our lives.' One source of tension was funding. The State training agency, FÁS, was the main financier of labour market initiatives, including the Social Employment Scheme (SES), which later evolved into the Community Employment Scheme.

The SES had been set up in 1985 to take long-term unemployed people off the Live Register and offer them temporary jobs in local schools, sports clubs and other community-based organisations. The aim was to give them some basic skills and a sense of work discipline that improved chances of finding 'real' jobs. At one stage 66,000 people were employed on the schemes.

The SES presented a particular challenge for the trade union movement. Des Geraghty, who was then with the ITGWU, was a representative on the first committee set up to oversee its operation. 'Nobody wanted to be on it. We were vetting schemes. The SES made the Live Register look good, but on the other side the fear was there of them providing jobs on the cheap and undercutting existing employment.' At the same time these temporary posts were having a beneficial effect, ensuring that local projects, including centres for the unemployed, could access resources otherwise out of reach of their shoestring budgets.

Geraghty was one of a number of senior figures in the ITGWU, and later SIPTU, who had put a lot of thought into social policy. He was one of the first to realise that national agreements made sense, not just from an economic point of view but because of the space they created to influence wider policies; and that concessions on social wage issues such as tax reform, welfare rates, child supports, education, health and housing could actually be worth as much, or even more in real terms than pay increases.

ICTU and the INOU parted company for a number of years on social wage questions such as tax reform, with some Congress affiliates more interested in negotiating reductions in tax rates and the INOU pushing for the emphasis to be on tax allowances. There were also tensions between the INOU and unions representing staff in FÁS, and in government departments providing services to the unemployed. Pickets, protests and press releases criticising shortcomings in the service inevitably bred resentment.

Likewise, Allen saw the Congress position as threatening at times, rather than as simply critical of the INOU. Some union leaders made no secret of their dislike for the INOU and for Allen. They pressurised ICTU funded unemployment centres to disaffiliate from the INOU. Similarly, the INOU would find EU funding it had expected to receive end up going to Congress sponsored initiatives. 'They were on the committees and they basically saw us as competition. . . . They didn't want this group of people that they couldn't control saying things about their business. And there were perceptions of us as anything from raving Trots to Provos.'

It was a somewhat schizophrenic relationship. While some trade unionists had serious reservations about the bona fides of the INOU, others actively supported them. For instance, SIPTU provided accommodation to the INOU in Fleet Street through ITUT, its social solidarity trust. When these premises were sold to Amnesty, the INOU found a new home in the TEEU premises on Gardiner Row. Even supporters of the INOU found their critiques of national agreements irritating, although other trade unionists argued that this was all the more reason for bringing them inside the tent. It was after the INOU moved to Gardiner Row that ICTU and the INOU finally began to mend their bridges. Allen met with the General Secretary of Congress Peter Cassells, and the latter signalled that Congress would not stand in the way of the INOU entering the social partnership process.

The INOU was not the only organisation seeking a place at the table. The Conference of Religious in Ireland (CORI) had similar ambitions. CORI, which represented the major Catholic religious orders, had been making policy pitches at senior civil servants, politicians, the media, and anyone else who would listen, for years. CORI's public face was Fr Sean Healy of the Society of African Missions (SMA), who became so synonymous with the organisation's social policies that he was eventually invited to address the Fianna Fáil parliamentary party 'think-in' at Inchydoney, in his native Cork, in September 2004. It added hugely to his profile as a leading advocate for those living in poverty. It was also a sort of homecoming, as his father, a CIE truck driver, had also been a staunch Fianna Fáil party member.

But it was Healy's experience as a missionary in Nigeria during the 1970s and early 1980s that had led him to reassess his attitude to social and economic issues. He returned to Ireland in 1983, armed with a doctorate in social policy, to take up his current position as co-director, with Sr Brigid Reynolds, of CORI's Justice Commission. He brought the same concentrated focus to the new job that he gave to his marathon running (he won the Long Island Marathon on 16 March 1975). Once the wider potential ramifications of the social partnership model became apparent, CORI made presentations to the Government in 1990, in relation to the PESP, and again in 1993 as initial talks began on its successor, the PCW. Healy recalls: 'Our view at the time was that there was a large group of people with a very strong interest in what was happening, who were not represented in the process. The groups we identified were the unemployed, the poor and women.'

Things became more formal in 1990 when CORI was invited to make a presentation to senior civil servants. Healy arrived to see the Secretary to the Government Paddy Teahon and sixteen assistant secretaries sitting neatly in two rows while Sr Brigid Reynolds and he made their pitch. Incidentally, there was only one woman in the audience, who was standing in as a substitute for her male superior.

In 1993, CORI was asked which departments it wanted to meet and identified ten, to whose representatives it made 'a fairly robust' presentation. The document was also circulated to the social partners. CORI made presentations to the Joint Oireachtas Committee on the labour market from 1992, as did the INOU. Although both organisations were brimming with ideas, there was relatively little interaction between them.

When the Rainbow Coalition came to power, both were given representation on the National Economic and Social Forum. It was composed of fifteen members of the Oireachtas, fifteen representatives of existing social partners and fifteen people from what would become the social pillar. Thirteen of the latter represented the unemployed, women, anti-poverty groups, travellers, people with disabilities, young people and the aged. Sean Healy was a government nominee, one of three experts it appointed.

The new Taoiseach John Bruton opened the first session of the NESF and Healy asked him to widen the social partnership process to allow in groups such as his own. Bruton demurred; although he had come around to the view that social partnership had created a positive dynamic between the Government, unions and employers, he had still to be convinced of the value of broadening the process.

While Fine Gael had opposed the PNR, as had the Labour Party, the third Rainbow Coalition partner, Democratic Left, and its predecessor the Workers Party had supported centralised bargaining. Ironically, while Fine Gael was reluctant to share power with Democratic Left, which had prevented Bruton forming a government with Labour in 1992, the smallest component in the new Government helped stabilise it and promote the partnership agenda. De Rossa, who was the leader of Democratic Left, was also Minister for Social Welfare and was one of the few people in government to think 'intellectually' about poverty issues, according to Allen, who came to know him well. He brought in Rosheen Callender, a senior SIPTU official, as his policy advisor. Callender was a long-time party activist in the Workers Party and Democratic Left but it was her widely acknowledged expertise in the areas of tax, pensions and welfare that led to her appointment.

De Rossa's commitment to fundamental reforms did not prevent serious political disagreements with the INOU when it was finally admitted to social partnership in 1996. But before that could happen the organisation, having served its term in the purgatory of the NESF, also had to serve an apprenticeship on the National Economic and Social Council. Representation on the NESC was another way of testing the capacity of the INOU, and of CORI, to contribute to the partnership process. The invitation to the INOU was somewhat unusual. Bruton's office contacted Allen and told him they wanted someone the Taoiseach could nominate to the NESC. But they also made it clear they did not want Allen. In fact they wanted the INOU's expert on welfare rights, Mary Murphy, who had already won the respect of senior civil servants in the Department of Social Welfare, through her grasp of issues and ability to point out potential flaws in initiatives being proposed to tackle unemployment. Sean Healy was invited to serve with other recognised figures from the voluntary sector such as Niall Crowley of the Community Workers' Co-op. Crowley later went on to become chief executive of the Equality Authority.

The INOU had also proven its worth in the Government's Task Force on Long-Term Unemployment, which had been an NESF initiative. If the organisation had mended its bridges with Congress it was equally important for it to win the support of IBEC for its social partner candidacy. 'The only real relationship we had with employers' organisations really . . . was meeting them to complain about their failure [to] create jobs or hire the long-term unemployed people,' Allen says. If the NESF created a context in which the INOU could get to know IBEC better on a less confrontational basis, the Task Force on Long-Term Unemployment was 'transformational'. Allen recalls that initially employer representatives 'thought it was a total waste of time. They couldn't see it having any impact whatsoever. It would be one case where they would say it proved its value for them because they came out, one, thinking that there were solutions to [long-term unemployment] and, two, that it mattered.' The INOU needed to demonstrate that tackling long-term unemployment was about more than just creating jobs and filling the vacancies, which was the initial employer focus. The Task Force forum allowed the INOU to point out that 'if it's always the guys from the front of the queue getting the jobs, the guys at the back of the queue get pushed further and further away so it does matter, both at an economic and social level.' One corollary of employers recognising this reality was the acceptance of the need to become more proactive with unemployed groups in identifying exactly who the long-term unemployed were and how best to tackle the barriers they faced in finding jobs. An important initiative to emerge from that learning process was the creation of the Local Employment Service, with its emphasis on one-to-one mentoring of unemployed people and putting in place supports to tackle problems such as numeracy, literacy and lack of personal development or self-esteem.

This occurred under the PESP in the context of twelve local area based pilot partnerships set up in some of the State's most depressed communities to create jobs. One of the most successful pilots was the Northside Partnership, which covered some of the worst unemployment black spots in north-east Dublin. The structure allowed for six community representatives, six social partners (comprising three trade union and three employer representatives), and members of the local authority. Former IDA chief executive Padraig White was persuaded to help get the project off the ground and found he was dealing with people from 'a different world'. He brought business people from large employers in the area, such as Cadburys and Tayto, together with Brendan Butler from IBEC and Paddy Coughlan from SIPTU and explained that, 'We had a certain core funding and it was up to us to find jobs. Here is the world of unemployment; here is the world of work. Our job is to get people to move from the world of unemployment to the world of work.'

According to White, instead 'of shunting people from scheme to scheme and going nowhere', the partnership decided to work on individuals and 'be person centred and find programmes and interventions to help that person become employable'. Contact centres and mentors were provided that individual unemployed people could relate to. This allowed for the development of individual strategies for joining the world of work.

White's recollections of relations between the local employment service and FÁS were more harmonious than Allen's. This may well have been because his experience was through a partnership process, whereas relations between the INOU and FÁS remained adversarial in many situations, especially over 'ownership' of the LES at local level. Certainly in the Northside situation it was accepted that FÁS would focus 'on the more employable' and the partnership on the rest. This meant that roughly half of the people coming off the register in places such as Bonnybrook and Darndale were going to FÁS and half to the Northside Partnership offices.

To a large extent, involvement in the Task Force and the NESC represented a coming-of-age for the INOU. It was far more important strategically than the NESF for putative social partners because it effectively set the policy parameters for negotiations. 'If you were in social partnership and you weren't in the NESC, you were picking up the pieces,' Allen says. Mary Murphy was able to 'create a context' for the INOU in which unemployment issues could be negotiated effectively at a strategic level, in the same way as wages.

It did not come a moment too soon, as far as the INOU was concerned, because long-term unemployment figures remained stubbornly high. This was in spite of the emphasis on 'work' in the successor to the PESP, the Programme for Competitiveness and Work. The very first section of the agreement was devoted to measures aimed at generating growth in areas of high unemployment. Overall unemployment fell by 4.6 per cent between 1988 and the conclusion of the PCW in 1996, but long-term unemployment only fell by 3.5 per cent. (The total drop in the unemployment rate was from 16.3 per cent to 11.9 per cent between 1988 and 1996. The fall in long-term unemployment was from 10.4 per cent to 6.9 per cent.) In other words, people out of work for less than a year were almost a third more likely to find a new job than someone out of work for more than a year. There was evidence that some of the replacements for the SES, such as the Community Employment Programme, while better structured and containing a bigger training component, remained little more than revolving doors, taking people off the dole for a few months before depositing them back where they started. A further problem was that long-term unemployed people tended to accumulate extra, secondary benefits to ease their hardship. These benefits were lost once they returned to work and this often negated the value of a wage, especially if the job was low paid, which it usually was. It was in areas such as the 'Back to Work' campaign that Mary Murphy proved the value of having an INOU input. It had developed an expertise on the ground that civil servants, employers or trade unionists could not match.

The Back to Work programme was the brain child of the Department of Social Welfare and flowed from the Employment Support Service, established mid-1993. It was one of the most successful initiatives undertaken under the ESS to combat long-term unemployment. Well over 110,000 people would eventually pass through the programme. Initially two-thirds of them were self-employed, for the simple reason that it was easier to help an unemployed person set up in business on their own than match them with an employer at a time of high unemployment. The programme phased out welfare benefits for participants over a four-year period and the Department's own job facilitators could help out with small discretionary payments.

These were recruited from among higher executive officers and all were volunteers. Although up to 50 job facilitators were authorised, the Department never received sanction for more than 33. The word 'job' was quickly dropped as the facilitators' role expanded to cover wider social, as well as employment initiatives. 'They went into areas other people had given up on,' recalled one official, 'and they learned to know what the likely options were.' Another said, 'they begged, borrowed and stole' to put programmes together for disadvantaged groups such as lone parents and early school leavers, as well as long-term unemployed.

Despite a widespread perception that there was rampant abuse of the social welfare system by people working in the black economy, only 15 per cent of participants in the first year were found to have been working illicitly while receiving welfare payments, and only 9 per cent had actually been earning anything substantial. The percentages in this category fell away rapidly in subsequent years. In its first year, 1993, some 6,000 people participated in the Back to Work scheme. That doubled to 12,000 in 1994 and peaked at over 39,000 by the year 2000. Today there are 8,500 participants, of whom 4,500 are self-employed and 4,000 are employees.

The Department of Finance was worried at the cost implications and suspected that some of those assisted in signing off the Live Register to start their own businesses would have left anyway. It was also unhappy, for the same reasons, about the subsidies offered to employers willing to take on the long-term unemployed. However, Social Welfare found political support for its argument that the scheme 'was doing good socially', and subsequent research showed that the Back to Work scheme was cost-neutral because it generated extra economic activity and tax revenue, while reducing social welfare expenditure. Fears about unscrupulous employers exploiting the long-term unemployed proved largely groundless. In fact, the Department found that at least one target employer body, the Small Firms Association, was largely ignorant of the subsidy until it was asked to participate in a publicity campaign to highlight it among members.

Despite the informal co-operation that was developing between the Department and groups such as the INOU, it could not evolve much further without more formal structures. Having secured the explicit support of Democratic Left and the implicit support of PD leader Mary Harney, who repeatedly asked in the Dáil why the unemployed were not invited to talks, Bruton agreed to meet an INOU delegation in May 1996. It was the first time in the history of a State where the unemployed had been a permanent ghost at the feast for over 70 years, that a Taoiseach formally met a body representing them. In July, Bruton attended the ICTU biennial conference in Tralee and announced his conversion to social partnership.

While he now accepted there were strong merits to partnership after all, Bruton remained sceptical about groups such as the INOU and CORI. He saw a fundamental difference between interest groups such as unions and employers 'who have to give up something in return for what they're getting and people who are really looking for a say without giving up anything . . . Obviously, in that context, the trade unions and the employers and the Government are in a different category to people who are simply looking to have their voice heard.' It tied in with one of his main reasons for attacking the PNR and subsequent agreements in opposition. 'I don't think social partnership can ever be a substitute for an elective democracy, because the people who sit as social partners, particularly those who come from the wider social pillar, are not necessarily representative of very large groups of people and they don't have to stand for re-election.' It was a view privately shared by several leading trade unionists.

Bruton's conversion to social partnership was as much for political as for economic reasons. He was bound to honour the terms of the PCW, negotiated by the previous Government, of which Labour had been a component, and he knew that he needed

> to find a deep accommodation with the Labour Party, not just on paper but in reality if we were to avoid Labour becoming a permanent partner in government with Fianna Fáil and Fine Gael becoming the permanent opposition. Probably, to the surprise of a lot of people in the Labour Party when they formed the Government with me as Taoiseach, they found that I was far more accommodating and consultative and anxious to find agreement with them than what they remembered [me being] like when I was Minister for Finance or Minister for Industry in the eighties and conflicting with them.

The change was possible because Bruton himself had changed and Labour Party policy had changed. The party was 'not pursuing the same statist ambitions that were implicit in some of their policy positions of the 1980s'. Bruton felt the change 'occurred because probably social partnership had worked and the trade union movement could see that it had worked'. Labour had to modify its own ambitions as a result. After opposing social partnership as a fundamentally flawed concept in a parliamentary democracy, he saw its value as a means by which harmony could be established between three very different political partners in government.

Once the strategic decision was made, Bruton's attitude towards including a Social Pillar was: 'There wasn't any great harm done by it. It made the thing more acceptable to a wider group and I suppose you could say that what the other social partners got was an ability to see what was going on [in other sectors of society], which is very important in a democracy.' The fact that other constituencies were 'being heard in a timely way and . . . getting information in a timely way, is good.' The business pillar was also extended at this time to include bodies such as Chambers Ireland. ISME rejected an invitation because it would not be involved in pay negotiations.

In October 1996, the Government formally invited eight organisations to join the social pillar. They were the community platform/pillar, an alliance of small and relatively new organisations, the Society of St Vincent de Paul, CORI, Protestant Aid, the National Youth Council, the National Women's

Council, the ICTU Unemployed Centres and the INOU. The latter resented the fact that, having led the public campaign for the voice of the unemployed to be heard in the social partnership process, a whole range of other organisations which had never sought membership were also invited to the table. Allen was severely critical of the Government's decision. It had created 'an awful hodge-podge which, whether deliberately or not, and we definitely thought deliberately at the time, ended up adding a wing of civil society to social partnership . . . which hobbled it'. Senior civil servants dealing with the new social pillar at the time certainly found it took the new social partners quite a while 'to learn the ropes'.

This was partly because the groups held a wide range of differing views, none more so than the INOU and CORI. Allen characterises them as, 'The two most fundamentally diverging views of unemployment that existed in Ireland at the time.' The INOU said unemployment 'was solvable, it was desirable; economic and social answers to unemployment were possible and people should work'. CORI had been campaigning for a basic income for everyone, a revolutionary concept based on a belief that unemployment could not be eliminated, but rather was a natural development of human society where technology signalled 'the end of work'. As far as Allen is concerned, 'the Government were saying, "Oh yeah, both [the INOU and CORI] are concerned about employment. They're one pillar and throw in the St Vincent de Paul, who want TV licences for the poor, and Protestant Aid because we don't have any Protestants . . .", and so on. So we were in this pillar and we had to have a position collectively, in order to improve the process.'

It was the classic Irish situation of the split being the first item on the agenda, if an agenda could be agreed. Thrown together relatively late in the talks, there was one powerful incentive that drove all the groups – the possibility of extracting more funds for their sector. The Government had earmarked between £250 million and £300 million in the new partnership agreement budget but there was unanimity that it was not enough. Healy argued that if the Government was serious about the redistributive functions of the State and creating a fairer society, it should agree to accept that welfare payments equate to at least half the amount earmarked for tax cuts, which would disproportionately benefit the better-off. The INOU was determined that the Commission on Social Welfare increases must be secured, or significant progress made towards attaining them.

'The government side was surprised we didn't collapse in disagreement,' Healy recalls. Instead, the Commission's recommendations became a focal point. The ESRI had produced a report updating the Commission's recommended rates. Healy and Allen drafted a memorandum to the other partners looking for a commitment that these revised rates would be achieved by 1999. This had been an objective of early drafts of the new agreement – which would become known as Partnership 2000 – but had slipped off the table, so the social pillar believed it was achievable. The simplicity, universality and common sense of the demand also made it easy for the other organisations to row in behind the INOU and CORI, which had the wit to provide secretarial support for some of the less well-resourced groups, as well as advice and technical expertise.

There was just one difference between the INOU and the rest and that was the length to which the unemployed organisation was prepared to go in order to achieve its objectives. With real unemployment still hovering around 20 per cent, when suppressed demand for jobs was taken into account, the INOU delegation felt it was worth walking out of the talks if necessary and doing as much political damage in the process as possible. While others, including Healy, threatened to launch public attacks on the Government, the INOU was the only organisation to storm out of Government Buildings on 19 December and announce that it was rejecting Partnership 2000. The agreement was due to be published on the following Monday, just two days before Christmas. Only a few hours earlier the Minister for Finance Ruairi Quinn had told the Dáil that, due to the new agreement, spending in the coming year would exceed the cap of £13 billion announced earlier in December and this included extra 'social inclusion' measures. But the Cabinet had signed off that day on a package that was still at least £25 million less than would satisfy the INOU.

The INOU delegation that gathered in the Davenport Hotel to issue a press release certainly felt lonely that night. Once more they were outsiders. It was not the actual amount that was critical but the need to show that their participation in the partnership process meant something. They wanted the extra cash and they wanted a commitment to implement the 1986 Commission on Social Welfare rates (index linked) by 1999.

Next morning, Allen accepted an invitation to a 'head-to-head' interview on RTE's *News at One* with the Minister for Social Welfare Proinsias de Rossa. De Rossa was willing to provide more money but he wanted to target it differently and, as he saw it, more effectively than had been envisaged in the Commission's report. As it happened, the INOU executive had decided to invest in a mobile phone during the talks, so that the negotiators could keep in touch with the outside world. As Allen went into the RTÉ radio building, the mobile rang. It was Mary Murphy and she said that the Secretary to the Government Paddy Teahon had been trying to reach him. 'The message was, "Don't do anything." And I said, "What does that mean?" and she said, "It's been agreed." ' Allen recalled later that De Rossa felt they were wrong 'but if that's what they want, give it to them.' The 'head-to-head' interview that followed the settlement was not riveting broadcasting.

Looking back, Allen believes De Rossa might have been right in terms of his approach to the question of income adequacy but, at that point in time, the INOU and the Social Pillar in general needed a victory to give them credibility: '[De Rossa] was more about restructuring it [income adequacy] and he's right, but there's negotiation and there's policy. And you had to walk out of the negotiations with some totems as well as with a policy.'

Allen does not totally discount the theory that the walkout was partly engineered by other social partners because 'in all negotiations you need to have a crisis and there might have been a sense that to bring the INOU into the process we need, not only to win something, but win something very publicly.' On reflection he feels this is too Machiavellian but the INOU negotiators found that their very public victory did not mean they had an easy time from delegates at the subsequent conference that voted on Partnership 2000. Allen thinks 'that it's true that when we went to our conference to get the thing through, the fact that we had been right up there willing to walk out . . . brought us over the line in a way that wouldn't otherwise have been possible.' According to Allen, many members still felt 'angry and bitter':

> They didn't have jobs and they were pissed off about it and wanted to do everything they could to articulate that. So it got through, in a very heated debate. We won with a clear majority but there was strong opposition because they wanted more money. There was still very heavy social welfare policing going on, in an intrusive and aggressive rather than in an effective way, and there weren't jobs. So, anyway, we got that through in the social partnership process. Then we had three years to try and get the pillar into more coherent shape.

Long-term unity was to prove elusive. The INOU was convinced it could have achieved more for the unemployed if it had been the only social pillar partner. It is certainly true that, if the unemployed had been the only group represented in the pillar then the interests of other groups representing Travellers, people with disabilities and the aged, would have been neglected by default.

As it turned out, the cumulative effect of labour market initiatives had finally begun to yield significant dividends. By the end of 1999, overall unemployment had fallen to 5.1 per cent and long-term unemployment had fallen to 2.1 per cent. From a situation where the long-term unemployed represented over 62 per cent of those on the dole when the PNR was negotiated, they now represented 41 per cent, well below the EU average of 49 per cent.

Cracks in the pillar were obvious in talks on the next agreement, the Programme for Prosperity and Fairness. The INOU peaked at this time organisationally. Unemployment was still a serious problem, especially long-term unemployment, and its team was strong enough to provide the secretariat to the pillar during negotiations and pursue their own agenda while Allen concentrated on his role as a neutral chair for the pillar. During the talks Allen was offered the job of general secretary of the Labour Party. He offered to step down but other members of the Pillar were happy to allow him to remain chairing the negotiations. He deferred taking up the Labour Party job until the PPF talks concluded.

When talks on a new agreement began, the social pillar discovered there was potentially €2 billion available, or seven to eight times as much as at the start of Partnership 2000 negotiations. The pillar had obviously come a long way but, according to Allen, 'we had no idea how to spend it, or how to monitor and ensure that it was implemented. And you had nonsensical processes like when we were preparing for the negotiations and I was saying, "Okay, what do we want to spend it on?" and lead people in other organisations would say things like, "It doesn't matter what we spend it on, it's more the process by which it's decided." And I'd say that if I was the Department of Finance I'd be rubbing my hands to that.'

Even more problematic was the row over child benefit, which revealed a chasm in attitudes towards a whole range of issues between the social pillar, the unions and employers. Social pillar organisations wanted a universal payment on the basis that parents in the home deserved to have the economic and social value of their work recognised and rewarded by the State. Parents in the home also tended to be those on the lowest incomes who needed the money most. Trade union negotiators wanted to reward working parents and argued that there were extra costs involved in working such as travel, food and, above all, childcare that parents in the home did not have to face. The unions also argued that these were precisely the sort of extra costs that acted as barriers to parents in the home entering the workforce and escaping the poverty trap. The INOU, which some trade unionists expected to take a similar position to themselves, stuck with the pillar. One of the senior union negotiators, Rosheen Callender, who was SIPTU's national equality officer and a member of the ICTU executive, described CORI's stance as 'very right wing on family issues', while Allen dismissed the ICTU position as 'workerist'. The issues were complex and, because negotiations were conducted behind closed doors, there was plenty of scope for media leaks and misinformation. The employers and the Government wanted greater benefits for working parents but Finance Minister Charlie McCreevy had already stirred up a hornet's nest with his controversial tax individualisation plans. Neither the Government nor the employers wanted to become embroiled in a debate between the unions and the social pillar that was clearly going nowhere.

In the end there were 'flaming rows' but no progress. The issue went by default, and so did much of the extra funding available from the exchequer.

Two members of the social pillar, the community platform and the National Women's Council, were so dissatisfied with the outcome of the Sustaining Progress negotiations that they refused to sign off on the terms. On 25 March 2003, the day before ICTU delegates and the IBEC council met to vote on the terms of the agreement, a spokeswoman for the Platform said the needs of people living in poverty had been 'completely ignored' in the process. The spokeswoman said, as noted by the *Irish Times* on 26 March: 'We are faced with an extremely socially conservative Government, where people are perceived as economic units and nothing more. The time has come for a new space and a new voice for radical social change.' However, IBEC and ICTU went ahead with their deliberations and the two social pillar groups had to sign the document they had rejected to regain their place at the table for the next round of talks. As Sean Healy puts it, 'If you do not sign an agreement you are not part of the process. You are not a social partner.' The logic was impeccable and having negotiations where social partners could walk in and out with impunity would have put the process on a par with musical chairs, or speed dating.

Healy, the longest surviving member of the social pillar, was sympathetic to the plight of the Community Platform and the National Women's Council: 'Sustaining Progress was extremely difficult because there was very little in it for us.' On CORI's negotiating stance he said, 'We made progress on some issues and decided to live to fight another day. The Government had won the election, comfortably. The opposition, to quote McCreevy, had been "fired".' CORI knew when it was time put its head down and do some research. One result of that research was that, when talks began on Towards 2016, it pushed hard for a ten year plan. It was necessary, Healy says, because a lot of the social engineering strategies in areas such as affordable and social housing, the National Spatial Strategy, the National Development Plan and the National Anti-Poverty Strategy needed longer time-frames than pay deals to deliver.

Healy is convinced that the Government has lost its bad habits whereby cost overruns, duplication and hasty decisions are subordinated to the electoral imperative. He points to the impressive progress made in basic income payments such as pensions since he spoke at Inchydoney in September 2004 – pensions up €51 a week in less than three years. This brought the contributory old age pension to the target of 30 per cent of gross average industrial earnings set by the Commission on Social Welfare in 1986.

It may be that the architecture of national agreements is changing, with longer social and economic planning requirements providing an overarching structure within which pay agreements can be negotiated. Whether power relationships are changing is another matter.

Mike Allen still believes that, 'Unless you are willing to walk under certain circumstances and you have the capacity to follow through [and bring the system down] . . . you shouldn't ought to be there. You're sort of trapped in the scrum for social change if you are so compromised, if your only reason for existence is to be there and you can't walk out.' Even if a figure as well known as Healy were to walk, it would not bring down the structures, only the unions and employers retain the power to do that. As Bruton points out, all social partners are not equal.

Involvement in the process also involves compromise. Allen accepts that the pillar has a significant capacity to influence policy and make other social partners aware of issues, but believes involvement also 'militates against the sort of developments in the 1980s of a radical, challenging, critical community sector'. The attitudes of other observers are not as bleak. They point out that, even in the 1980s, there had been initiatives to rebuild communities and tackle problems such as drug addiction, early school leavers and illiteracy. By the 1990s, the regularisation of local area based partnerships that involved unions, employers and community groups had entered the policy-making mainstream through the NESC.

NESC Director Rory O'Donnell feels the social pillar has increased in importance to the process. 'They undoubtedly bring an air of legitimacy', he says. 'I think . . . they have got to a position where, if they were to walk away from an agreement, they could damage its legitimacy for the other actors. Maybe not fatally, and maybe not in all circumstances, but I think to a significant degree. So it is a kind of power.' He also believes that, at its best, the social pillar can focus on issues that other partners miss. Most importantly of all, 'They can bring . . . information into the process where they are trapped into genuine social activism.' Critical information on what schemes really work and why others do not is brought back to the process. O'Donnell says, 'They feed a whole collection of material into the system that in the ordinary course . . . wouldn't figure.' However he does share Allen's concerns that the more integrated community and voluntary groups become in the national partnership structures, the more likely they are to become institutionalised, with Dublin-based bureaucracies mediating between members on the ground and bodies such as the NESC.

One of the ironies of the success of social partnership is that many of the leading activists in the pioneering days of the social pillar, such as Allen, have moved on. It may be that the radical edge challenging complacency has been dulled and that, while there are still enormous problems facing some individuals, families and communities, the raw mass unemployment, abysmal social welfare rates and lack of supports that characterised the economic wasteland of the 1980s are gone.

It is also unlikely that the sort of adversarial relationship which existed in previous decades would return, at least in the short term, even if social partnership collapsed. This is because of other institutional changes. The Department of Social and Family Affairs, into which the Department of Socil Welfare has evolved, continues to develop strong relations with the voluntary sector. Back in the 1980s, reform in the social welfare codes was largely determined by EU law and battles in the courts, where campaigning lawyers such as Alan Shatter, Mary Robinson and Gerry Whyte, and organisations such as FLAC fought for the rights of groups denied basic entitlements. The most important case involved Cotter and McDermott, two married women who were made redundant and then denied the same entitlements as a married man in similar circumstances. Some 70,000 women were affected by the outcome. The legal battle dragged on from 1986 for a decade when the then Minister for Social Welfare Proinsias de Rossa finally authorised a compensation package of £265 million (see *Sex*

Equality, Community Rights and Irish Social Welfare Law edited by Gerry Whyte and *The Irish Social Welfare System: Law and Social Policy* by Mel Cousins).

It was a sign of the changed times when, in 1997, the new Minister for Social Community and Family Affairs Dermot Ahern appointed the former Director of FLAC Mel Cousins as his policy advisor. Cousins was effectively doing the same job as Rosheen Callender under De Rossa, but he had no previous connections with Fianna Fáil or with Ahern. He was recruited simply because Ahern wanted expert, independent advice in his new brief and thought that the best place to look for it was among those who had spent their lives fighting to reform the system.

Cousins found senior officials in the Department were open to ideas and were interacting already with a wide range of voluntary and community groups. In fact, one of the major tasks he faced as Budget day approached each year, was to wade through anything up to 50 submissions. He did find, like Healy, that the Government was determined to batten down the hatches in the Sustaining Progress talks, largely because the pre-election splurge in 2002, coupled with fears of recession, meant there was little appetite for lavish public expenditure.

In many ways the Department had anticipated change. As far back as the PESP, it had become involved in the area based partnership initiatives and it also embraced the proposals in the EU White Paper on *Growth, Competitiveness and Employment*, which argued that the market alone could not tackle unemployment and associated social problems. Since 1993, the creation of the Employment Support Service had led to major initiatives such as the Back to Work Scheme, second chance education for the long-term unemployed and similar supports for lone parents, people with disabilities and students seeking summer work. Many of the roles it took on came about by default, with other departments such as Health, Education or Enterprise, Trade and Employment showing little interest in what were then seen primarily as social problems.

De Rossa substantially strengthened links between the Department of Social and Family Affairs, other government departments and the voluntary sector when he introduced the National Anti-Poverty Strategy (NAPs) in 1997. This provided a social audit mechanism for government policies to ensure they reduced, or at least did not exacerbate, levels of poverty in Irish society. The NAPs has been continued and regularly updated by his Fianna Fáil successors and is now seen as an intrinsic tool of social policy planning.

The attitude of Mulherin and his colleagues is to 'continually look at policies and ways of helping to make them work'. He sees the voluntary and community sector as allies in identifying problems early and tackling them. Much of the work is labour intensive, but there are far more resources to deliver services than in the 1980s, making the task of delivery much easier.

Even if the overarching social partnership structures collapse, these strong networks will survive in the sector and ensure social dialogue continues. Whether such a dialogue can survive a serious economic downturn is another question, as is the question of how sustainable the new contributory old age pension of 30 per cent of the gross average industrial wage would be in such circumstances. With an ageing population, pensions, both private and public, are likely to loom large in any future national agreements, and so is the role of the social pillar.

Addendum

GIVING A ROLE TO FARMERS

This book focuses primarily on the role of successive governments, trade union and employer leaders in the new generation of national agreements since 1987. However the involvement of other groups such as the farmers has been crucial to their success. The decision by Charlie Haughey to include farmers in the process from the beginning was an indication that he intended to create something more than a simple wage deal.

Michael Berkery, chief executive officer of the Irish Farmers' Association (IFA) since April 1983, recalls the immense changes and challenges which have taken place in primary agriculture. Post-war Ireland was a very difficult place for agriculture. From 1955 on, adult education and the evolution of Macra na Ferime helped lift agriculture out of a climate where there was little or no investment. In time, the IFA became a major campaigning organisation for farmers, adopting a defensive position on some issues and a more forward looking strategic approach to others.

The Irish Farmers' Association (IFA) had been excluded from the National Wage Agreements of the 1970s and early 1980s, even though the agenda had broadened over time into decisions on national social and economic policy that affected members of the farming community. Farm leaders had to deal with the consequences, in terms of higher costs to agriculture and the food sector in general, while their vital interests were effectively ignored. The inference they took from the process was that, while the Government was happy to recognise employers and the trade unions as having a major input into policy, the farmers and agriculture in general were 'unapologetically excluded from the process'. That, at least, was how one IFA document of the time put it.

During 1985 and 1986 in particular, the relationship between the IFA and the FitzGerald Coalition deteriorated. A number of factors contributed to this situation. One was the progressive reduction in expenditure by the Department of Agriculture on services and supports for agriculture, leading the then President of the IFA Joe Rea to publish what he termed 'the Deasy Decline Index'. This was a deprecatory reference to the stewardship of the Minister for Agriculture Austin Deasy. Deasy had been a surprise appointment and was seen as a relatively unknown backbencher lacking any particular knowledge of the sector.

The introduction of the land tax caused significant difficulties and was seen by farmers as inequitable and divisive. Finally, the weather in 1985 and 1986 was extremely bad and the IFA was very critical of the slow response of the Department of Agriculture to the plight of farmers, particularly in respect of a fodder crisis in the West of Ireland. On top of this, new difficulties were emerging over problems of oversupply by producers at EU level.

The Government's proposed 'farm tax', better known in farming circles as a land tax, was meant to apply from 1986 and extend ultimately to all agricultural holdings of 20 acres or above. Plans to increase yields from farm taxation ran into huge opposition from the IFA, which launched a high profile campaign against the proposals in 1986 and 1987. Fianna Fáil gave a commitment that, if elected to government, it would repeal the land tax.

In a similar fashion to his high profile visit to the ICTU headquarters on Dublin's Raglan Road, Charlie Haughey visited the IFA headquarters in the Farm Centre at Bluebell, off the Naas Road, to enunciate his new approach to farmers. At that meeting, on 26 February 1986, the IFA put forward its Survival Strategy for Farm Families. The main elements of the plan were:

   i.   a corrective devaluation of the punt (£) by 8 per cent to 9 per cent to restore competitiveness;

   ii. renewal of the euro currency exchange rate guarantee scheme to provide loans for farmers at nominal rates of 6.5 to 8.5 per cent;

   iii. a government expenditure policy which ensured agriculture did not suffer a disproportionate share of the spending cuts;

   iv. restoration of the three year TB eradication scheme; and

   v. strong and resolute rejection by the Irish Government of the EC Commission proposals on beef, cereals and milk.

The IFA felt badly about being excluded from the National Understandings. According to Berkery, while they did not have a seat at the national talks they were involved in the NESC, which was a very important forum for input. The IFA had representation and recognition as regards agriculture dating from a statement by former Taoiseach Jack Lynch in 1966. In Berkery's view, Irish social partnership was born 'out of necessity; it was not people waking up one morning and saying this is the way we do it and here are the benefits.' The IFA in turn had to shoulder major changes in relation to taxation. Berkery recalls the influence of Austria and Sweden on Padraig O'hUiginn: 'O'hUiginn had the structure and the model and he reconstructed the model for Ireland,' according to Berkery.

The IFA was coming from being an organisation of protest and the PNR represented a shift of gear: 'Suddenly we were on the top platform of the Burlington Hotel while people were telling us we should be with the opposition.' Berkery suggests that leaders had to highlight the potential for tangible gains and show that the IFA could make specific gains from being 'inside the tent'. Securing agreement for the PNR meant winning support from the 100 member IFA National Council. As Berkery notes, the shift for the organisation amounted to 'moving from protest to the briefcase'.

The main commitments on agriculture in the PNR were:

- a new grant/loan scheme to increase the national suckler cow herd;
- new arrangements on bovine TB eradication;
- a pilot programme on integrated rural development;
- a ministerial office for horticulture and a five-year development plan;
- an action programme to develop forestry;
- development of the marine sector including farmed fish.

The PNR duly committed the Government to defending the Common Agricultural Programme (CAP) commitments to Irish farmers and to ensuring that any 'system of budget discipline' did not impact adversely on the sector. There were also commitments to developing the food industry and producing a plan for an 'aggressive international marketing strategy' built around core companies. This would eventually lead to the Goodman controversy and Beef Tribunal, but also to strong growth in exports. At a more mundane level, the PNR contained provisions for developing confidence within the farming community through supports for beef cow producers, measures to tackle bovine TB and establishment of integrated rural development programmes.

The PNR provided a template for future agreements where agricultural issues were negotiated largely on a bilateral basis between farming organisations and the Government, but within the context of wider economic and social policy. While this arrangement generally worked well, it left the farming organisations with a semi-detached attitude towards the wider process at times. This came to the fore most notably in 2003 when the IFA withdrew from talks on Sustaining Progress. The then President of the IFA John Dillon expressed his members' frustration with the way pay negotiations, particularly over benchmarking, were dominating the agenda by stating: 'The reality is that this is an agreement on a €2 billion public sector pay bill.' However the withdrawal was temporary.

Coupled with the temporary withdrawal of the Community Platform and National Women's Council from the process, the IFA protest led the *Irish Times*, which traditionally supported social partnership, to describe 'Sustaining Progress' as 'a two tier agreement' in an editorial on 4 February 2003. While all three parties eventually returned to the partnership process, it showed that a tri-partite deal between government, unions and employers would not have the same credibility or widespread support as one involving all the social partners.

Radical changes to the CAP and to trade policy, caused by the World Trade Organisation Doha Round and EU expansion, has seen policy priorities change. The NESC Strategy 2006 Report provided a comprehensive analysis of the challenges facing the sector. In Towards 2016, the development of a National Strategy for Rural Development and measures to improve competitiveness and productivity in the agri-farm sector were identified as essential agents for future development. The aim remains to maintain a vibrant rural economy and sustain the family farm model, albeit in fewer but larger units. The longer timeframe for the Agri-Vision 2015 Action Plan converges with that of Towards 2016 in regard to the National Development Plan and suggests that, whatever the future for national pay agreements, there will remain a need for holistic planning for agriculture on a national level.

CHAPTER 8

The People Factor – The Dynamics of Social Partnership

It's a social mechanism, it's part of governance, it's a cultural accomplishment, it's an instrument of social learning, it's a variety of things but, at the end of the day, it's about relationships between people.

Dermot McCarthy, secretary general of the
Department of the Taoiseach

The Irish model of social partnership is not really a model at all. Academics have tried in vain to place it within a European framework, to shoehorn it in somewhere between Berlin and Stockholm. But it won't fit. It contains some elements of models from other countries, but perhaps what it has most in common with European experience is that, at the outset, it was a response to an economic and social crisis. In this respect, the parallel lies more with how other countries responded to their post-World War Two devastation than with any other so-called corporatist style model. The crisis of the 1980s was so all-pervasive that it undermined the political system, seeming to shatter any confidence that Ireland could save itself, never mind build a future. Social partnership was a pragmatic response to finding a way out of that trough, helping – as the title of this book suggests – to 'save the future'.

In the Ireland of the 1980s, there were few of the ideological class divisions that existed elsewhere, especially in Britain, from whom we inherited our industrial relations system. The lack of a clear left-right divide has often been blamed for holding back our development. The catch-all nature of the larger parties, Fianna Fáil and Fine Gael (themselves a result of a division dating back to the civil war), seemed to many observers to put a break on 'real politics'. In 1987, however, this perceived ideological weakness turned into a strength, enabling the main social partners, with their broad political support, to establish a system or model that remains at the centre of decision-making to this day. Just two years later, the Berlin Wall was to come down, further signaling the end of old and distinct left-right divides in mainland Europe.

Perhaps Ireland, unburdened by the divides that had been central to much of the European experience for so long, actually held an advantage. It was also, as it turned out, ideally positioned to become one of the success stories of an increasingly globalised world economy, possessing as it did a key ingredient to capitalise on this: a young well-educated workforce waiting to join the modern world.

Politics in much of the Western World has been gravitating towards the centre over the past decade or more. Arguably, Ireland got there first, perhaps by accident, but in no small measure helped by the ability of key interest groups to reach a pragmatic consensus on the big issues facing a country in crisis. And at the heart of that process has been the dynamic that drives social partnership, namely a web of both formal and informal links between influential people and their social partner bodies and government. One social partnership insider has described this as a 'social capital network'. The process also demonstrates an ability on the part of the social partners to renegotiate the scope of the agreements to reflect the realities of a small open economy. Employers and investors have secured some of the changes they need to maintain competitiveness, and in return trade unions have been able, thus far, to deliver pay increases and a social wage dividend for their members. HR Director of Penneys Breege O'Donoghue believes partnership has helped to give the trade unions access to a wider agenda. And it has 'forced unions and employers to be seen to have a united front, held together by the experience of the negotiators'.

As the central figure in the current process, the Taoiseach's Secretary General Dermot McCarthy says social partnership is more than a social mechanism or part of governance, 'at the end of the day it's about relationships between people.' Many of those people had similar backgrounds. Phil Flynn, former IMPACT general secretary and president of ICTU, says this may be because 'a significant number of us were peasants, just one generation from the land. We're a small country, not as class ridden in hierarchical terms as others.' Labour Court Chairman Kevin Duffy, a former ICTU assistant general secretary, says good relationships between people were significant: 'It's much easier to deal with somebody with whom you have an ongoing working relationship than somebody you have to ring up and meet for the first time.' It was not unusual for Duffy, and other key union or employer leaders, as he says, 'to pick up the phone and talk one-to-one' to Bertie Ahern when he was Minister for Labour.

All of these people were operating under the big tent of partnership. These relationships, set within the context of a small intimate country with a talent for conversation, drive the model. They have made it into the thing that today is frustratingly difficult to describe to outsiders. 'Rarely a week goes by that we don't have a delegation from some country, coming here to look at it. It is hugely valued outside the country, more than it is internally,' says David Begg. Perhaps it is inevitable that outsiders may miss what is probably the key ingredient in the process, namely the people factor, because it is so specific to the local culture. Having put their stamp on the social partnership system that has evolved, a combination of these same people and emergent leaders will drive and shape the model into the future.

LEANING TOWARDS THE CENTRE

A very important figure throughout the twenty-one years has been Dan Murphy, a relatively dispassionate observer on the trade union side. Within the process that is partnership, his role in devising the nuts and bolts of the various deals has assumed legendary status. Murphy has always held the view that, because Ireland is a small country, this makes it far easier for people to relate, at national level, than would be the case in a larger country. On the left-right issue, Murphy agrees that the lack of a real cleavage between the two may have helped: 'It means we recognise that a lot of our members vote for all sorts of political parties and there is no point in trade unions pretending that their members are militant left, because clearly they are not. If they were, the political "scenery" would be different.'

This view dovetails with the perspective of IBEC's John Dunne, a key player from the outset of the process. Dunne says the Thatcherite solution to Ireland's difficulties in the 1980s would not have been the way to go. According to Dunne, Irish employers did not have the appetite for such an approach, at least at that time, even though it may have seemed like the only possible option for dealing with the fiscal crisis that loomed in 1987.

Con Power, then director of economic policy with the Confederation of Irish Industry, concurred that Thatcherism was never an option for him.

The ability of quite different interests, albeit interests which held their ideological baggage lightly, to come together enabled all sides to find a way of reaching consensus on a range of contentious issues. This consensus also prevailed at a political level, although not everyone would agree. SIPTU's President Jack O'Connor takes the view that former Fine Gael leader Alan Dukes, who devised the crucial Tallaght Strategy, did so to provide the opportunity for the minority Fianna Fáil Government led by Charles Haughey to take a Thatcherite approach: 'The Tallaght Strategy was about signaling to the Government of the day that they had a blank cheque. It was about a licence to undertake a Thatcherite assault on organised labour. That's what it was about, I've no doubt that it was a licence to screw the unions.' Dukes denies Fine Gael would ever have gone down that road. It is his view that former Taoiseach Garret FitzGerald had no intention of breaking the trade unions. Looking back, Dukes says tellingly, 'the pity is that we didn't really start it before 1986.' Peter Cassells concurs: 'I don't think that in Ireland there was ever any appetite for Thatcherism or any of that.' Former IMPACT General Secretary and one-time ICTU President Phil Flynn believes that Dukes was 'hugely underestimated in terms of his contribution' and for the 'courage and foresight' he had, particularly in relation to the Tallaght Strategy.

Although some may disagree with O'Connor's perspective on the Tallaght Strategy, there is perhaps more consensus with the line he takes on the potential for instability in the Republic at the time. There was certainly a fear in establishment circles that discontent with high unemployment and disillusionment with politics generally, could have added to the attractiveness of more extreme political positions. The influence of the troubles in Northern Ireland was never far from the thoughts of politicians. Jack O'Connor says that Haughey recognised that the consequences for the country of undertaking a Thatcherite approach 'would have been dire, with no guarantee of success given the strength of our labour movement'.

Looking back with the benefit of her extensive knowledge of workplace industrial relations, Breege O'Donoghue believes that the Thatcherite experience in the UK may have actually helped bring employers and trade unions together in 1987, 'and go for a national initiative, as opposed to going for the sort of damage they had in Britain'. In a way, she says, it was an 'Irish solution for an Irish problem' and suited the economic circumstances of the time.

LABOUR MISSES OUT

The Labour Party was also a backer of centralised deals, but was perhaps jealous of the ability of the trade unions to do deals with Fianna Fáil, particularly Charles Haughey. This testiness between the two wings of the broader labour movement was a peculiarity of the time. Labour, led by Haughey's political bette noir Dick Spring as Tanáiste, with John Bruton as Taoiseach and Fine Gael leader, subsequently negotiated the P2000 agreement in 1997. In fact, as we have already seen, all of the mainstream parties have negotiated and overseen one or more of the seven programmes.

The 1980s was a particularly tough time for Labour to be in government, and it was also a time when the trade union movement had to reassess its basic strategies. The dynamic between the two left a lot to be desired, particularly in contrast to the relationship between the trade unions and Fianna Fáil. Relationships between Labour and the unions improved markedly in later years, with Dick Spring and Ruairi Quinn (Minister of Enterprise, Trade and Employment, 1993–94 and Finance Minister, 1994–97) operating social partnership under the PCW and negotiating the P2000 agreement.

SIPTU's Jack O'Connor provides an intriguing perspective on the Labour Party, which he believes made 'a disastrous decision' in 1994 not to go back into government with Fianna Fáil under Bertie Ahern. The Taoiseach Albert Reynolds (1992–94) had insisted on appointing the former Attorney General Harry Whelehan as President of the High Court. Whelehan had been attorney general when that office had made a botched effort to extradite a paedophiliac priest to the North. Reynolds apologised before the Dáil, but Labour left government and Reynolds resigned. Bertie Ahern, who succeeded Reynolds as leader of Fianna Fáil in 1994 and looked on the verge of becoming Taoiseach, tried to mend the coalition, but was unsuccessful. Labour decided to form an alternative 'rainbow' coalition with Fine Gael and Democratic Left. For O'Connor, not going into government with Bertie Ahern was a huge missed opportunity: 'I would say it was one of the two worst decisions the Labour Party made in its history.'

Many trade union leaders like O'Connor were Labour supporters but, unlike their colleagues in the UK, they were guided by pragmatism more than ideology. Most of them saw no difficulty in doing business with Fianna Fáil, in fact some preferred it. Their ability to do this arises out of

Ireland's electoral system of proportional representation (PR), which makes it difficult for one particular political position or ideology to dominate. In Jack O'Connor's view, this allows the broader labour movement to influence the direction of government policy 'to the extent that they could ameliorate the worst effects of what the other side was contemplating'.

THE HEART OF THE AFFAIR

The critical relationship in the social partnership story, therefore, is the one between Fianna Fáil and the trade union movement. At the heart of the relationship lies a deep affinity with pragmatic solutions, rather than ideological ones, at least on the part of a majority of Congress unions. The deal between Haughey's 1982 Government and left-leaning independent TD Tony Gregory, and his community based coalition, may have been opportunistic on both sides, but it was also indicative of the sort of political pragmatism that a small country with weak political cleavages can produce. The cost of the 'Gregory Deal' ranged from £80 million to £150 million, to be spent on inner city projects in Dublin. It was witnessed by Mickey Mullen, General Secretary of the ITGWU, and was read into the records of Dáil Éireann.

NESC Director Rory O'Donnell says that there was also a sense in the late 1980s among the central players in the drama that 'they were stuck with each other'. They were also tied to a 'consensus oriented political system, not a conflictual one in the same mould as Britain's, even though Ireland's industrial relations system has been fundamentally based on that of the UK.'

In a political culture where pragmatism was valued so highly, therefore, the individuals with leadership roles within government, the apparatus of government, and in IBEC and ICTU, were even more important than they might have been in a larger, industrialised nation with a more traditional left-right divide. Personal preferences and attachments were, and still are, important. Padraig O'hUiginn, who chaired the NESC at the time of its critical 1986 report, was also secretary general of the Department of the Taoiseach under Charles Haughey. As one observer puts it, O'hUiginn was more closely associated with Haughey 'than would have been the norm for Irish civil servants'. Former Finance Minister Charlie McCreevy recalls that Haughey, many years after his departure from the national scene, considered O'hUiginn to be 'as wise as old sin himself'. This was, of course, delivered as a compliment.

Charlie McCreevy says Ireland has been lucky to have a 'long line of great civil servants'. He recalled that he used to say in his speeches at one stage, 'there's only two good things the Brits left us – good buildings and a good ethos in the public service.' Dermot McCarthy is the latest in a line of three such talented and respected secretary generals in the Department of the Taoiseach, following Paddy Teahon and O'hUiginn. Other key civil servants have played vital roles, such as Kevin Murphy, Kevin Bonner, John Hurley and Philip Kelly, to mention a few. What is instructive is the huge respect the other social partners have for individuals within the government apparatus who handle the process. They also know that the enhanced role given to his own Department by Haughey when he became Taoiseach in 1987 was, and remains, a clear signal that social partnership is at the centre of the action. This makes an enormous difference when seemingly intractable problems arise, such as the Irish Ferries dispute in 2005.

Jack O'Connor regards secretary generals like Dermot McCarthy as possessing more than just enormous ability: '[McCarthy's] outlook is one of strong commitment to the public interest. He is a public servant in the truer sense of the word and has the capacity to balance so many angels and devils on the head of a pin.' McCarthy is a man with an extraordinary level of patience, Dan Murphy says. He describes how he reacts when two sides are in conflict: 'When one group says, "black, black, black" and another group says, "white, white, white", Dermot says, "that's been a very useful exchange and I think we should now reflect on the position and see if we can move towards a greater degree of understanding." ' Peter Cassells says that each of these pivotal civil servants is associated with a particular achievement: Padraig O'hUiginn with national debt crisis; Paddy Teahon with economic development; and Dermot McCarthy, who has integrated all of the elements and 'had the patience to be able to bring in and involve the community sector'.

CARRYING THE TORCH

At a political level, we have seen how employer and trade union leaders have shown a remarkable degree of consensus in praising Haughey's role, both in deciding to opt for the partnership route, and for his management of that process during the PNR years in particular. Both Haughey and Finance Minister Ray McSharry were crucial in persuading, not just the social partners, but the country at large, that they were serious about tackling the fiscal crisis in 1987, says Paddy Teahon. Not everyone might have believed that Haughey 'had a complete change of heart relative to his earlier positions on public expenditure. If you hadn't had a Minister for Finance that was as strong as Ray McSharry, it would have been very difficult to carry the day.'

Such unwavering leadership was crucial in establishing the consistency that is one of the bedrocks of social partnership, from compliance with the pay deals to adherence to fiscal targets, or tax reform commitments. And yet there has also been considerable subtlety at the heart of the process, which allows for enough flexibility within the system as long as it does not damage it. The nurses' dispute in 1999 demonstrated what can happen when one group manages to subvert the pay agreements but, that apart, many major disputes were handled with a level of skill and patience that would have done credit to the Northern peace process. No-one, at least at a political level, was more adroit at this ability to smooth over tensions while maintaining the integrity of the various partnership agreements than Bertie Ahern.

Dan Murphy describes the role of Bertie Ahern who, even more than Charles Haughey, is the politician most associated with social partnership: 'He doesn't take a decision unless he absolutely has to. The effect of that is that he doesn't antagonise people – unless he has to. He has enormous patience and he's always available. He is extremely good at trying to knit situations together, extraordinarily good.' Ahern, in various roles as Minister for Labour, Minister for Finance and as Taoiseach, has spanned all twenty-one years of the process. Billy Attley recalls Ahern's ability to calm a dispute. One of Attley's officials, 'who hated employers, hated Fianna Fáil' met Ahern in his local pub, Kennedy's, in Drumcondra during a dispute: 'All the hostility went out of it. He went up to him and he was "yes Bertie, no Bertie, kiss my arse Bertie." [Ahern] is that type, but having said that you wouldn't want to underestimate him. Mary O'Rourke [former Fianna Fáil Minister] summed him up when she said, "The only person who knows Bertie Ahern is Bertie Ahern."'

Phil Flynn says Ahern's 'brilliance' was based on good intelligence, which meant he 'knew exactly the correct moment to intervene in a dispute'. A story Flynn relates about Ahern tells us something about the personal nature of the Irish social partnership process, and just how accessible even the leader of the country could be: 'I used to have foreign trade union

leaders here and they just could not just believe it. On the way to the airport you would take them for a pint in Kennedy's pub where Ahern would
sometimes be. You would say to them, "that's our Prime Minister." '

Ahern's ability to act as a facilitator is legendary. Peter McLoone says
Ahern 'never gets upset, never fights with you'. Ahern might mean to say
'no', but he would never say it 'like that'; 'then again he might say "yes"
and you wouldn't know it was "yes". And it worked. His was the first
Government to be re-elected in thirty-three years.' And McLoone recalls a
comment made by Labour Leader and former union official Pat Rabbitte
who opined that 'Bertie is better than any opposition'. In other words, he
could seem all things to all people. Billy Attley asks what other Prime
Minister would spend three hours every Sunday knocking on doors in his
constituency? 'That's the way he works.'

Ahern himself tells a story about trying to help resolve an issue in the
Dublin Port and Docks Board, which sums up how extensive his intelligence sources are, and just how deep Fianna Fáil's roots are within all
segments of Irish society. His 'buddy' is the Chairman of the Board, the
senior shop steward is one of his Fianna Fáil activists in East Wall, and
another friend works in management: 'All of them are politically supportive of me, from one extreme to the other. So I can sit here in my office and
get the three views: the board's, the management's and the trade union's.
We have that all the time. Probably the only sector we tend not to influence is the legal sector. We tend not to be in that game. In every other part
of Irish life I think we are the predominant group.'

Ahern also believes that in many respects Fianna Fáil is to the left of the
Labour Party. 'Dare I say it, the Fianna Fáil parliamentary party are a long
way left of Labour who tend to get involved in ideological arguments. Our
people get involved in practical arguments because they are down at the
post office, the pub, the old people's home. It might not be the greatest
ideological, intellectual thing. But it's a pragmatic thing.'

Fianna Fail's Albert Reynolds, who oversaw the PESP and was Taoiseach
for the PCW negotiations, was not as patient with the process as Ahern,
who played a direct role in delivering tax reductions and other commitments as Reynolds' Minister for Finance. Reynolds, who was also a successful businessman, was very much a pragmatist. He would not have
described himself as a socialist as Bertie Ahern once described himself.
But Reynolds oversaw partnership at an important time, a time that Dermot
McCarthy describes as the period when partnership moved from the 'fiscal

adjustment stage' to the next phase. This produced, not just a focus on incomes policy towards employment creation, 'but also a very active period of policy innovation'.

With Reynolds it seems 'what you saw was what you got.' Phil Flynn explains Reynolds' character through the lense of the Northern Ireland peace process: 'In relation to the North his attitude was: "this is an awful problem and it's got to be sorted. It's bad for the economy, bad for the country. We'll sort it out." He was totally pragmatic, no baggage, no ideology. [His attitude] was the same with social partnership: "That's a damn good idea. It seems to work. Let's get on with it." '

THE REALITY OF POWER

Some politicians were seen as sceptics, for instance Charlie McCreevy as Minister for Finance. But this was a misconception, says Peter Cassells. '[McCreevy] embraced it very quickly, and saw the value of it once you weren't trying to write the Budget!' Cassells describes two types of Ministers in his experience: 'You had ones like Mary O'Rourke, when she was in Education, who understood fully that, unless it got into the national programme, it might never happen, whereas others would be inclined to look at it and say, "well, I want to announce that initiative, I'm not going to hand it over to the national programme." '

The role of Fine Gael's John Bruton as Taoiseach has often been neglected, even undervalued. Not only did Bruton preside over the negotiation of Partnership 2000, which was an extremely difficult deal to guide through choppy union waters, he also introduced various community and representative groups via the social pillar. Bruton, a one-time critic of the process, saw its value when in a position of real power. According to Dermot McCarthy, 'It was a pragmatic more than an ideological conversion, the agreement was there. The processes were in place.' Peter McLoone recalls Bruton's conversion and how he broadened it by introducing the social pillar. According to McLoone, it was in Bruton's nature to be innovative, a feature that has marked his political career. Jack O'Connor says Bruton's participation showed that there was a dynamic about social partnership that had developed by then: 'It's not a unique claim of Fianna Fáil.'

Phil Flynn, McLoone's former boss, says John Bruton not only has a 'great mind' but he has always been very open and brims with new ideas: 'His problem was actually, at times, he was slightly too open. You would meet him one day and he'd open up on you like a machine gun with ideas. He'd be spewing out ideas all over the place and you would meet him a few weeks later and he'd have a whole new set of ideas!' But Bruton seemingly could also exhibit a common touch, which is often so necessary, not just for a politicians, but for the social partnership process. Bruton was 'very socially conscious and caring', according to Flynn. While Bruton was Taoiseach, Flynn, in his capacity as ICTU President, invited Bruton to an ICTU conference. 'I asked him to come down the night before. He spent it drinking with shop stewards in the bar. They couldn't believe it. They couldn't believe that this guy John Bruton, Taoiseach, was amongst them, trading punches and drinking pints with them.' (Bruton's brother Richard, also a key figure in Fine Gael, is critical of partnership; but rather than wanting to jettison it, he wants to reform it.)

THE COMMON TOUCH

This level of informality is something Phil Flynn observed first hand on numerous occasions. Trade unionists from outside Ireland 'could not get their head around it, particularly our [UK] colleagues from across the water. They thought this was an El Dorado, a paradise.' The non-ideological nature of Irish politics was a cause of further confusion in Europe. Flynn recalls an episode when his namesake, Padraig Flynn, was EU Commissioner for Social Affairs. A former Fianna Fáil Minister, often satirised in Ireland as a conservative on family and social issues, Padraig Flynn was invited to address the British Trade Union Congress: 'They asked me what he was like. I said, "It would be better for you to decide, but he's certainly not to the left, but we will see." Anyhow, Flynn came and he delivered this incredibly progressive speech, ringing all the fucking bells. And in the bar afterwards they were saying to me: "If he is right wing, what's the left like?" He made an incredible impression. They didn't understand us really.'

IBEC leaders like Dan McAuley, John Dunne and Turlough O'Sullivan have also made their particular contributions to the process. According to one insider, 'IBEC has no ideology.' Translated, this means that IBEC will go for what works, placing no intrinsic value in the idea of partnership per se. Its members have little real interest in areas covered by the social pillar and in many of the wider non-core elements of the agreements. That is not to say that IBEC and employers generally do not value the access and enhanced influence that social partnership gives them with government and State agencies. They certainly do but, unless the pay and related aspects of the deals are sound in their eyes, then the process is not worth it. They have the standing to influence key policy areas anyway.

An example of how closely influential leaders on each side can manage the process was shown through the long-standing working relationship between Labour Court Chairman Kevin Duffy, when he was ICTU Assistant General Secretary, and IBEC's Director General Turlough O'Sullivan, when he was in charge of industrial relations in the confederation. Well before the establishment of the National Implementation Body, this duo operated almost like an emergency response unit, helping to resolve difficult disputes that had the potential to upset the agreements. Now that task is performed by ICTU General Secretary David Begg and O'Sullivan within the NIB, usually assisted by IMPACT's Peter McLoone and IBEC's Brendan McGinty.

THE BIG UNION

The character and personality of these influential people have been important. Personal ties and friendships are not usually built into academic models of social partnership or corporatism. But in Ireland, as we have seen, they form a crucial element and have been critical in the dynamic that has developed within the process. The standing of the main leader of SIPTU (formerly ITGWU and FWUI), given that union's size and prominence within ICTU, has always been critical. John Carroll and Billy Attley, who were the main architects in creating SIPTU out of an amalgam of their respective unions – the ITGWU and FWUI – were key figures in securing the breakthrough PNR agreement, and critical persuaders at a time when the membership of the ITGWU and the FWUI would not have been as strongly supportive of the agreements as SIPTU members later became. SIPTU Regional Secretary Patricia King believes that Attley simply realised that Ireland had to be made attractive to secure inward investment. It was pragmatic, not ideological. 'There was a lot of change and pain, yet the leadership was prepared to stand up and say, "this is where we have to go to get the place we need to be."' It would have been easy to 'stay running with the members. The hardest thing is to lead.' She said that Attley was a 'big character at a time when he needed to be'.

King describes Des Geraghty, who followed Attley in the top SIPTU leadership role, as someone who was full of innovative ideas and with acutely developed political antennae. Geraghty was able to bring these talents to bear on the talks and, over the years, his relationship with the 'other side' was a well honed one. His major talent was his ability to work ideas like the social wage through to a concrete conclusion.

The current President of SIPTU Jack O'Connor took over the leadership mantle held by Geraghty and Attley at a particularly important time. One employer describes Jack O'Connor as the sort of leader that the employers might not want, but 'he may be the leader that his members need.' Certainly O'Connor, who can seem diffident, came across as a reluctant leader at the outset. But he commands huge respect within SIPTU, particularly due to his stance on pursuing the employment standards agenda in the wake of the Irish Ferries dispute. His sure-footedness on that crucial case cemented his stature within the union, earning him the genuine affection of activists and members. Ultimately, O'Connor sees social partnership as part of a journey in pursuit of social democracy 'as conceived by Larkin, Connolly, and all the other visionary pioneers of the labour movement'.

O'Connor and Patricia King operate as a very effective team in the social partnership process, complimenting one another. Vice President Brendan Hayes tends to operate more behind the scenes, acting as a crucial interpreter of events and as a strategist, while General Secretary Joe O'Flynn looks after the union's internal affairs. While King maintains a close link to the grass roots herself, she is also more comfortable mingling with the other big fish of partnership than is O'Connor. She is convinced that O'Connor deserves to 'go down in history as one of the great trade union leaders', believing him also to be an excellent strategist. As one employer who believes the trade union movement needed a 'result' from the Irish Ferries row puts it, the 'SIPTU card was well played'.

LINKING THE GENERATIONS

Playing that card in the lead up to the Towards 2016 talks did frustrate some of the public sector union leaders. But, during the Irish Ferries dispute, and in the long-running talks that later emerged, a strong relationship was forged between three of the key players on the trade union side. ICTU General Secretary David Begg, IMPACT General Secretary and ICTU President Peter McLoone, and Jack O'Connor were a formidable triumvirate, effectively leading the ICTU talks' delegation. It was over the course of almost nine months of on-and-off again talking that respect was sown between each of these central players. David Begg, whose previous job was as regional director of Concern Worldwide, works closely with O'Connor and McLoone. McLoone himself is the link back to the first agreement, the PNR. His boss at that time was Phil Flynn, who also served as President of ICTU and played a very central role devising trade union strategies around the process, particularly in its early years.

Of course, among those with a link back to the first agreement is Bertie Ahern and, on the employer side, Turlough O'Sullivan. For the smooth operation of the process, this linking of the past and present generation of social partnership figures at the top is crucial. If leaders emerge at the top of ICTU or IBEC who are less sympathetic to the process then it may not survive. The same applies in the political sphere, which reinforces the argument that individuals have been one of the core ingredients of social partnership from the outset.

If the PNR was a rescue operation then Charles Haughey was the man with the lifeboat and union agendas were adjusted so that the scramble aboard would not capsize the vessel. Ireland today is very different. There is a tighter labour market, but also far greater pressure from the effects of globalisation, competitiveness and migration in areas such as job security, pensions and real employment standards, as opposed to those presided over in the highly regulated public sector.

THE TRADITIONAL OPPOSITION

The pragmatic consensus developed in the crisis of the 1980s was never unanimous, but the main critics on the union side then came largely from the old left within the movement, such as Brian Anderson and Joe Bowers of the Amalgamated Union of Engineering Workers (AUEW) and the Technical Administrative and Supervisory Section (TASS), Michael Brennan of the EETPU and Mick O'Reilly of the ATGWU. O'Reilly saw the main threat from social partnership as a 'depoliticisation of members', who needed class conflict on the shop floor to be constantly reminded of the importance of union organisation and, ultimately, of political mobilisation against the capitalist system.

Partnership reduced trade union activity to 'a fire brigade service' and members became 'consumers of trade unionism, not producers'. O'Reilly's answer, a grand alliance combining trade union militancy with Labour Party radicalism, never saw fruit. Many trade union activists clung stubbornly to the material benefits of partnership, in large part because of the strategic shift in the trade union movement, led by union leaders like John Carroll, Billy Attley, Dan Murphy, Phil Flynn and Peter Cassells. Many of them, like Attley, Carroll and Murphy, were Labour supporters, but they helped to create the dynamic for social partnership along with Fianna Fáil politicians like Haughey and Ahern, and civil servants like O'hUiginn. These were, ultimately, joined by IBEC leaders like John Dunne and Turlough O'Sullivan.

The O'Reilly approach had no real chance in a country with such weak ideological underpinnings. Its day also looks to be past in the UK and in mainstream Europe, where the clamber to the centre ground of politics continues largely unabated. Media labeling of German Chancellor Angela Merkel as the German Blair (incidentally not Thatcher) signals a move toward the centre, be it slightly centre-right or centre-left, or even the 'third way', as championed by former US President Bill Clinton and UK Prime Minister Tony Blair.

THE NEW OPPOSITION

Arguably, Ireland was in the centre ground before any of them, or, at the very least, she was pragmatic at a time when this was the only possible response to the 1987 crisis. It has remained there ever since, as evidenced by the ease with which parties interchange in government and by the social partnership model itself. So there is a dynamic of the centre at play, one that the social partners act out within their sphere of influence, which must be considerably enhanced by the relationships that the players have with one another. This may not sit well with all trade unionists or some on the employer side. But it is clear that there is little room at the table for traditional far-left or far-right solutions.

Of course, this is not to suggest that any of the social partners have abandoned their particular political perspectives or long-term goals, whether these be disposed, for example, towards social democracy or Christian democracy. What it does mean is that decisions are made on pragmatic grounds and judged according to how much of one's particular agenda is achievable within the process. This leaves it up to the leaders of ICTU trade unions and IBEC, at least every three years, to decide whether staying with partnership is the best option. For twenty-one years they have said 'yes', and their respective members have endorsed their judgement.

What is fascinating today, however, is that the stronger ideological push against partnership is coming from the right. While much of this is based on media contributions with an inbuilt prejudice against social partnership, there have also been many weighty contributions to the debate by its opponents. In tandem with this, there is an emerging group of employers who may be outside IBEC or the partnership mainstream. They simply do not believe in social partnership. They also have a diminished respect for the State's dispute resolution agencies like the Labour Relations Commission or the Labour Court.

At a political level, this emerging constituency has yet to fully find its voice, simply because the political parties have, with the occasional exception of Fine Gael, been advocates of social partnership. The PDs may be regarded by the trade unions as far to the right, but they have operated and worked the social partnership system. Former Tanáiste, Mary Harney, herself a former Fianna Fáiler, introduced that policy no-go area for right wing parties – a statutory national minimum wage. Meanwhile, although Fine Gael has been hostile to partnership, it has never sought to ditch the process, merely reform it – a position that any opposition party would be expected to adopt. In fact the phases in their history when Fine Gael and the PDs have been most critical of the process also happen to coincide with their periods in opposition.

Nonetheless, there may be an emerging anti-partnership vacuum in the political arena, possibly built around opposition to issues like public service benchmarking. This could find a political voice and create a political dynamic around a range of anti-partnership issues, posing a challenge for the social partner leaders. Their biggest task will be to convince the doubters that social partnership suits this modernising economy, and that it has the ability to deliver reform.

FORGING A NEW DYNAMIC

The underlying core of pragmatism at the root of Ireland's social partnership system has been sustained by a core group of leaders within ICTU, IBEC and at government level, whether through senior politicians or by key civil servants. In other words, by the social capital network referred to earlier. Its legitimacy is founded on the trade union side by an often tortuous process of consultation and union-wide balloting. IBEC relies on its own sounding boards, from regional meetings to informal contacts. On the government side, there is little interest in the Oireachtas, apart from some honourable exceptions, in more open debate and consideration of the programmes and what they mean for society and the democratic system.

The main players understand very well the language of social partnership. It is something they have created themselves, and nourished and extended over twenty-one years into the relatively sophisticated system it has become today. However they know that, not only do leaders move on, but the know-how they have acquired moves with them. So replacing the current network with equally astute leaders is critical if social partnership is not to stagnate. Partnership is facing an enormous task to establish its capability to meet future challenges. We now turn to the final chapter to survey the emerging themes and questions that the partners must answer. They must attempt to forge a new dynamic to cope with what lies ahead, one that exhibits greater openness and transparency in tune with the greater openness and accountability expected of all institutions that operate in the public eye.

CHAPTER 9

Can Social Partnership Survive into the Future?

The winners of today are tomorrow's losers.

Breege O'Donoghue, HR director Penneys

Twenty-one years on from the launch of the Programme for National Recovery, it is evident that Ireland more than recovered its bounce in the decades that followed. It stepped confidently into the future, a future saved by the policy decisions taken and acted upon from 1987 onwards. The social partnership agreements played an important part in that achievement. While the weight that commentators have given to that role has varied, few have dissented from the view that the PNR was a catalyst for the creation of the Celtic Tiger. This book does not claim that social partnership was solely responsible for the Irish economic miracle. Rather it suggests it was a vital ingredient that became part of the fabric of our political, economic and social life and it has made a significant contribution to shaping modern Ireland.

The titles of the six programmes that followed the first one have reflected the mood of the times in which they were negotiated, from the aspiration to greater social progress in the PESP, to the lofty aim of moving 'Towards 2016' under the banner of the NESC. A broad consensus has been in operation, one that none of the main players will walk away from lightly. This in itself is a testimony to how the process remains at the heart of policy and decision making in 2007. To justify its existence, however, social partnership must constantly renew itself, which is the challenge it faces again this year.

By the early summer of 2007, many of the commitments on employment standards in Towards 2016 were on their way to being delivered, and there was little sign of problems regarding the application of its pay terms. Inward migration looks set to continue, even though the rate of increase is expected to fall off. But the challenge remains of how to integrate a new and vibrant workforce within society, and how to ensure that the employment standards regime that the social partners have agreed is fully up and running. It is vital that the new system is seen to be credible. The demand for the Rights Commissioner Service under the Labour Relations Commission has 'increased exponentially', according to LRC Chief Executive Kieran Mulvey. Mulvey has noted the increased use of legal representatives on behalf of all parties and the rising number of complaints from non-Irish nationals of the EU and other nationalities on a range of employment rights issues. Further enforcement of employment rights and improved services like those provided by the Rights Commissioner Service, would ensure that the social partners, in particular the trade unions, would enter a new set of talks in a positive frame of mind.

Ireland must improve its performance in a whole range of areas such as education, workplace change, productivity and modernisation, particularly in key areas of public service delivery. Other emerging themes include the conundrum of how to deal with the unresolved issue of trade union representation and recognition in the workplace; the general direction in which our industrial relations system is heading; and how to meet the growing calls for social partnership to be more accountable to the electorate and the Oireachtas.

A central question is, can social partnership endure? Key questions on this point centre on the longevity of the key relationships themselves and their evolution across different generations of union and employer leaders, the state of the economy and finally the mood and outlook of the political system towards the process. And can the key backers of partnership continue to persuade their own constituents, be they union members, individual firms, the voluntary and community sector or farmers, that staying the course is the best option.

There is a growing awareness in employer and trade union circles that a broad range of competitiveness challenges in the private and public sectors are forcing a re-think on all sides. The emergence of separate pay agendas in the FDI sector, despite their initial backing for partnership, presents a new backdrop which may lead to reduced support. Equally, there are voices and positions emerging from within the unionised sector of the economy which are more hostile and these have, if anything, increased following the Ryanair and Irish Ferries cases.

Social partnership has never been a substitute for conflict. As ICTU President Peter McLoone puts it: 'The opposing interests are real and they've had to be faced up to.' But what the process has done, according to advocates like McLoone, is to provide mechanisms that are able to handle disagreements without, in most cases, the necessity of conflict: 'What we have developed is a process, not simply a series of seven successive agreements, and it's certainly not some sort of lazy alternative to real industrial relations.'

MAKING DISTINCTIONS

On the immediate industrial relations front, there appears to be an emerging trade union consensus, articulated by SIPTU President Jack O'Connor. This advocates trade union co-operation with good non-unionised employers, but would challenge those he labels as 'tyrants'. The SIPTU leader was careful in setting out his union's stall, to make a clear distinction between non-union and anti-union employers. He said he had no problem with companies that offer good terms and conditions and 'treat their employees with respect'. This was a clear message for FDI companies: trade unions would not target those who engaged in best practice sophisticated HR policies. Effectively, this was an historic acknowledgment by a senior trade union figure of the good quality terms and conditions that apply in many 'high end' companies.

This apparent repositioning appeared to be well-timed. It coincided with the growing concern in the FDI sector, as articulated by voices in the influential US Chamber of Commerce, as well as by IBEC. Forfás Chairman Eoin O'Driscoll, with his vast experience of that sector, believes that 'every strength ultimately gives way to a weakness.' Although a backer of partnership, he suggests that, in its current form, 'extrapolating forward, the structure we have from the past is not the right way. Productivity is fundamental.' He identifies major problems in the public sector and warns that it is now 'cheaper to put a factory in California than in Dublin'. Partnership, he believes, has to look at how it can help us revive our competitive edge.

O'Driscoll is also worried that the momentum for change that social partnership has helped to generate is being lost or forgotten. There is still a recognition that it is beneficial, he says, but there is an emerging concern among those in the US FDI sector that partnership now centres around public servants who are 'the ultimate employer negotiating with themselves.' According to O'Driscoll, partnership is starting to become a closed club, is public service dominated, and semi-State dominated: 'IBEC are part of the same system as the public service unions. They are mirror images of one another; they both have the same dependence on larger State or semi-State groups of employees.' O'Driscoll, however, is not demanding the abandonment of partnership, rather he would like a rekindled version, one 'that is highly competitive' and that ensures reform in the public sector.

Breege O'Donoghue, HR director of the hugely successful Penneys chain, and who operates in the unionised private sector, comes at social partnership from a different angle. She believes that, without partnership, 'we would not have achieved as much change on the ground.' It brought a stability that is needed when the 'pace is changing worldwide, the price of technology is coming down and the product cycle is getting shorter.' She says that, if one looks at past agreements, walking away would have been difficult for any one party, given that there are three parties involved. 'It comes down to value for money and the price we put on certainty.'

Rory O'Donnell, the NESC chairman, shares some of Eoin O'Driscoll's concerns about the perceived lack of depth to the change delivered in the public sector, the area of social partnership that has attracted most criticism in recent years. O'Donnell says this poses a real challenge for the trade unions, who are faced with 'an interesting tension to say the least, which is, on the one hand, a widening of the Irish agenda from just achieving competitiveness to balancing that with more social investments. That brings the focus right back to the quality of the public services and flexibility and responsiveness.'

The Benchmarking Challenge

Ensuring the continuation of and compliance with the public service pay benchmarking system is part of this challenge. The protracted nurses' dispute in 2007 has shown how determined the Government is to defend the hard-won benchmarking process and avoid a return to the relativities culture of the past.

The first Benchmarking Report was all about putting in place a framework, even if there is a perception in some quarters that the price paid was higher than was strictly justified. Benchmarking is also an enabling process in the pursuit of reform. So it must be seen to deliver, not just on payments to public servants, but in assisting in the delivery of ongoing change and in the push for better public services.

To do this, the Public Service Benchmarking Body must attempt to forge real links between change in the private and public sector. If certain job skill sets, performance criteria and productivity are being met in related private sector jobs, then they need to be matched in the public sector. But if benchmarking was to become an exercise in phoney relativity, then it would only fall into disrepute. This would also act as a disincentive to investors and make Ireland less competitive. Our public service pay system needs to be coherent, transparent and capable of delivering on the promises that the social partners have invested in it.

Genuinely confronting the modernisation agenda will be important into the future, not alone for the unions, but for the credibility of the change process itself. It is clear that in the private sector, employers are able to secure change without major upheaval in many instances and that, in a sense, it has become the norm. So much so that change has almost become a given and the key issue is what level of national settlement secures it.

In the public sector, the issue is more complex. As Rory O'Donnell acknowledges, while the public service unions have become the strongest supporters of partnership, their system has been the slowest to adjust to modernisation. Future development will require balancing economic success with more social investment in infrastructure such as better social services and childcare. However O'Donnell is careful to note that the slowness to modernise is not simply an issue of union resistance but, like John Dunne – formerly of IBEC and also a former member of the Benchmarking Body – he highlights that you need a 'much more articulated management agenda'.

Peter McLoone laments the fact the trade unions seem to be alone in defending benchmarking, a view that we have seen is shared by John Dunne. When the PPF was negotiated in 2000, it was the politicians who pushed for benchmarking to replace the old pay links. 'It was senior civil servants who drew up the management agenda for modernisation and change,' McLoone says. 'You can count on one hand the number of managers or politicians who are now prepared to defend the outcome on the airwaves or elsewhere.' He says there is no stomach for any return to the pre-benchmarking days, but he does agree that a better way needs to be found to link benchmarking to better services 'if we are to rebuild public belief in both'.

195

In short, he says public servants have co-operated with change, but their managers have sought the wrong changes. The big flaw in the management agenda for change has been to focus on industrial relations issues exclusively, instead of targeting proposals that put the emphasis on customers and service users. This is what he wants to see emerge out of the current benchmarking round.

FACING UP TO CHANGE

The small scale of Irish society, as referred to earlier, has facilitated the evolution of such shared agendas and understandings of the key challenges facing it. In some ways it could be argued that there has been 'a cross pollination' between key members of the bargaining elites which has brought the process to the stage it is at now. What was striking from the 1980s on, and even in advance of it, was the emergence of a modern and economically literate body of trade union leaders. Their thinking was influenced, not alone by national economic discourse or newspaper headlines, but by deeper analysis of what was happening elsewhere and by developments in other union worlds.

This approach in turn fed into their analysis of the situation which they connected in turn with the type of social agenda they thought was worth pursuing and developing. Figures like Donal Nevin educated a generation of trade unionists on economic analysis and, in the process, laid the ground for the sort of strategic shifts which were to emerge in the NESC. What is clear in recent years is the way in which trade union leaders themselves recognise that, while the public are happy to support unions and see people properly paid, in turn they demand the modernisation of services, better customer services and more flexibility. There is a general intolerance of inadequacy or inconvenience.

By not tackling these problems in an upfront way, the unions have seen public demand and public cynicism about public servants grow, despite very general claims about long-term improvements in services. In this context, most public service trade unions recognise that it is now time 'to stand and deliver on the modernisation agenda' and demonstrate their credibility in seeking wider levels of public investment and funding of particular sectors. Meanwhile, it is increasingly clear that the public has little or no tolerance of industrial disputes, especially in areas such as transport or energy. The strike weapon has become largely outmoded – there were just

196

ten industrial disputes in 2006 – and it is seen by most strategic thinkers on the union side as a last resort. The cost of strikes in terms of trade union credibility, or damage to the reputation of specific categories of employee, has to be weighed up by trade unions.

However, this is not a one-way street. Some private sector disputes in companies such as Gama, Irish Ferries and in the mushroom industry are examples of unions getting back to basics. They also see it as a way of mobilising public support and combating any image there might be of trade unionists as just another interest group. Many of the workers involved are migrants from new EU accession states and even non-EU states. Unions argue that, in order to head off a backlash against foreign workers, better organisation and recruitment strategies are critical in the private sector. SIPTU, for example, has recruited foreign language organisers, with 10 per cent of its membership now made up of migrant workers.

If greater flexibility is a prerequisite of public service reform, many private sector unions see greater regulation and enforcement in areas such as construction and services as essential to their own future growth. They are concerned that regular unionised employment is giving way to a more disposable workforce provided by labour agencies. There are 520 such agencies currently registered in the Republic, according to the European Foundation for the Improvement of Living Standards and Working Conditions. It says that Ireland is 'the country with the highest percentage of those employed with a temporary agency employment contract in the EU'. Jack O'Connor has described the proliferation of these agencies as the 'key instrument for exploitation and reducing employment standards generally in our economy'. To a large extent, the future of the trade union movement in the private sector is in its own hands. Unions are now arguing that long-term growth, and relevance, can only be achieved by developing more effective organising models to build membership.

KEEPING THE PRICE RIGHT

IBEC as a social partner will not be overly perturbed by a declining role for unions in the private sector but it does back public service benchmarking. It wants it to achieve more. We have heard how John Dunne has expressed frustration with senior civil servants for not exploiting its potential for real and enduring change. In their own area of direct concern, namely private sector pay, IBEC knows that were a 'free-for-all' to re-emerge in the private sector then some unions would, in all likelihood, be able to secure above average pay rises that might set a benchmark.

Of course, the unions know that extending any such pay deals down the line would be extremely difficult in today's more competitive climate, with workers less willing to engage in industrial action. One employer close to national pay talks over the past decade or more suggests that IBEC members are still inclined to avoid such a scenario, as they may not want trade unions to get such a close connection to their own members: 'National deals may be worth paying, even if the price is a little high, to avoid the prospect of renewing the unions at local level.'

So, in the same way that FDI companies track the partnership pay agreements, employers across the economy may be happy to pay a little above the odds to avoid heading back to what they see as higher trade union involvement with their own members at local level. For the trade unions, there is an obvious balance to be struck in this delicate equation, one of which they are acutely aware.

There is a view emerging, expressed in particular by Jack O'Connor, that private sector unions must break the old habit of simply servicing members in unionised firms. But they face a tough task in hostile workplace environments where unions are actively discouraged. This may not be very appetising for a generation of union officials reared on operating a service model in a social partnership environment, but many trade unionists argue that this is where their future lies – if unions are to have a future.

MORE OR LESS REGULATION?

The description of Ireland's industrial relations system as a voluntarist one (i.e. it is based on negotiated settlements between unions and employers rather than binding arbitration or legal codes) is under serious scrutiny. Powerful and persuasive evidence has been produced recently by experienced actors and analysts, including Labour Court Chairman Kevin Duffy, that what we have today is a highly regulated system. Duffy and former senior SIPTU official Martin King have broadly concluded that such is the scale of the encroachment of employment law – and other quasi-regulatory mechanisms on the terrain of traditional industrial relations – that the system can no longer be accurately portrayed as voluntarist.

The wider explosion in labour law, much of it generated at EU level over several decades, has meant an increasing level of encroachment on much

of the industrial relations terrain. This has included a greater use of mandatory outcomes in cases involving collective bargaining. Kevin Duffy says
that, while the bulk of the Labour Court's work is still on IR disputes over
'issues of interest', it now has an expanding role in adjudication on disputes over 'issues of right'. There are now well over two dozen separate
pieces of employment legislation and the volume of cases referred to third
party institutions has increased year on year. Employers say they are finding it difficult to cope with the mounting burden of compliance. The volume of employment legislation now means that virtually no aspect of the
employment relationship is completely free from regulation.

Speaking at a IRN conference in 2005, Martin King stated: 'The ultimate
test of a voluntarily negotiated collective bargaining agreement is whether
the employees covered by such proposed agreements are at liberty to reject
the outcome of those negotiations.' One of the main consequences of the
shift from voluntarism to the greater use of binding procedures, King suggests, has been greater predictability. This is greatly valued by employers
and government, and has been consolidated by national social partnership
agreements. The upshot of all this, King concludes, is that 'the voluntarist
emperor is threadbare if not totally naked.'

ICTU's David Begg suggests that, at social partnership level, the trade
unions actually should endeavour to formally move towards binding outcomes and not seek to pull back from them. He says it is a paradox that the
main vehicle for the development of social protection – the European social
dialogue – is a process that has been based in law in most of Europe, but has
no legal basis in Ireland. This suggests that the trade unions could move in the
direction of more enforceable mechanisms, rather than less. Begg says that
institutions such as the Labour Court and the Labour Relations Commission
have been effective in maintaining industrial peace because, 'with occasional
aberrations, both sides of industry accepted their authority'. But now he says
that employers of 'substance and strategic importance, acting together in an
apparently deliberate manner, are choosing to no longer recognise this authority and [this] calls into question the continuation of a voluntary system.'

IBEC's Turlough O'Sullivan disputes this contention. He says the reality is
that compliance by employers with Labour Court findings is 'substantially
more positive than the record of trade unions'. Looking back at the history
of compliance and the attitudes of the unions and employers on binding arbitration, O'Sullivan recalls with some irony, 'a time going back to the
Commission on Industrial Relations when employers were very positively

disposed to having the Labour Court as the court of final appeals and having recommendations binding. But trade unions wouldn't have it.' Everyone then went 'through a stage, coincident really with the birth of partnership, when the trade unions wanted it, across a whole range of issues, including union recognition. [But] by then employers wouldn't have it!'

In recent times, O'Sullivan says he would like to think that both sides see the benefit of having more certainty in the process as it now stands:

> The fact is, we have got more certainty and it's working. Whether you call it a trend or not, the bottom line is that both sides are happy with it. Everyone was fed up, including the Labour Court and the public, with the fact that parties were going into those institutions and coming out the other end and not getting solutions. You seem to have a more stable approach to problem solving in other parts of the world. People were wondering, why can't we have it here? So I think it's a positive development. The fact that it works is the important thing.

RULES OF ENGAGEMENT

The reason for David Begg's growing preference for more enforceable industrial relations outcomes from the State's dispute resolution agencies may lie in his perception of an emerging trend towards a disregard of these bodies by some employers. Notwithstanding the very considerable achievements in improved employment standards in 'Towards 2016', Begg claims the minimum wage has become the 'default wage' for many people who come to work in Ireland. The absence of legally enforceable wages in many sectors of the economy and the lack of legal enforcement of the pay terms of 'Towards 2016' itself suggests that this trend will continue, he says.

Taken together, Begg believes that these factors build into a persuasive case for a move towards a more legally based system of industrial relations. It is hard to argue, he suggests, that in the present context at any rate, collective agreements should not be binding and use of the Labour Court in industrial disputes mandatory. Begg realises that these ideas might give rise to reservations in trade union ranks. 'Frankly, I do not want to abandon the voluntary system myself but if employers are no longer willing to accept its authority then it cannot function.'

Turlough O'Sullivan agrees that there have been a few exceptional cases, but says the vast majority of employers accept the status quo. Moreover,

IBEC would be strongly opposed to any suggestion of collective bargaining norms being enforced by the Labour Court. It remains to be seen whether ICTU puts this idea forward in the next round of national talks, but it is one that would face huge resistance from employers, who would see it as interfering with the marketplace.

TROUBLESHOOTER'S ROLE

Apart from a number of isolated cases, the troubleshooting National Implementation Body has managed to channel most difficult disputes towards finality. It is playing an ever more important role, arguably emerging as a first port of call for many major disputes. It is acutely aware of the danger that parties in disputes may see it as the main arm of the State's dispute resolution system. This is why it has been careful to refer the vast majority of cases back through the formal industrial relations processes.

The Independent Newspapers case in 2005 was its first real failure. Management had already secured a controversial redundancy plan, but the NIB had wanted the company to attend the Labour Court, effectively to provide something close to a fig leaf for partnership. The NIB's failure to influence the company's position showed that itself, as well as IBEC, ICTU and the Government, were unable to exert their combined influence over a powerful company that had decided the cards were stacked in its favour.

It was an indication that the informal rules of engagement, under which IBEC member companies have traditionally accepted voluntary Labour Court recommendations, even if trade unions sometimes reject them, could be changed. Were it to take root, this has the potential to undermine the standing of the State's dispute resolution agencies. It is something that even Taoiseach Bertie Ahern saw fit to comment on and is sure to inform much of the background debate within the social partner bodies themselves in the build up to talks on the next agreement. It is also worth asking whether IBEC could sustain a position whereby some firms secured competitive advantage by breaking these informal rules.

STANDING ALONE

Looking back after two decades, it is striking that – despite being one of the three arms of the social partnership process – the trade unions have yet to achieve a statutory right to be recognised in the workplace for collective bargaining purposes. Part of the reason for this state of affairs is that, along with IBEC and the government side, ICTU opted to go down the route that led to the 2001–04 Industrial Relations Acts. These provide the right for employees who join a union in workplaces where collective bargaining does not exist, to be represented on workplace issues as far as the Labour Court. But, as we have seen, largely because of the 'Ryanair' Supreme Court case, the long-term future of these provisions is now in doubt.

The Supreme Court ruling in the 'Ryanair' case has put the focus firmly back on the issue of statutory union recognition. That the trade unions in Ireland have failed to achieve this basic right must stand as a signal failure of the system from their perspective. It is a right that most employees in the Western World enjoy. In Britain, for example, once employees reach a certain proportional strength in a company they are, after a ballot, entitled to collective bargaining rights. But in Ireland, a Constitutional referendum would most likely be required to make this a reality. This would clearly be a bridge too far for IBEC, and perhaps the Government – as well as our job creation agencies. They would be concerned that a referendum might attract the unwelcome attention of potential overseas investors, and be exploited by rival inward investment agencies. It would, of course, also represent something of a risk for trade unions who might be fearful that such a change could open up the prospect of de-recognition ballots in some workplaces.

In this highly sensitive area, it seems Ireland may yet again have to wait for a solution to arrive courtesy of the EU. When that might happen is anyone's guess. In the meantime, the partners know they must tread carefully around the issue in the run-up to the next national talks. If the problem has not been resolved after twenty years, it is very unlikely to be settled over the next six months or so. That said, it does need to be resolved in some rational fashion. Ultimately, this surely must be achieved in a way that puts Ireland broadly into line with our peers in Europe. Statutory union recognition would not mean the end of civilization for employers. They live with it in the US, the UK and in many other countries. It is unlikely to make much difference to falling trade union density, but it would certainly add to trade union credibility and the standing of the trade union movement.

Breege O'Donoghue certainly believes in doing business with trade unions. But she warns that Penneys management would have a problem if the unions were to put a brake on change. In Ireland, she says, 'we stick together and kick together.' According to O'Donoghue, 'There is a solid trade union tradition here. You walk down our capital street and you see the statue of Jim Larkin. Freedom of association is very important. There needs to be checks and balances on those who wield the power.' The role of trade unions 'is to ensure that good jobs are provided and decent wages are paid. And that this is done in a good environment. In future, jobs are going to be more fluid and more global and the unions are going to have to get ready for this. They will need to be more open and democratic and more participatory.'

O'Donoghue says the unions won't 'wither on the vine', even though she does observe that collective activity is weaker these days, making it harder for trade unions generally. But for O'Donoghue it seems, the right to join a trade union and have those rights recognised should be one of the cornerstones of a healthy democracy. She would, of course, like the trade unions to exercise those rights in a manner that accommodates necessary change.

KEEPING THE SHIP AFLOAT

Critics of social partnership might rail at the 'insiders' who protect the process. But few could doubt its durability and its ability to sustain itself by circling the wagons. The crisis that surfaced before the talks on Towards 2016 was just the latest, albeit one of the most serious threats, to its continuation. The social partners have, however, been through two decades where a whole range of problems, at one time or another, seemed set to finally sink it below the waterline. Almost weekly, the NIB deals with disputes, processing them on to the LRC and the Labour Court, often unknown to the media. Even before the NIB was established, the process handled disputes more informally, regularly availing of the services of a seemingly unlikely partnership, IBEC's Turlough O'Sullivan and Kevin Duffy (formerly of ICTU, now chairman of the Labour Court).

Peter McLoone says there have always been disputes capable of knocking partnership off course: 'If you don't see social partnership as a process, then you are missing the nuances and the important subtleties that are necessary to understand why this has sustained.' According to McLoone, the model has been able to adapt itself to different conditions. The way in which the NIB channelled the ominous An Post and Irish Ferries disputes to an outcome that left social partnership intact showed how agile it could be: 'I think this process we have created has certainly shown itself not just resilient, but capable of getting engaged with most intractable disputes.'

THE BIG PICTURE

Under the leadership of David Begg, ICTU knows that big ticket issues like pensions, the future of the State sector, health care and so forth can get lost in immediate demands for better employment conditions and pay increases. This is why, in the run-up to talks on Towards 2016, Begg pressed for a revision of how the social partners do business. Begg would like to see greater use being made of the NESC strategy reports, which have traditionally provided the backdrop for talks since 1986. Signed by all the social partners, the latest report, *Strategy 2006: People, Productivity and Purpose*, provides a blueprint for social and economic development that, theoretically at least, all sides can live with.

Begg's idea is that, instead of arguing over the text of a national agreement in the relatively short period of time allowed for talks on complex issues, the national talks should focus on the narrow, but vital, issues of pay and employment-related matters, leaving the broader social and economic issues agreed within the NESC to be monitored regularly by the social partners in an ongoing process. The most immediate challenge facing such a construct for social partnership into the future is that the NESC reports would be fought over much more than they are at present. If they were to become the blueprint for future political and social development without a wider debate, this would inevitably raise the unresolved issue of where social partnership fits within a parliamentary democracy.

Concerns have been raised by many, from Richard Bruton of Fine Gael to influential employer voices, that the net is now cast far too wide. Former Finance Minister and EU Commissioner Charlie McCreevy, a supporter of the process, warns that it must not become a 'monster that could become part of the problem, rather than part of the solution'. Alan Dukes believes partnership is worth retaining, but argues that it should be simplified, with some way found to give both Houses of the Oireachtas a degree of 'political oversight'. Bertie Ahern, the strongest political supporter of partnership, has actually suggested a role for the Senate in this regard, but this proposal has yet to be embraced within the Oireachtas.

Can partnership maintain the authority needed to ensure that social and economic development occur on converging lines, or will the gap between social and economic imperatives become too wide for consensus to be maintained? For the system to work requires some approximation in the strength of the partners and this will always be problematic in a small, open economy where there are limited domestic markets to provide a buffer against global forces.

DEFINING DEMOCRACY

Charlie McCreevy is very aware of what he sees as 'the trade union movement trying to establish that the partnership process would become the process where all kinds of decisions would be made'. Although an advocate of the process, he is wary about the direction in which it is headed: 'You can't take away the rights of Dáil Éireann and the Government to make the big decisions.'

Former Taoiseach John Bruton was very sceptical of the democratic credentials of social partnership before entering government: 'My view would be that policy should be made in the Dáil and not outside the Dáil with people who haven't been directly elected,' he said, 'but I think, with the benefit of hindsight, we can see that, in any event, policy isn't actually made in the Dáil. In the Irish system the government makes policy and the Dáil approves it, or disapproves it, and if it disapproves it there is a general election.' He believes any attenuation of the democratic process 'as a result of these agreements was a price well worth paying in the light of the improvements in competitiveness that were as a result of wage restraint.' He sees unions and employers as less of a problem, in terms of democratic credentials, than the social pillar, which brings nothing to the table in terms of economic resources and whose representatives do not always have clear cut democratic mandates from constituents.

NESC Director Rory O'Donnell, who has been closely involved with the social partnership process from the beginning, feels that the main reason the debate about the democratic deficit 'hasn't really caught fire' is that social partnership has delivered for the ordinary person in the street, as well as for the elites. If the 'argument is articulated by anyone in the political system it tends to be backbenchers. But once people are ministers they don't feel cut out of the action.' He also points out that the declining role of parliaments in political decision-making processes is an international phenomenon, as governments everywhere assume greater executive powers. Like many participants in the process, O'Donnell believes the relatively small scale of Irish society makes partnership work and provides a democratic dimension to how decisions are taken and their implementation monitored; this would not be possible in larger economies such as the UK.

Union leaders are very mindful of the charge that social partnership is undemocratic but, as we have seen, most ICTU affiliates now ballot members. Jack O'Connor describes social partnership as 'the greatest example of participative democracy we have in Ireland today.' He regards membership of a social partner organisation as an 'admission ticket' to what he regards as a participatory democratic process. O'Connor points out that each union reports back on the outcome of negotiations to its members. 'In our own case we hold a further consultative conference to debate the merits of the deal on offer and the alternatives, before putting the issue to ballot. Turnouts in such ballots have been high. I think what is important to stress here is that it is a process with a strengthening democratic dimension over the years.'

ENHANCING THE PROCESS

After twenty-one years, social partnership has secured its own distinctive space within the political system. The government parties aside, however, members of the NESC are not directly answerable to the electorate. But the various partners, the social pillar included, do articulate the concerns of their respective constituencies. Arguably, social partnership enhances democracy rather than diminishes it, by giving an effective voice to these interests. It may also favour the weaker groups who, if left outside, may protest vociferously, but often quite ineffectively.

Certainly a role for elected representatives could be a step in lifting the veil on social partnership, pushing it out into the open, although the actual negotiation of deals will, inevitably, be done in private. Theoretically, the Oireachtas has the ability to address its own lack of involvement in the partnership process by a variety of means, such as specialist committees to interact with the social partners or increased representation on partnership bodies. This could boost democratic accountability and develop social partnership at the same time, rather than undermine either. After all, social partnership has been central to Ireland's social and economic development for over two decades, operating deftly behind the scenes. Whatever its critics might say, the process has been at the heart of the Celtic Tiger, but too often its workings – and its achievements – have been hidden from view. It has been close to the heart of the Celtic Tiger, a key valve or channel in a story that may have some distance to run.

THE PNR GENERATION

Assessing the role of the different generations of leaders who have maintained and developed social partnership across seven agreements is a difficult, if not hazardous task. However, what is clear is that the roles of the 'founding fathers' of the social partnership of the late 1980s stand out.

In terms of relative risk-taking, leadership and making the crucial calls which risked putting them at odds with their own constituencies, those involved in the formulation of the 1987 agreement deserve the highest accolade and probably the greatest credit. People like Peter Cassells, Phil Flynn, John Carroll, Billy Attley and Dan Murphy, on the union side, became key advocates and persuaders, modifying and developing their thinking as they went along. They clearly understood the scope and evolving shape of the economic crisis of the 1980s and the opportunities and risks it presented.

Equally, on the employer side, people like Dan McAuley, John Dunne, Turlough O'Sullivan and Tom Toner became key figures in shaping what emerged, and brought their own side aboard, 'reading the tea leaves' on the changing union agenda. It is clear that, over subsequent agreements, trade unions and employers have had to take risks and confront difficult issues in securing and getting these deals across the line. But the contribution of those involved in 1987 probably stands out above all.

Equally important was the role of civil servants, particularly Padraig O'hUiginn as chairman of the NESC and secretary general of the Department of the Taoiseach, a dual role later assumed by Paddy Teahon and Dermot McCarthy. Substantial inputs also came from the top of other key departments like Finance, Social Welfare, and Enterprise, Trade and Employment.

It is important to remember that, if anything, there was an institutional bias against the sort of formulations and structures which partnership represented. Dealing with unions in the way that is now normal under social partnership was anathema to many senior civil servants, a point conceded by Bertie Ahern himself when he made an early effort at forging an agreement in the Mansion House in 1987.

Assessing the political connections which made it work is probably both the easiest and the most difficult task. What is clear is that there were people who were ideologically open to bringing the unions in from the cold, but many in the Fine Gael-Labour Coalition of the 1983–87 period did not see it either as a runner or a possibility. This may have something to do with the culture and background of Fine Gael. It is probably fair to say that Fianna Fáil were always closer to organised labour, deriving much of their support from traditional working-class areas. And in this context, the role of people like Charles Haughey and Bertie Ahern was crucial and central in understanding that a deal could be done via their networks of key union leaders and others. Later, politicians from other parties, most notably John Bruton as Taoiseach, took the pragmatic option of sticking with social partnership.

THE BIG ISSUES

When the 2007 general election got underway, all the main political parties remained committed to the process although there were some misgivings about the details of specific agreements. But, as the social partners contemplate talks on a new agreement at the end of 2007, they have plenty of big issues to consider, along with specific concerns from their own constituencies. They have clearly given some thought to many of the individual issues, but it is less apparent that they have seriously considered the threat some of these factors pose to the continuance of social partnership.

The success of social partnership, so far, has hinged on the ability of the partners to reach agreement on a shared set of issues, in other words, to sing from the same hymn sheet. That is becoming increasingly difficult. It is worth encapsulating some of these challenges because the social partners may face an even greater challenge in making the process work today than 21 years ago:

- There is an emerging gap between those employers who insist on fewer employment regulations and maintaining Ireland's 'light touch' employment law legislation, and the trade unions, many of whom tend towards greater regulation of industrial relations matters and further extending employment rights. Irish business is ideally positioned to benefit from the opportunities of globalisation, but the corollary of this is that workers are faced with the prospect of less secure employment and worsening pay and conditions in some areas. The large body of migrant workers in Ireland from EU and non-EU countries has added to the potential for exploitation. The social partners will have to come to some *modus vivendi* around this issue of competitiveness versus regulation and enforcement. Can they produce outcomes that ensure gains for both sides?

- The public service pay benchmarking process has attracted adverse comment and controversy but, despite considerable turbulence and efforts to undermine it, most of the key actors acknowledge that it is better than the chaos it replaced, which was described in Chapter 6. Benchmarking is still being 'bedded in'. Apart from its aim of providing a fair comparison with private sector pay movements, it must also be understood as an enabling instrument through which reform and the delivery of efficient public services can be pursued. This is now a major issue for government and the trade unions – both of whom face the task of building on the benchmarking process – not to mention those who use and pay for public services. It is time, as Peter McLoone has said, for all sides 'to stand and deliver' by using benchmarking to help modernise public services and make them more accessible. Are both sides up for the challenge?

- Over the course of the various social partnership agreements, the industrial relations system has been drifting in the direction of greater regulation, particularly over the past decade. Through the creation of the National Implementation Body, as their own elite watchdog on the partnership agreements, the social partners have created a powerful instrument for conflict resolution at the centre of the process that can assist in bringing critical disputes to finality, thus ensuring the integrity of the process. Meanwhile, the development of instruments, such as Labour Relations Commission appointed pay assessors, to deal with 'inability to pay' cases has further added to the stability of the pay agreements. The social partners need to decide whether they want to push harder in this direction: do they want to further erode the voluntarist nature of the industrial relations system, or do they want to put a brake on compulsion and enforcement?

- The impact of the 2001–04 Industrial Relations Acts has been altered significantly by the Supreme Court ruling in the Ryanair–Labour Court–IMPACT case. The social partners will have to carefully monitor developments in the wake of the finding, and decide whether to consider amendments to the legislation. The legislation has not been popular with employers and, since the Supreme Court ruling, several unions believe it has been rendered toothless from their perspective. Should the social partners review the legislation? Should they leave well enough alone for now? Or should they look for an entirely different approach to dealing with employee representation rights in the workplace, such as opting for the more conventional model used in other democratic societies – straightforward statutory union recognition rights in the workplace?

- The latest NESC report underpins the Towards 2016 agreement. ICTU General Secretary David Begg sees the current social partnership process as a vehicle for a gradual move towards a Scandinavian-type social democratic model, based on many of the social and economic platforms spelled out by the NESC. This is certainly not a view shared by IBEC, or even some trade unions, which retain an essentially pragmatic approach to social partnership, and are wary of it becoming a wider political project. The role of the Oireachtas is important in this area, opening up the question of the accountability of social partnership to the primary democratic body in the country. The social partners are clearly not singing from the same hymn sheet in this area, something they will have to examine closely in the lead up to talks. They must also consider whether the process would benefit from more openness and scrutiny by elected representatives and media.

- The generation of leaders that oversaw and led the social partnership process since the 1980s has practically left the stage. Are the leaders of today capable of identifying areas of common concern, and have they the same ability as that shown by the founding fathers of social partnership to make strategic decisions? This is critical if the process is to maintain the cohesion it has demonstrated thus far. The talks on the Towards 2016 agreement were considerably protracted by the fallout from the Irish Ferries dispute, a trend that had already been established by the extended talks on the previous deal, Sustaining Progress. Will social partnership survive the crisis atmosphere that now seems to almost inevitably pervade national-level talks, and which is usually triggered by an unforeseen dispute? Can the social partners come up with a better way to handle the negotiations phase of the process, while maintaining their focus on the bigger picture and the goal of a pragmatic consensus?

WILL THEY WALK AWAY?

Social partnership is still not so firmly embedded that one or more of the partners cannot up and leave if they believe it is putting too much of a brake on change, or stymieing their particular interests. Rory O'Donnell says that, if one of the parties was diminished in importance or influence, it could not be said the others wouldn't take advantage but, having said that, 'partnership has been amazingly institutionalised. Everybody accepts this and does business.'

In other words, the pragmatism that lies at the heart of the process remains the key ingredient for the main actors. It started out as a problem-solving exercise and it will only remain relevant if it continues in that vein. The challenges are entirely different in 2007 compared to 1987, but they are no less vital, and social partnership must demonstrate a continuing capacity to meet them.

Dermot McCarthy, the figure currently at the heart of the process, provides one final analogy that best sums up how its supporters would like social partnership to be understood:

> It's like a muscle, the more it's used the stronger it gets . . . . it brings people together and encourages them to be minded to solve problems, rather than [to] create or exacerbate them, and do it in a way which respects parameters that everyone agrees are either necessary or desirable.

Appendix: Summary of the main points in the social partnership agreements, 1987–2007

PROGRAMME FOR NATIONAL RECOVERY, 1988–90[1]

1988	2.5%	3% on first £120 a week and 2% on pay above this. Minimum payment of £4 a week increase.
1989	2.5%	Tax cuts of £225 million.
1990	2.5%	Special pay awards for public servants dealt with on deferred basis.

PROGRAMME FOR ECONOMIC AND SOCIAL PROGRESS, 1991–93

1991	4%	£5 minimum for low paid in year one.
1992	3%	£4.25 minimum for low paid and 3% local bargaining available for workers in private sector and semi-States.
1993	3.75%	£5.75 minimum for low paid, 3% local bargaining in public sector and £400 million in tax cuts aimed primarily at lower paid.

---

[1] Dates are approximate. The pay phases of agreements sometimes ended at different times for different groups of workers and therefore expired in the lifetime of the next agreement – most notably with Partnership 2000. The difference in phasing is particularly marked between private and public sectors.

PROGRAMME FOR COMPETITIVENESS AND WORK, 1994–96

1994	2%[2]	Public sector pay deal for 3.5 years, starting with five-month pay pause, then 2% for 12 months.
1995	2.5%	Tax cuts for low paid. Public service 2% for 12 months. Minimum increase of £2.80 a week for low paid.
1996 I	2.5% for six months	Minimum increase of £2.10 for low paid. Public service 1.5% for four months.
1996 II	1% for six months	Minimum increase of £2.10 for low paid. Public service 1.5% for three months and 1% for last six months.

PARTNERSHIP 2000, 1997–2000

1997	2.5%	Public service: 2.5% of first £220 a week for nine months; 2.5% on balance of basic pay for three months.
1998	2.25%	The 2.25% applied across public and private sector, with 2% local bargaining in private sector and 3% in public sector. Minimum increase £3.50 a week for low paid.
1999 I	1.5% for 9 months	Minimum increase of £2.40 a week for low paid.
1999 II	1% for 6 months	Minimum increase of £1.60 a week for low paid.

---

[2] Construction sector had separate phasing of increases from the rest of the private sector.

PROGRAMME FOR PROSPERITY AND FAIRNESS, 2000–02

2000	5.5%	Twelve months. The National Minimum Wage (NMW) was introduced from 1 April 2000 at £4.40 an hour.
2001	5.5%	Twelve months. The NMW increases to £4.70 an hour from 1 July 2001. First instalment of 25% of Benchmarking agreement increases to be backdated to 1 December.
2002	4%	Nine months. The 4% in the public sector is dependent on meeting performance indicators. General commitments on improvements in transport, social and affordable housing, and childcare provision by Government. The first Benchmarking Report is issued on 30 June. NMW increases to £5 an hour from 1 October.

SUSTAINING PROGRESS, 2003–05

2003 I	3%	The agreement provides for a mid-term review in 2004 because of uncertainty over inflation. The first increase is paid as the PPF expires in each employment or industry and applies for nine months.
2003 II	2%	Next six months of agreement.
2004 I	2.5%	Next three months of agreement. Public service to receive 50% of Benchmarking award from 1 January, plus backdating.
2004 II	1.5%	Next six months of agreement. This is conceded under the Mid-Term Review of Sustaining Progress and provides a 2% increase for workers on less than €9 an hour. The outstanding 25% of Benchmarking award to be paid from 1 June.

2005 I	1.5%	Next six months. The Mid-Term Review provides for statutory redundancy payments to be increased to two weeks per year of service from 1 January 2005. The NMW is increased from 1 May to €7.65 by Labour Court.
2005 II	2.5%	Next six months.

TOWARDS 2016, 2006–07

2006 I	3%	First six months of the agreement. The overall agreement is for ten years in terms of delivering non-pay aspects in areas such as the National Development Plan. This is to develop a longer-range focus for partnership agreements. It is also agreed to introduce wide-ranging measures to protect employment rights and enforce them in the wake of the Irish Ferries dispute.
2006 II	2%	Next nine months. Workers on €10.25 an hour, or less, to receive 2.5%.
2007 I	2.5%	Next six months of agreement.
2007 II	2.5%	Next six months of agreement.

Works Cited

Allen, Mike (1998), *The Bitter Word*, Dublin: Poolbeg Press.

Chubb, Basil (ed.) (1992), *Federation of Irish Employers 1942–1992*, Dublin: Gill & Macmillan.

Cousins, Mel (1995), *The Irish Social Welfare System: Law and Social Policy*, Dublin: Round Hall Press Ltd.

FitzGerald, Garret (1992), *All in a Life*, Dublin: Gill & Macmillan.

Garvin, Tom (2005), *Preventing the Future*: *Why was Ireland so Poor for so Long?* Dublin: Gill & Macmillan.

Hardiman, Niamh (1988), *Pay, Politics and Economic Performance in Ireland, 1970–87*, Oxford: Clarendon Press.

Mansergh, Martin (1986), *The Spirit of the Nation: the Speeches and Statements of Charles J. Haughey 1957–1986*, Cork: Mercier Press.

O'Neill, Cathleen (1992), *Telling it Like it is*, Dublin: Combat Poverty Agency.

Roche, William K. and Murphy, Tom (eds.) (1998), *Irish Industrial Relations in Practice* (2nd edition), Dublin: Oaktree Press.

Sheehan, Brian (1996), *Crisis, Strategic Re-Evaluation and the Re-emergence of Tripartism in Ireland*, unpublished MComm.

Sheehan, Brian (2002), 'Irish Industrial Relations and HRM: An Overview of the "Lovett Years"', in Parick Gunnigle, Michael Morley and Michael McDonnell (eds), *The John Lovett Lectures*: *A Decade of Developments in Human Resource Management*, Dublin: The Liffey Press.

Tansey, Paul (1998), *Ireland at Work*: *Economic Growth and the Labour Market*, Dublin: Oaktree Press.

Whyte, Gerry (ed.) (1988), *Sex Equality, Community Rights and Irish Social Welfare Law*, Dublin: ICEL.

Glossary

'Above the Norm' 'Above the Norm' (ATN) pay deals are those involving pay rises in excess of the basic terms negotiated in a national pay agreement.

Amicus Union created by merger of AEUW-TASS and MSF. Now part of Unite.

AnCo State training agency that combined with Manpower and the Youth Employment Agency to form FÁS.

Arms Trial 1970 trial in which Charles Haughey and others were accused of attempting to import arms for Northern republicans. Haughey was sacked as a government minister but was subsequently acquitted.

ASTI Association of Secondary Teachers Ireland

ASTMS Association of Scientific, Technical and Managerial Staffs (now part of Unite)

ATGWU Amalgamated Transport and General Workers' Union

AUEW Amalgamated Union of Engineering Workers

Back to Work Scheme Programme introduced in the 1990s which allows previously unemployed people to retain some social welfare entitlements for four years after they find a job or set up their own business.

BATU	Building and Allied Trades' Union
Beef Tribunal	A tribunal of enquiry into irregularities in the beef industry established to examine the relationship between Charles Haughey and the 'beef baron' Larry Goodman.
benchmarking	A system of comparing public service pay grades to related levels in the private sector.
'blue flu'	Unofficial industrial action by gardaí (police) in 1998 in pursuit of pay increase.
'buy-in'	Signing up for an agreement.
C&A System	Public service pay system based on conciliation and arbitration.
CCR	Cost and Competitiveness Review
CII	Confederation of Irish Industry, which represented employers on issues of trade, economics, taxation and development (now part of IBEC).
Commission on Industrial Relations	Established in 1978 to make recommendations on the system of industrial relations in Ireland.
community platform	An alliance of smaller groups within the social pillar to ensure their more effective participation in the social partnership process.
Congress	Irish Congress of Trade Unions
CORI	Conference of Religious, Ireland (represents major Irish religious congregations within the Catholic Church)
CPSU	Civil Public and Services Union
CRC	Central Review Committee, which monitors the implementation of social partnership agreements. Includes representatives of all partners.
CWU	Communication Workers' Union

Dáil	Lower chamber of the Irish parliament, equivalent to the House of Commons at Westminster
DBG	Policy document: *Delivering Better Government*
democratic deficit	Social partnership is sometimes characterised as undemocratic because public representatives are not involved in negotiating the terms of national agreements, and the agreements are ratified by the government rather than directly by members of the Oireachtas (Irish Parliament).
EBR	Exchequer Borrowing Requirement
EETPU	Electrical, Electronic, Telecommunications and Plumbing Union (now part of Unite)
ELC	Employer-Labour Conference. Industrial relations conflict resolution body established in the 1970s and now defunct.
ERC	Employee Representative Committee
ESB	Electricity Supply Board
ESOP	Employment Share Ownership Plan
ESRI	Economic and Social Research Institute
ETU	Electrical Trades Union (now part of TEEU)
'excepted body'	a body whose members are employed by the same employer and which carries on negotiations for the fixing of the wages or other conditions of employment for its own members (but not for other employees).
FÁS	Foras Áisenna Saothair, the Irish Training and Employment Authority
FDI	foreign direct investment
Fianna Fáil	Ireland's largest political party.

FIE	Federation of Irish Employers, which represented employers on industrial relations issues (now part of IBEC).
Fine Gael	Second largest Irish political party.
Forfás	Irish policy and advisory body for enterprise, trade, science, technology and innovation.
'free-for-all'	Also free collective bargaining. Local bargaining on a company-by-company basis.
FUE	Federated Union of Employers, renamed Federation of Irish Employers (FIE).
FWUI	Federated Workers' Union Ireland (now part of SIPTU)
GDP	Gross domestic product: Total value of goods and services produced within a country during one year, excluding net income from foreign investment.
GNP	Gross national product: Total value of goods and services produced within a country during one year, including net income from foreign investment.
Goodman controversy	see Beef Tribunal
GPC	General Purposes Committee of the ICTU
GRA	Garda Representative Association
HRM	Human Resource Management
HSEA	Health Service Employers' Agency
IBEC	Irish Business and Employers' Confederation, Ireland's main employers' body.
IBOA	Irish Bank Officials' Union
ICTU	Irish Congress of Trade Unions. Umbrella body that represents most Irish unions, North and South.

IDA	Industrial Development Authority. Official agency responsible for securing foreign investment in Ireland.
IFA	Irish Farmers' Association
IMPACT	Irish Municipal Public and Civil Trade union. Largest public sector union in the Republic of Ireland.
INO	Irish Nurses' Organisation
INOU	Irish National Organisation of the Unemployed
INTO	Irish National Teachers' Organisation. Represents teachers in primary education.
IPA	Institute of Public Administration
IR	Industrial Relations
IRN	*Industrial Relations News*, specialist weekly journal covering Irish industrial relations.
ISME	Irish Small and Medium Enterprises
ITGWU	Irish Transport and General Workers' Union (now part of SIPTU)
'jobless growth'	Misnomer that describes apparent failure to reduce unemployment after the PNR in 1987. In fact, employment creation did gradually pick up, but it was not until 1996–97 that unemployment started to fall away dramatically.
Labour Court	Statutory body for investigation and resolution of industrial disputes.
'leap-frogging'	Occurs when unions are able to build on one pay agreement (involving one group or company) and use this to build a follow-on higher wage increase.
LGMSB	Local Government Management Services Board

LGPSU	Local Government and Public Services Union. Now part of IMPACT.
Live Register	List of those entitled to statutory unemployment benefits.
LRC	Labour Relations Commission, Irish statutory body providing non-binding dispute resolution services.
Maastricht	Reference to the Maastricht Treaty (1992), which led to the creation of the European Union.
MSF	Manufacturing, Science and Finance union. Now part of Unite.
NAPs	National Anti-Poverty strategy
National Understandings	Formal incomes policy agreements in 1979 and 1980.
NCP	National Centre for Partnership
NCPP	National Centre for Partnership and Performance
NERA	National Employment Rights Agency
NESC	National Economic and Social Council. Statutory body, with representatives from government and the social partners, which develops the strategic economic and social framework that informs negotiations on national agreements.
NESF	National Economic and Social Forum. Advises government on policies to achieve greater equality and social inclusion.
NIB	National Implementation Body. High level body established under the SP to deal with intractable industrial disputes.
NSS	National Spatial Strategy. A twenty-year strategy launched by the Government in

	November 2002. It is a strategic vision for the spatial development of Ireland, designed to enable every place in the country reach its potential regardless of size or location.
NUJ	National Union of Journalists, Ireland
Oireachtas	Collective term for the Upper and Lower Houses of the Irish parliament
P2000	Partnership 2000. National partnership agreement in force between 1997 and 1999.
PCW	Programme for Competitiveness and Work. National partnership agreement in force between 1994 and 1996.
PESP	Programme for Economic and Social Progress. National partnership agreement in force between 1991 and 1993.
PNA	Psychiatric Nurses Association
PNR	Programme for National Recovery. National partnership agreement in force between 1988 and 1990.
PPF	Programme for Prosperity and Fairness. National partnership agreement in force between 2000 and 2002.
process, the	Often used as shorthand to describe social partnership in operation.
Proportional Representation (PR)	A decision-making process which, in Ireland, is based on the single transferable vote system used at general elections.
PSBB	Public Service Benchmarking Body which, since 2000, has made periodic reviews of public service pay through making comparisons with the private sector.
PSEU	Public Service Executive Union

PTWU	Postal and Telecommunications Workers' Union
PVG	Performance Verification Groups. Verify staff and union compliance with modernisation requirements in later national agreements.
R&D	research and development
SES	Social Employment Scheme, forerunner to Community Employment Scheme.
SIPTU	Services, Industrial, Professional and Technical Union. Ireland's largest trade union.
SMA	Societas Missionum ad Afros (Society of African Missions)
SMI	Strategic Management Initiative
social dialogue	Provision whereby the European Commission must consult the European Social Partners before presenting proposals on social policy.
social partnership	Consenus between government, main trade union and employer bodies, farming organisations and other community-based organisations.
social pillar	A new strand to social partnership introduced in 1996. Provides for structured participation in negotiations on national agreements by organisations in the community and voluntary sectors.
SP	Sustaining Progress. National partnership agreement in force between 2003 and 2005.
SPD	Social Democratic Party of Germany
SUI	Services Union International (USA)
T16/T2016	Towards 2016. National partnership agreement in force between 2006 and 2007.

Tallaght Strategy Named after a speech in the Dublin suburb of Tallaght where then Fine Gael party leader, Mr Alan Dukes, promised his party's support for the minority Fianna Fáil Government so long as it pursued spending cutbacks designed to reduce borrowing.

Tánaiste Irish deputy prime minister

Taoiseach Irish prime minister

TASS Technical Administrative and Supervisory Section

TEEU Technical, Engineering and Electrical Union

TGWU Transport and General Workers' Union

TUI Teachers' Union of Ireland. Secondary and third-level teachers' union.

UCATT Union of Construction Allied Trades and Technicians

Unite Union formed by the merger of the British Transport and General Workers' Union and Amicus.

'virtuous circle' Describes the improvement in the public finances, rising incomes and improving employment situation after the PNR in 1987.

voluntarism A system of industrial relations based on negotiated settlements between unions and employers rather than binding arbitration or legal codes.

Index